TOWARDS A THEORY
OF SCHOOLING

Deakin Studies in Education Series

General Editors: Professor Rob Walker and Professor Stephen Kemmis,
Deakin University, Victoria, Australia

Deakin Studies in Education Series: 4

TOWARDS A THEORY OF SCHOOLING

David Hamilton

 The Falmer Press

(A member of the Taylor & Francis Group)
London ● New York ● Philadelphia

UK   The Falmer Press, Falmer House, Barcombe, Lewes, East Sussex,
            BN8 5DL

USA   The Falmer Press, Taylor & Francis Inc., 242 Cherry Street,
            Philadelphia, PA 19106-1906

First published 1989

**Library of Congress Cataloging in Publication Data is available
on request**

ISBN 1 85000 480 3
ISBN 1 85000 481 1 (pbk.)

Typeset in 12/13 Garamond by
The FD Group Ltd, Fleet, Hampshire

Jacket design by Caroline Archer

*Printed in Great Britain by Taylor & Francis (Printers) Ltd,
Basingstoke*

Contents

Domestic education is the institution of nature; public education the contrivance of man.

(Smith, A. (1759) *The Theory of Moral Sentiments*)

The great proliferation of historical writing has served not to illuminate the central themes of western history but to obscure them.

(Bailyn, B. (1982) *The challenge of modern historiography*)

The concept of a historically based (investigation) is misunderstood by most researchers. For them, to study something historically means, by definition, to study some past event. Hence, they naively imagine an insurmountable barrier between historic study and study of present day behavioural forms. To study something historically means to study it in the process of change. Thus, historical study is not an auxiliary aspect of theoretical study, but rather forms its very base.

(Vygotski, L. (1932-33) *Problems of method*)

Pedagogical instruction should propose, not to communicate to future practitioners a certain number of procedures and formulae, but to give them full awareness of their function.

(Durkheim, E. (1905)
The evolution and role of secondary education in France)

Preface

Schooling is not the same as education. Schooling is an extensive and elaborate human institution. It began to take its present shape in the Middle Ages, and it has been repeatedly reformed since that time. In the process, schooling has emerged as a malleable instrument of the political state — an agency charged with the transformation of immature human beings into appropriately-socialized adult citizens. It is perhaps no exaggeration to say that, on an international scale, schooling was conceived by christianity and raised by capitalism.

This book, then, is about schooling. Inspired by works written by two non-historians — Emile Durkheim's *The Evolution of Educational Thought* (a course of lectures originally delivered in 1904-05) and Maurice Dobb's *Studies in the Development of Capitalism* (originally published in 1946) — it examines long-term changes in the form and function of schooling. In summary, the work falls into three sections: an introductory chapter; five historical essays — which can be read on their own; and a concluding chapter. Chapter 1 (Setting the Agenda) unfolds the theoretical and practical considerations that governed the selection and organization of the historical essays. The historical essays (chapters 2-6) address notable and pivotal episodes in the history of school organization (for example, the introduction of classes and class teaching). And chapter 7 (Notes Towards a Theory of Schooling) builds upon the essays by advancing a range of general propositions about the relationship between 'schooling', 'society' and 'educational change'.

The manuscript for this book was largely prepared between 1977 and 1986. I regret, therefore, that it does not profit more fully from recent publications such as Connell (1987) *Gender and Power;* Corrigan and Sayer (1985) *The Great Arch: State Formation, Cultural Revolution and the Rise of Capitalism;* Courtenay (1987) *Schools and Scholars in Fourteenth Century England;* Goodson (1988) *The Making of Curriculum;* Kliebard

(1986) *The Struggle for the American Curriculum 1893-1958;* Maynes (1985) *Schooling in Western Europe: A Social History;* and Morgan (1986) *Godly Learning: Puritan Attitudes Towards Reason, Learning and Education.*

Just as schooling did not evolve in an ideological vacuum, so this book owes much to an unfinished dialogue that I have shared with colleagues and friends. For their forebearance, counsel and support, I would particularly like to thank Clem Adelman, Richard Aldrich, Susan Bain, Leo Bartlett, Wilf Carr, Anne Currie, Donald Broady, Margot Cameron Jones, Michael Clanchy, Bruce Curtis, Mary Finn, Simon Frith, David Gough, Nigel Grant, Elisabet Hedrenius, Keith Hoskin, Walter Humes, Ervin Johanningmeier, Stephen Kemmis, Ulf Lundgren, Andrew McPherson, Philip McCann, Kerstin Mattsson, Margaret Nieke, Hamish Paterson, Tom Popkewitz, Margaret Reid, William A. Reid, Richard Selleck, Harold Silver, Brian Simon, Joan Simon, James V. Smith, Louis Smith, Robert Stake, Lawrence Stenhouse, Rob Walker, Gaby Weiner, Ian Westbury, Jack Whitehead, Donald Withrington and Michael F.D. Young.

And just as schooling did not evolve in an economic vacuum, so this book also owes much to the supplementary financial support I have received from the British Council, the Social Science Research Council (grant No. HR/5127), the Swedish Institute and the University of Glasgow.

David Hamilton
Glasgow
October 1988

Chapter 1

Setting the Agenda

Any description of classroom activities that cannot be related to the social structure and culture of the society is a conservative description.   (Walker (1970) *The Social Setting of the Classroom*)[1]

To explain any educational process we must have a conceptual apparatus that relates the economic and social structure of society to the teaching process.
(Lundgren (1979) *School Curricula: Content and Structure*)[2]

Education is not simply shaped in a general way by the imperatives, arrangements and logic of the capitalist system. Education is *specifically articulated* with this system in certain very definite ways.   (Hall (1981) *Schooling, State and Society*)[3]

I

This book has its own history. Its origins lie in the study of a new open plan school that I conducted in 1975-76.[4] At that time, the individualized methods proposed for such schools were repeatedly contrasted — sometimes unfavourably — with the class teaching methods deemed typical of older settings. Very often, too, such debates about educational innovation were conducted as if the status quo — classrooms, desks, blackboards etc. — had existed since time immemorial. In fact, the multi-teacher, multi-room school is of recent vintage — a monument to the educational reforms of the late nineteenth century. Indeed, if the history of school innovation is traced back to the end of the eighteenth century, an even more subversive claim can be made — that class teaching had, in its turn, grown from an earlier pedagogy that was just as 'individualized' and 'open plan' as anything offered in the 1970s.

Yet, on what basis could I claim a pedagogic similarity between eighteenth and twentieth century schooling? And why did classrooms and classroom methods emerge in the intervening years? Taken together, these two questions gave a new direction to my research interests: if one-to-one instruction is deemed to be the most 'natural' teaching method, then perhaps it is class teaching, not the individualization of open plan schooling, that is most in need of explanation.

Until the open plan study I had regarded myself as a classroom researcher. I had spent a number of years absorbing, recording and making sense of contemporary schoolroom life. But my glimpses into the pre-history of open plan schooling had an unnerving effect. They made me realize how little I knew about long-term pedagogic change. Clearly, I needed to make a more sustained examination of the historical record. At first, the task seemed relatively trivial. Surely, educational historians had already explored and documented the pedagogies of the past. My optimism, however, was unfounded: no one seemed to have looked in that direction, at least not in terms that I found congenial.[5] Slowly, I began to appreciate that the weak sense of history shown by classroom researchers was matched only by the weak sense of the classroom shown by educational historians.

An opportunity to address this intellectual tension came within a few months of publishing the open plan study. In October 1977, I received a one-year grant to investigate 'Classroom life and the evolution of the classroom system'. Using West of Scotland data, my intention was to focus on the educational changes that had brought about classrooms and class teaching. Already, my attention had been drawn to the seminal influence of local figures such as Robert Owen (1771-1858) of New Lanark and David Stow (1793-1864) of Glasgow. Moreover, I was equally aware that David Stow's name had been linked to an early form of class teaching known as 'simultaneous instruction'.

Besides investigating the work of these innovators and their Scottish contemporaries, the initial phase of my investigation was also steered by a chronological question: 'When did the term "classroom" first appear in the educational record?'.[6] This train of inquiry led me to Samuel Wilderspin's *On the Importance of Educating the Infant Children of the Poor* (1823).[7] Yet, along the way, my concentration was somewhat disrupted when a postgraduate student (Maria Gibbons) drew my attention to the fact that the term 'classroom' was still used within the University of Glasgow's Department of Humanity (i.e. Latin).

I had not anticipated this datum. It seemed unlikely that such a high-status institution (and such a long-standing subject-area) would have adopted the terminology of nineteenth-century elementary schools.

So where had the University of Glasgow's usage come from? Turning from speculation to investigation, I searched the University's records and found uses of 'class room' that stretched back more than sixty years beyond Wilderspin's. And further investigation revealed no earlier uses in any of the other Scottish universities (Aberdeen, Edinburgh and St Andrews).

These unexpected findings gave my investigation a new edge. If Glasgow was, in fact, the ultimate English-language source of 'classroom', then its educational institutions deserved a more exhaustive examination than I had originally envisaged. I would have to extend my remit and grapple with an earlier set of educational innovations — those that occupied Scottish university teachers during the period of the eighteenth-century Enlightenment. In turn, of course, I would also need to explore the connection, if any, between the eighteenth-century Scottish universities and nineteenth-century elementary schools.

These were not easy questions to address, not least because they cut across a variety of disciplinary boundaries (for example, those that separate economic history from the history of ideas). Meantime, too, the boundedness of my case study was under revision in another direction — a chance remark (from Herbert Kliebard of the University of Wisconsin) drew my attention to the fact that the seventeenth-century records of the University of Glasgow provide the *Oxford English Dictionary* with its earliest source of the word 'curriculum' (1633). Should my case study also extend to this earlier educational innovation?

Within the timescale allowed by my research grant, there was no possibility of tackling all these questions — except, perhaps, in the same kind of hit-and-run manner that I had used with the open plan study.[8] In the event I was able to prolong my investigations through other circumstances — I was appointed to a tenured lectureship at the University of Glasgow that was to commence immediately my research fellowship expired.

II

During my fellowship year I gathered large amounts of data — enough possibly for a book entitled *On the Changing Disciplines of Education: Schooling in Glasgow During the Industrial Revolution.* But the prospect of writing such a book did not exactly fill me with excitement. Its style and content would have been too reminiscent of the antiquarian tomes I had been warned against.[9] I did not want to produce a book simply about the past: I wanted, instead, to produce something that could illuminate the continuous present.

To this end, I needed something more than a chronological, one-thing-after-another framework. I had to find a way of talking about schooling that was as valid for the twentieth century as it was for the Industrial Revolution. In logical terms, the solution to my problem boiled down to the creation of two complementary theoretical frameworks. The first of these would help me to differentiate between schooling and other social institutions (for example, the Church, the family); while the second framework would help me to differentiate among forms of schooling (i.e. among different pedagogies). In effect, the first framework makes it possible to answer the question 'What is schooling?'; while the second framework makes it possible to answer the question 'What is a pedagogy?'. Armed with this double differentiation, it becomes possible to acknowledge the long-term persistence of schooling yet, at the same time, identify certain of its internal pedagogic discontinuities. Together, these frameworks began to act as the long- and short-focus lenses with which I repeatedly scanned the educational record.

Initially, I tackled the issue of pedagogic differentiation. I began to link the pedagogic variations I had noted during the open plan study to changes in the organization of economic production. Was the changeover from individualized to class teaching anything to do with the contemporaneous switch from 'domestic' to 'factory' production that had been discussed, for instance, in Maurice Dobb's *Studies in the Development of Capitalism* (1946)[10] and in the introduction to George Unwin's *Industrial Organisation in the Sixteenth and Seventeenth Centuries* (1904)?[11] Similarly, was the twentieth century changeover to forms of individualization anything to do with the introduction of 'scientific management' into industrial production (cf. the arguments of Clarence Karier, Paul Violas and Joel Spring's *Roots of Crisis: American Education in the Twentieth Century* (1973)[12]; and David Tyack's *The One Best System: A History of American Urban Education* (1974)[13]). If so, how were the rationales that underpinned the organization of schooling connected to the rationales that underpinned the organization of manufacturing (cf. Sidney Pollard's *The Genesis of Modern Management: A Study of the Industrial Revolution in Great Britain* (1965)[14])?

In this last respect, it was particularly important to consider the work of those, like Robert Owen[15], who figured both in the history of schooling and the history of management. Another such personage — of local as well as international significance — was Adam Smith. Indeed, Adam Smith's educational credentials include the fact that, while a professor in Glasgow (1752-64), he was present on the occasion of the first recorded use of the term 'class room'.

Although Smith's most noted work is *The Wealth of Nations* (1st edn, 1776), it is the preparation of his earlier treatise — *The Theory of Moral Sentiments* (1st edn, 1759) — that most closely corresponds to his sojourn in Glasgow. *The Theory of Moral Sentiments* was Smith's attempt to put the moral sciences on the same footing as the physical sciences. He claimed that civil society was held together by an ethical bonding agent analogous to the force of gravity that held together the material world. Further, Smith chose the terms 'fellow feeling' or 'sympathy' to label this universal moral sentiment.

Smith's use of 'sympathy' caught my eye. Did it have any connection with the concept of 'sympathy of numbers' that, sixty years later, David Stow used to justify the grouping of pupils for 'simultaneous' instruction? Certainly, the circumstantial evidence was persuasive. Like Smith, Stow accepted that 'sympathy' was a 'principle of our nature'. Similarly, Stow held that its bonding effects were 'more or less powerful' in proportion to the 'proximity and concentration of *numbers*'. In pedagogic terms, then, Stow believed that the 'power in numbers' unobtainable through 'individual teaching' made possible a moral machinery adequate to the social problems created by the Industrial Revolution. With 'proper management' and the correct 'moral atmosphere', simultaneous instruction could promote the moral and intellectual 'elevation' of the 'sunken masses' that had accumulated in the manufacturing areas of Great Britain.[16]

Here, then, was a basis for linking the eighteenth-century Scottish Enlightenment to nineteenth-century elementary schools. Gradually, I traced out an intellectual genealogy that linked Adam Smith, via Robert Owen, to David Stow. And, as important, I was able to cite Adam Smith's moral philosophy in support of the idea that early class teaching had an integrity of its own — it was not just the insertion of factory methods into the organization of schooling. Exploration of the Smith-Stow connection also had another practical consequence: it gave me a better grasp of the connections between economic history and the history of ideas. The central feature of both schools and factories is that they are as much about the management of people as they are about the design of a technical 'machinery'. Hence, the social philosophies that inform their respective management practices are just as important as the technological developments that govern their choice of material resources. Indeed, educational production, like its industrial counterpart, entails a fusion of both technical and social considerations. By 1979, this general idea — that educational practice lies at the intersection of economic history and the history of ideas — had become an important organizing principle in the conduct of my research programme.

5

Detailed analysis of the Smith-Stow connection also enabled me to strengthen my earlier ideas about the periodization of pedagogic change. I began to claim that modern (i.e. post-medieval) schooling can be divided into three broad pedagogic epochs: (i) a period when the dominant pedagogy comprised the 'individualized' (i.e. 'in turn') processing of learners; (ii) a period (commencing around 1840 in Great Britain) when the dominant pedagogy hinged upon the 'batch' processing of groups of learners: and (iii) a period (commencing around 1890) when pedagogic practices began to be re-ordered in the light of new notions about the evolutionary significance of individual differences.

In turn, I used this three-stage model to organize the remainder of my research programme. Resetting my chronological boundaries at the late Middle Ages (c.1400) and the First World War (c.1916), I was able to envisage the history of post-medieval schooling in terms of three 'revolutionary' phases and two intervening 'transitional' periods. Successively, these five 'episodes' comprised: (i) the 'revolutionary' emergence of modern schooling and the associated stabilization of an individualized pedagogy; (ii) the seventeenth-century elaboration of this pedagogy as schooling began to incorporate the children of wage labourers; (iii) the 'revolutionary' change-over from 'individualized' to 'batch' production at the time of the Industrial Revolution; (iv) the nineteenth-century elaboration of 'simultaneous' methods alongside the growth of 'elementary' schooling; and (v) the 'revolutionary' change-over from batch processing to new forms of individualization at the beginning of the twentieth century.

In one sense, of course, a sixth 'episode' should be added to this chronology — the elaboration of individualization in the remainder of the twentieth century. From the outset, however, I decided to limit my study to the pre-first World War period. In part, this arose because I regarded the open plan study as already occupying the territory marked out for episode 6. But an additional reason was that a re-evaluation of episode 6 (for example, a study of 'progressive' teaching practices) would extend the timescale of my research programme beyond tolerable limits.

III

After completing a version of the Smith-Stow connection[17], I returned to the word 'curriculum'. By this time I had begun to bracket it with the word 'class'. Both terms, it seemed, had come into prominence around the same time; and both, through their adoption, had helped to make 'schooling' recognizably different from other social institutions.

Much of my initial knowledge about the emergence of class was drawn from Philipe Ariès' *Centuries of Childhood* (1962).[18] Ariès suggested that 'class' was of Renaissance coinage. It made its appearance, he noted, in one of Erasmus' descriptions (c.1519) of St Paul's school — an institution founded some ten years previously by the Mercers' (i.e. cloth-merchants') Company of London. Further, Ariès also claimed that such 'classes' had been prefigured in earlier pedagogic reorganizations — notably those associated with the University of Paris and with the schools founded by the Brethren of the Common Life (a religious community based in the Low Countries). Yet, in posing these relationships, Ariès failed to clarify the lines of descent from one to the other. Equally, in claiming this connection, Ariès neglected to explain why the term 'class' appeared some eighty years after the Brethren were claimed to have sub-divided their schools into smaller units.

While browsing in the University library one day, I found the word 'class' in an English-language version of a 1517 account of the University of Paris — Robert Goulet's *Compendium Universitatis Parisiensis*. If accurate, this translation predated the earliest usage reported in Ariès. But I was well aware, from examining W.H. Woodward's *Desiderius Erasmus Concerning the Aim and Method of Education* (1904), that translators are not always faithful to an author's original text.[19] Eventually, however, it turned out that 'class' had, indeed, been a faithful translation.

At that stage in my investigation, the historical significance of the sixteenth-century adoption of class was still unclear in my mind, but I was pleased to have supported and, to some extent, extended Ariès' original commentary. Eventually, these different pieces of data about Paris and the Low Countries began to fall into place when I considered the emergence of classes within a broader context — the cluster of new educational practices, known as the *Modus et Ordo Parisiensis,* that spread from Paris to universities, colleges and schools throughout sixteenth-century Europe. Pedagogically, the *Modus* combined the sub-division of schools with the retention of individualized pupil-by-pupil instruction.

Whilst reflecting on this relationship, I was reminded of the fact that 'order' has two distinct meanings in the english language: it can refer either to sequence (for example, an 'order' of events) or it can refer to coherence (for example, an 'ordered' society). The *Modus* clearly had links with the former, but could it also be construed in the latter sense? Were Renaissance schools therefore, to embody a new sense of social order? If so, the combination of individualized instruction and class grouping could serve such a purpose. Whenever groupings were reduced in size (sixteen pupils was the recommended figure for St Paul's), pupils were brought more frequently under the direct control of their teacher(s); and whenever classes were constrained to follow a pre-arranged sequence of texts, teacher deviation from recommended practice was made more visible to those, like the Mercers' Company, who patronized, financed and 'visited' such schools.

By this stage in my research I began to feel that Renaissance schooling was particularly noteworthy for the attention it gave to pedagogic order and administrative control. And the same feeling also made me more comfortable about bracketing class with curriculum, since the latter — derived from a latin root meaning an athletics track or circuit — had similar resonances with 'order as sequence' and 'order as structure'.

I found this connection between class and curriculum to be logically appealing; but I could find no other historian or educationist who had drawn the same inferences. I was well aware, too, that on the available data I was bracketing events that took place more than 100 years apart (viz. 1517 and 1633). Were there any earlier uses of 'curriculum'? I turned to the statutes of the sixteenth- and seventeenth-century European universities. Unfortunately, references to curriculum were much rarer than I had expected. Indeed, I found nothing to improve upon the Glasgow date.

In the absence of fresh data I was forced back to my original sources. The question 'What was happening in Glasgow in the period leading up to 1633?' finally broke the impasse. As soon as I registered an answer — 'the Calvinist reformation' — possible explanations began to emerge. My background reading in books like Richard Tawney's *Religion and the Rise of Capitalism* (1928)[20] suggested a possible convergence between the educational concept of 'curriculum' and the Calvinist concept of 'discipline'. Could it be that curriculum brought the same kind of order to Calvinist educational practice as the concept of 'discipline' brought to Calvinist social practice?

Having sketched out this argument, I subsequently learned (from Maria Gibbons) of a reference to curriculum in the 1582 records of the University of Leiden, an institution founded by Calvinists some seven years previously. Two data sightings are not exactly overwhelming yet, as with the Smith-Stow connection, I felt that the associated arguments were sufficiently 'newsworthy' to be circulated in a mimeo form.[21]

IV

While awaiting reactions to these early drafts, I returned to the theme of simultaneous instruction and class teaching. The Smith-Stow paper had excavated the transition from individualized- to batch-production; but it had stopped short of a full examination of class teaching's subsequent career. Why, for instance, had the one-room, one-teacher school of the 1830s turned into the multi-room, multi-teacher school of the 1890s? Further, what data were relevant to this question? Was it necessary to wade through such sources as the multi-volume reports of the school inspectorate and through the equally voluminous minutes of the major school boards? If so, the prospect of a life-time's work unfolded uncomfortably before me. A definitive analysis was out of the question, but could I prepare a defensible account?

In effect, I had to find a way of sampling the available sources. Gradually, a practical solution emerged. I realized that the 'manuals of method' produced for nineteenth-century teacher training students might give me reasonably sensitive access to the changing practices of schooling. The first problem, however, was to track them down. Various histories of education (for example, Selleck (1968) *The New Education*)[22] had made passing use of such manuals but no one seemed to have studied them systematically. Using secondary sources like Selleck, the bibliographies of Higson and Craigie, cross references in the manuals themselves, and three or four volumes found on the shelves of secondhand bookshops, I managed to assemble a primary database — of little more than a dozen volumes — that ranged from Henry Dunn's *Principles of Teaching* (c.1837)[23] to J.J. Findlay's *Principles of Class Teaching* (1902)[24].

The pedagogic diversity portrayed in the manuals far exceeded my expectations. To reduce my perplexity I began to trace certain phenomena through time. Did the manuals refer to teaching groups as 'classes', 'divisions', 'drafts', or 'sections'? Was simultaneous instruction envisaged as occupying the main schoolroom or an adjoining anteroom? And how did simultaneous and individual methods correlate with the different labels used to describe nineteenth-century teachers (for example, 'monitor', 'pupil teacher', 'assistant teacher' and 'head teacher')?

Aided by such prompts, I began to see some patterns in the data. The earliest simultaneous instruction (i.e. in the 1830s) typically took the form of a gallery lesson conducted with relatively large numbers of pupils (for example, a 'division'). If a school had a classroom — an exceptional state of affairs in the 1830s — it was used for the individualized instruction of smaller groups of pupils (for example, a 'class' or 'draft'). On the other hand, if there was only one schoolroom, the schoolteacher and his or her assistants (if any) conducted 'collective' and 'individual' lessons side by side in the same room. Thus, it is important to note that although simultaneous instruction could be deemed an early form of class teaching, it was not associated with classrooms. Rather, classes taught in classrooms continued to receive their instruction 'in turn'. Indeed, it was not until the 1860s and 1870s that teachers, rooms and classes began to converge into a one-to-one relationship. Equally, it was not until this later period that 'class teaching' began to take on its twentieth-century connotations.

The patterning reflected in the manuals of method also gave me a strong sense of the reasons underlying the emergence of multi-room, multi-teacher schools. It is insufficient to explain them merely in terms of a growth of the school population — the construction of more and more one-teacher schools would have satisfactorily accommodated the same problem. Rather, they evolved — architecturally and organizationally — to accommodate contemporaneous assumptions about the control and efficiency of schooling. In short, it seemed to me that the historically significant feature of the urban schools built in the 1870s was not so much their size as their embodiment of assumptions about hierarchical management.

Again, I committed these tentative ideas to paper.[25] Besides establishing a provisional chronology of changing events, I also speculated as to the connections between pedagogic change, changes in the structure of schooling (for example, the feminization of elementary teaching), and changes outside the school system (for example, governmental attitudes towards working class education). In other respects, however, my account of nineteenth-century pedagogic shifts remained theoretically impoverished. It made no comment, for instance, about the (then) popular explanations for nineteenth-century educational change. My silence, however, was deliberate. On the one hand, I felt unable to subscribe to the view that changes in elementary schooling were engineered solely to serve the 'social control' interests of the ruling class. And, on the other hand, I was equally unattracted to the idea that the transformation of elementary schooling arose merely from the internal momentum of the education system.[26]

Typically, 'social control' has been portrayed as a set of structural constraints that can be tightened or loosened according to the malevolent (or benevolent) intentions of the educational state. In reacting against this viewpoint, I took a different view of social control. I saw it not as something imposed from outside schooling but, rather, as something that is intrinsic to all institutionalized pedagogic processes (and, hence, to all forms of schooling). Indeed, it is the presence of social control assumptions that makes 'schooling' something rather different from 'education'. For me, then, the important issue was not to identify the presence or absence of social control — I took its occurrence to be axiomatic. Rather, I was more interested in the different ways that social control is expressed in the pedagogic lives of teachers and learners. Equally, I was unwilling to presume that all such influences are necessarily negative.

Taking these problems into account, I began to search for an alternative organizing concept. Eventually, I chose the term 'social efficiency'. Guided by the general question 'What conception of social efficiency does this pedagogic form express?', I found myself better able to reconstitute the broader political meanings of schooling. Moreover, a social efficiency framework also offered a wider range of explanatory shadings than the black and white pigments popular with social control theorists.

The problem of one-dimensionality also arose in respect of 'internal momentum' theories of pedagogic change. These tend to give the impression that succeeding pedagogies flow from one another in a unilinear evolutionary sequence? For my part, I had developed a rather different view of pedagogic evolution — namely, that the events of the last 500 years represent one developmental career among a myriad that might have been. I was happy, that is, with the notion that pedagogies are shaped by their predecessors; but I felt little sympathy with additional appeals to an underlying 'grand design'.

My own resolution of this problem was as follows: I began to assume that all pedagogic forms — whatever their degree of institutionalization — embody 'degrees of freedom' which allow for the possibility of subsequent change. Knowingly or unknowingly, teachers and learners exploit these degrees of freedom as they work, day by day, to realize their own pedagogic goals. In turn, educational 'drift' sets in which, if consolidated, may culminate in the establishment of recognizably-altered pedagogic practices.

Nevertheless, the descriptive language of schooling responds unevenly to these changes. At least three possibilities can be envisaged: (i) that practice changes while terminology stays the same; (ii) that terminology changes in concert with changes in practice; and (iii) that terminology changes while practice remains the same.

The last of these relationships is particularly important to my argument. It points to instances where the goals of educationists — as revealed in their choice of new labels — remain unrealized. Yet, the mere existence of these labels (for example, in pedagogic manifestos) serves to remind us of the many unfulfilled aspirations that exercised the past. In the process, too, it also confirms that the history of pedagogic developments is not quite so straightforward as is sometimes assumed.

V

By this stage in my research programme, I had reported upon three investigations. Two of these — the sixteenth-century uses of 'class' and 'curriculum', and the nineteenth-century evolution of class teaching — had been primarily concerned with unravelling the chronology of pedagogic change. Both, however, needed to be placed more adequately within the general social currents of their respective epochs. More specifically, my investigation of class and curriculum had had very little to say about the contemporaneous transition from feudalism to capitalism. As I read further in economic history, I began to realize that, geographically and chronologically, my research programme traced out not only the cutting edge of schooling, but also the cutting edge of capitalism itself. There seemed to be some merit, therefore, in searching a little further for earlier (i.e. pre-Renaissance) connections between schooling and capitalism. In doing so, I returned to a theoretical issue raised earlier — the differentiation of schooling from other social institutions.

In the 1970s, English-language discussions of the links between capitalism and schooling usually took their starting point as the Industrial Revolution. But such accounts were necessarily foreshortened: capitalism's roots go back much further in time. Accordingly, I began to seek out studies that incorporated this longer-term perspective upon schooling and capitalism. But again, nothing came to light. With a certain reluctance — I was unsure where the investigation would lead me — I set about reconstructing the relationship myself.

In searching for the origins of schooling, I began by identifying a suitable 'tracer' — in this case the medieval Latin term for school, 'schola'. Etymologically, the word 'schola' derives from a classical greek root that, like its latin counterpart (ludus), denotes 'leisure' or 'play'. But when did it begin to take on its modern meaning? Should I conduct a chronological search through 2000 years of history? Or could I, once again, use some kind of sampling procedure? I chose the latter approach — building upon a conceptual analysis of 'socialization', 'education' and 'schooling' that I had developed previously.

My starting point was the premise that, while all three processes — 'socialization', 'education' and 'schooling' — yield a common output (viz. 'learning'), there are important differences in the manner by which such learning is acquired. 'Socialization', so I argued, is a relatively diffuse process; it generates learning that is 'picked up' or 'rubbed off' in the course of human interaction. By comparison, 'education' is a 'stronger' and more visible process; it yields learning that has been deliberately promoted through 'teaching'; and, finally, 'schooling' is even more socially-visible; it produces learning that, in its turn, has been shaped by formalized and institutionalized modes of teaching. In these terms, then, there are grounds for claiming the existence of 'schooling' whenever there is evidence, among other things, of distinctive educational personnel (for example, 'teachers'), distinctive educational instruments (for example, 'textbooks') and distinctive educational premises (for example, 'schools').

By holding this analytic framework up to the educational record, I felt able to narrow my enquiries to the period between 1000 AD and 1250 AD. In Britain, for instance, these years witnessed the first appearance of a vernacular grammar of 'standardized linguistic forms' (c.1000 AD)[27]; the first occasion when teachers were required to be licenced by the church authorities (c.1100 AD)[28]; and the first record of separate premises being allocated specifically for educational purposes (c.1150 AD)[29].

There is room for debate about these criteria and their significance.[30] Nevertheless, further investigation suggested that they were not random occurrences but, rather, part of a general medieval interest in the design and deployment of administrative apparatuses. For instance, Maurice Keen's *A History of Medieval Europe* (1969) speaks of a 'twelfth century revolution in government'[31]; Richard Southern's *Western Society and the Church in the Middle Ages* (1970) refers to a 'steady elaboration of a machinery of government' in the two centuries after 1058[32]; and Michael Clanchy's *From Memory to Written Record* (1979) notes that, between 1066 and 1307, the 'most decisive' increase in English bureaucratic documents occurred 'within a decade or so on either side of 1200'[33].

Indeed, the connection between schooling and administrative reform is one of the themes in Alexander Murray's *Reason and Society in the Middle Ages* (1978). 'Roughly up to 1250', Murray claims, the church lacked 'properly educated recruits'. 'Endowment of schools was the outcome', he continues, an 'act not just of philanthropy but of long-term planning'. Elsewhere in the same volume, Murray also points to the new social efficiency considerations that these schools were designed to address. They were to turn adolescents 'not born and bred for supreme rule' into personnel who could be fitted easily into the 'ever-developing structures of centralized government'. Thus, as Murray indicates, the new schooling was designed more around texts for the training of administrators rather than around the manuals ('miroirs') used earlier for the education of hereditary princes.[34]

The general background to these innovations in education and government seems to have been a bid by the church for political (and economic) control over the fragmented authority of Western Europe's feudal rulers.[35] Headed by a succession of lawyer-Popes[36], funded by the fruits of 'prolonged prosperity in the countryside'[37], and armed with the newly-proclaimed doctrine of papal supremacy[38], the church set about reorganizing its resources to achieve this goal. Most notably, it sought to tighten its central and provincial administrations. Among other things, a sustained attempt was made to eliminate self-perpetuating (and self-aggrandizing) clerical dynasties. Thus, post-ordination celibacy was made compulsory by the Second Lateran Council (1139)[39]; child recruitment oblation was banned by twelfth-century reformed orders (for example, the Cistercians and Cluniacs)[40]; and the purchase of direct entry to monastic houses (simony) was outlawed by the fourth Lateran Council (1215)[41].

While these activities gradually purged the church of unwelcome and/or reluctant members, they also created new problems of recruitment and training. If simony and clerical marriage were to be abandoned, where was the church to obtain its new personnel? And if admission was to be restricted to near-adults, how were these raw recruits to be trained for ecclesiastical office? The first problem was easily solved. According to Murray, the elimination of dynasties opened up many new and attractive careers in the church. The problem of delayed recruitment, however, yielded less easily. Previously, recruits had been socialized into their ecclesiastical roles from an early age; but near-adults needed a more condensed form of training. To facilitate this latter process, the church developed new educational initiatives. For instance, the third (1179) and fourth (1215) Lateran Councils, respectively, agreed that masters should not be required to pay for their licences and that cathedrals and other large churches should make special financial provision to support in-house teachers of grammar (i.e. latin) and theology (cf. canon law).[42]

At one level — namely the spread and stabilization of cathedral schools — these changes might be regarded simply as the culmination of centuries of official exhortation.[43] But at another level (viz. schooling's new purposes) they represented a clear break with the past. Earlier cathedral schools (for example, Chartres) comprised a circle of disciples who, gathered round an influential leader (for example, Bernard of Chartres), had devoted themselves to the examination and interpretation of religious texts. Indeed, the major philosophical movement of the Middle Ages — scholasticism — took its name from such schools. The newer cathedral schools, however, had a less-elevated educational mission. Their products were not so much philosophers as field officers (for example, bishops) and troops (for example, parish priests) trained to superintend the 'front lines'[44] of the church's political campaigns. From these changes in organizational purpose came a new meaning for 'schola': whereas earlier schools had been populated by 'disciples', the new cathedral schools were populated by an alternative translation of 'discipuli' — 'pupils'.[45]

VI

By courtesy of this detour into medieval history, I acquired a better sense of 'schooling'. At the same time, however, I realized that my account was incomplete. It is relatively easy to explain the church's adoption of schooling in terms of the enforcement of celibacy and the reform of administrative procedures. But the same explanation cannot be used for the medieval merchants who took to schooling in the wake of the church. The merchants pose a different problem. If they reproduce biologically, why should they have sought to augment their within-family sociali-zation practices by means of education purchased (or acquired) from outsiders?

In addressing this issue I was able to strengthen my earlier ideas about 'social efficiency'. Like the church leaders, the merchants began, it seems, to pay greater attention to the consolidation of their present and future prospects. They regarded education as an investment — a means of managing (and expanding) their social capital.[46] If nothing else, it enabled them to acquire new skills (for example, 'arithmetic' practices derived from astronomy and astrology)[47] and new dispositions (for example, 'manners' drawn from courtly sources)[48] that gave their progeny an advantage in the inter-locked worlds of business and marriage.

The merchants seemed to have extended their socialization practices in at least four ways. First, by sending their children to be brought up in the families of their superiors; secondly, by patronizing existing cathedral schools; thirdly, by bringing cathedral-trained clerics into their own homes as tutors; and fourthly, by acting in a corporate manner and establishing schools for the collective upbringing of their young.[49] These options, however, differed widely in their control implications. High-cost solutions — for example, the employment of tutors — allowed high merchant control; whereas the lowest-cost solution — the use of existing cathedral schools — entailed a risk that children would be drawn into the church rather than returned to their parents.[50] In these respects, then, corporate-run merchant schools, using clerical teachers, represented a cost-efficient compromise. Inevitably, however, residual control problems remained. And it is these problems, I suggest, that help to explain the subsequent (i.e. sixteenth-century) introduction of 'classes' and 'curricula'. Renaissance merchants, like their medieval counterparts, continued to 'put out' the education of their young; yet, as in the wider conduct of their affairs, they developed new managerial techniques (cf. new accounting procedures) to increase the profitability of their investment.[51]

With these arguments about the efficiency of 'classes' and 'curricula' I moved, chronologically speaking, into the sixteenth century. But there was still some 200 years to explore before the onset of the Industrial Revolution. What intervening pedagogic transitions, if any, remained to be identified? One answer to this question had already been prefigured in my arguments about the connection between Calvinist discipline and the idea of a curriculum. If the medieval church had adopted schooling merely to discipline its cadre of teachers and preachers, Calvinists (and to some extent Lutherans) began to use schooling for a broader political purpose — the disciplining of the population at large.

Schooling, that is, underwent its own reformation. It took on an additional social mission — the ideological incorporation of the subordinate members of society. At one extreme, it continued to develop pedagogic forms suitable for those children whose social expectancy was to manage and to govern; while, at the other extreme, it began to develop new pedagogic forms — strongly catechetical[52] — for those whose social destiny was to obey and to follow. It seems, however, that these different pedagogic forms did not immediately yield a corresponding differentiation of school types. Just as the (smaller?) medieval cathedral schools had prepared children for either clerical or secular life, so post-Reformation schools seem to have accommodated a range of social fractions. In such schools, therefore, pedagogic practice may have been only weakly linked to social status.

In one sense, the resultant mismatches (for example, low-status pupils enjoying high-status pedagogic practices) might be regarded as socially inefficient. Yet, such mismatches could also be deliberately engineered in the interest of upward (and downward) mobility. If this was in fact the case, then seventeenth-century schooling was designed not so much to conserve the status quo as to accommodate a much more sophisticated model of social regulation (cf. the meritocratic ideals of the catholic and protestant reformers). But social regulation was not a new educational purpose. For a century or more the apprenticeship system had been managed along such lines. That is, successive revisions in guild statutes had been designed, among other things, to limit or to increase access to the social capital that accompanied guild membership.[53] Apprenticeship controls, however, were relatively guild-specific; whereas broad-based schooling had a much wider regulative potential. Its gradual adoption, I would suggest, gave the merchant and craft guilds — acting in concert as a kind of 'local' state — a more powerful instrument with which to administer the affairs of their own communities.

VII

Through identifying a possible link between schooling and social regulation, I also began to realize how schooling articulated with the early capitalism of the sixteenth and seventeenth centuries. Schooling became socially important because it offered a means of managing the 'common' (cf. unskilled)[54] labour market that had grown up outside the medieval guilds.

To understand this relationship between schooling and the labour market, it is necessary to distinguish feudalism from capitalism. Under feudalism, the labour market played a weak role in social affairs. The bulk of the population were directly socialized into their adult occupations. That is, men and women merely took up the tools, land etc. passed on by their forebears.

In the transition from feudalism to capitalism, however, this lifestyle was interrupted. The immediate and/or ultimate causes of this destabilization are a matter of controversy among historians. One line of argument, however, points to imbalances that arose between the food produced in the countryside and the population it was expected to support. To overcome food shortages, marginal landholders had a limited number of options: they could acquire more land, they could adopt more efficient forms of agriculture, or they could seek additional sources of income.

These options were taken up in different ways, and at different times in different parts of Europe. But their general effect was the same: landholdings grew in size; agricultural production changed in favour of cash crops that could be sold in urban markets; and squeezed-out landholders were driven to take up part-time employment as day-labourers for their more successful agricultural neighbours and/or as 'outworkers' (for example, spinners and weavers) for urban-based guild masters.[55]

In extreme cases, small landholders were entirely deprived of their land and their tools. They were left, therefore, to sell their only remaining asset — their capacity to work. Accordingly, a 'labour market' emerged where raw materials and equipment possessed by potential employers were matched to the 'labour power' of individual workers. If a successful match was obtained, the workers received a wage for the duration of their employment. If not, they were forced back to the labour market in search of another employer. For those without land, therefore, the only peaceful alternatives to wage labour were starvation and migration.[56]

As capitalism grew, the unwanted consequences of the labour market (for example, unemployment, mass migration and social unrest) became political as well as economic issues. Clearly, there was much to be gained in capitalist terms if the labour market could be more adequately supervised. Indeed, it was this political agenda that helps to account, on the one hand, for the emergence of strong centralist (i.e. 'absolutist') governments in the sixteenth and seventeenth centuries and, on the other hand, for the wave of national social legislation subsequently sponsored by these governments (for example, with respect to poverty, employment, apprenticeship and schooling).

Through these reforms — discussed, for instance in Catherine Lis and Hugo Joly's *Poverty and Capitalism in Pre-Industrial Europe* (1979)[57] and Wilbur K. Jordan's *Philanthropy in England 1480-1640* (1959)[58] — the capitalist 'state' emerged as a national political force. It acted, often through the agency of a national church, to maintain and advance the social order. Further, as the state's sphere of influence extended from 'local' to 'national' labour markets, so questions of social efficiency became issues of national efficiency (cf. the sixteenth-century appearance of the political concept of the 'commonwealth').[59]

It was at this time, too, that theorists of national (or 'universal') schooling came into their own. For instance, a disciple of Comenius — John Dury — made a direct connection between schooling, social regulation and the labour market in *A Supplement to the Reformed-School* (1650):

> In a well-reformed commonwealth . . . all the subjects thereof should in their youth be trained up in some schools fit for their capacities, and that over these schools, some overseers should be appointed to look to the course of their education, to see that none should be left destitute of some benefit of virtuous breeding, according to the several kinds of employments, whereunto they may be found most fit and inclineable.[60]

Diffusion of this concern for the integration of 'unskilled' labour into a wider system of social welfare was, I maintain, the background to an important seventeenth-century educational development: national support for the notion of 'charity' schools (i.e. schools designed for the poor and funded by the rich). But national support did not automatically result in the creation of a national (or unified) system of schools. In fact, different charity schools seem to have served contrasting social purposes. Some for instance, fostered upward social mobility by equipping children with the attitudes, tools, clothes and financial premiums necessary for admittance to craft and related occupations. Others, however, served conservative purposes by seeking to keep families from falling below the subsistence threshold (for example, by providing food for their pupils).

Despite these internal variations, the general institution of charity schooling served a unified purpose. It stood between family socialization practices and the labour market. In times of high unemployment, for instance, charity schooling could conserve a local pool of labour by reducing migration out of a district; and in times of labour shortage it could lower the barriers that, otherwise, kept poor children from becoming apprentices.[61]

By the early eighteenth century, then, the spread of the charity school idea meant that embryonic school systems could be found in a range of European countries (for example, England, France, Holland). Within a capitalist framework, such systems had the important social function of regulating access to adult labour markets. Indeed, through their accompanying processes of pedagogic and structural regulation, such systems helped to maintain, and even create, specific configurations of the labour market.

VIII

To arrive at this appreciation of schooling I had made a lengthy detour into the realms of educational history and educational theory.[62] En route, my attention had been focused upon the link between schooling and the labour market; and upon the ways in which schooling served (or was intended to serve) different interpretations of social efficiency. Not surprisingly, these new insights served the next stage of my inquiries.

In August 1983, I returned to one of the pivotal 'episodes' identified in my original framework — the pedagogic transformations that, at the end of the nineteenth century, accompanied the transition from batch to individualized production. The account of this episode had been taking shape in my mind for a number of years: I had already decided to follow the cutting edge of capitalism across the Atlantic to the

USA; I had selected a focusing framework — the association between pedagogic changes and innovations in industrial management; and I had discovered a corpus of source material — the University of Glasgow's almost unbroken run of US Commissioner of Education Reports (viz. 1873-1916). By 1983, too, I was well aware of the discussions stimulated by Raymond Callahan's account of scientific management in *Education and the Cult of Efficiency* (1962)[63] and by Harry Braverman's analysis of industrial change in *Labour and Monopoly Capital* (1974)[64]. Yet important issues still remained to be tackled. For instance, Callahan's argument had paid very little attention to the period before 1900; and Braverman's work (and that of his critics and followers) had been relatively silent about the connections between the labour market and schooling.

To bridge these gaps I began with a systematic search through the US Commissioners' Reports, noting the ideas and material that seemed relevant to my overall scheme. Ultimately, this material proved very useful but, at the time, I found it contained very little overt discussion of the broader social and economic changes that accompanied the transformation of late nineteenth-century American schooling. Once again, I had to step back from my pedagogic sources — this time to take a broader look at American history.

The subsequent detour enabled me to tie together some hitherto disparate phenomena. First, I noted an association, prominent in the 1880s and later years, between the outbreak of 'labour problems' and the spread of machine-paced production lines. Secondly, I discerned a connection between these labour problems and the 'progressive' proposal that regulation of the labour market should be the overall responsibility of the state. And, thirdly, I realized that Darwin's biological theory (viz. that successful evolution rests upon the exploitation of differences among members of the same species) had focused greater attention on the promotion of individualization in schools.

Within this economic and ideological climate, American school authorities had the two-fold task of responding to the social problems created by the spread of wage labour while, at the same time, making a general contribution to the advancement of 'progress' (i.e. social evolution). How, then, were these different tasks to be reconciled in pedagogic terms? Slowly, I put together a defensible story using the US Commissioner's Reports; the extensive range of nineteenth-century US educational pamphlets held in the University of Glasgow's Library; a range of documents sent to me by correspondents in the USA; and additional material furnished by the British Library inter-library loans service.[65] Particularly useful were works written by school superintendents who, in common with British 'masters of method', were in touch with both schoolroom practices and the ideological currents that informed them.

The pedagogic 'tracer' that I used for this investigation was a form of class teaching known in the USA as the 'recitation'. In that country the 'simultaneous' class recitation had, in the 1830s and 1840s, begun to replace earlier individualized forms of instruction. Like its British analogue — with which it presumably shared a common Enlightenment ancestry — the simultaneous recitation was claimed to effect a more efficient moral supervision of a citizenry increasingly disrupted by the spread of industrialization. In turn, this class-based supervision was further strengthened in the 1850s and 1860s as pupils from one-teacher schools were regrouped within the hierarchical structures of the 'graded' or 'union' school.

By the 1870s and 1880s, however, the 'lockstep' methods that grew from these economies of scale began, themselves, to come under attack. Calls were made (for example, by William T. Harris, Superintendent of St Louis) for more 'elastic'[66] promotion of pupils — a proposal that resonated not only with social-Darwinist calls for greater individualization but also, at a more mundane level, with the difficulties school managers faced in maintaining efficient teacher-pupil ratios in the sparsely-populated upper grades. Finally, opposition to the class recitation widened again in the 1890s. Teaching 'individuals not classes' became a new goal for schools — a means of 'breaking up the masses'[67] whose presumed propensity towards unsocial group behaviour was held to be a threat to industrial peace.

In many cases, such appeals in favour of pedagogic individualization were part of a more general opposition to state intervention. From such a standpoint, the 'survival of the fittest' was deemed to be as applicable to the management of schooling as it was to the organization of industry. By the second decade of the twentieth century, however, such free-market policies had become less popular. It was widely recognized that their adoption created a range of secondary social problems (for example, poverty, unemployment) whose remediation proved costly to the state and its tax-payers. A new solution was canvassed. 'True' individualism was to be achieved, not through unbridled competition but through role-differentiation.[68] Every child had a different place in the sun, and it fell to the state to help them find it.

The 'comprehensive high school' (c. 1918) was the outcome of this new thinking. It was intended not merely as an agency of individual citizen formation, but also as an instrument of structural harmonization. Moreover, a balanced and socially-coherent society was also deemed to be a united society. Further, these revised goals for schooling were to be achieved through new pedagogic procedures. Again, the recitation was remoulded to these ends. It re-emerged in a 'socialized' form. Class teaching was designed around group-based conversations and discussions that, so its protagonists believed, would cultivate an ethos of collective responsibility appropriate to the functioning of a socially-efficient capitalist democracy.

Overall, the Progressive aspiration seems to have been realized. The state did, indeed, take on a coordinating and regulatory role, finding its voice in a series of quasi-official committees that reported in the period between 1890 and 1920 (for example, the 'Committee of Ten' on the high school, 1893; the 'Committee of Fifteen' on elementary education, 1895; the Committee on 'The Economy of Time in Education', 1913; and the 'Cardinal Principles' Committee on Secondary Education, 1918). The general tenor of the committees' proposals was towards the creation of an integrated school system. Three associated innovations reflected these concerns. First, the accomplishment of compulsory schooling — largely completed by 1918[69] — which brought all children within the legitimate reach of the state. Secondly, the establishment of the comprehensive secondary school that brought a range of differentiated 'curriculums' under the same roof[70]. And thirdly, the creation of pedagogic forms that blended an appeal to individual differences with a concern for social adjustment and 'social unification'[71].

In turn, schooling took on a new historical significance. Its importance derived not simply from its ability to transmit particular occupational skills, to create a morally-trained labour force, or to mediate access to the labour market. Rather, its importance in the twentieth century resided in its capacity — backed up by the power of centralized governments and the welfare state — to take a much more interventionist role in shaping (and reshaping) the labour market. Indeed, events in the USA prior to 1920 marked only the beginnings of these closer state/school/labour market relationships. A full analysis, which would examine more recent Keynesian and monetarist views of state intervention, lies beyond the scope of this book.

IX

The final phase of my research programme coincided with a twelve-month period of study-leave that commenced in October 1984. By this stage I had one remaining 'episode' to explore: the pedagogic circumstances surrounding the emergence of 'charity' schooling in the seventeenth century. Earlier, I had been drawn by the claim, originally made in the nineteenth-century, that simultaneous instruction had been invented by Jean Baptist de la Salle (1651-1719), a French priest who, in turn, is also remembered as the founder of a teaching order (The Brothers of the Christian Schools) and the compiler of a minutely-choreographed pedagogic manual — *The Conduct of Christian Schools*.

I was curious about the nineteenth-century claim. If true, De la Salle's batch production methods anticipated the factory system by about 100 years. In the light of this apparent anomaly, and in the light of the earlier difficulties I had encountered using texts in translation, I searched out the French original of De la Salle's manual. I soon recognized, first, that *The Conduct of Christian Schools* does not contain the term 'simultaneous instruction'; and, second, that De la Salle's pedagogical methods make no appeal to the kind of intra-group psychological processes that were central to David Stow's conception of class teaching.[72] Yet, I was still unsure how the confusion had arisen. I needed to search out further French sources — a process that took several weeks.

In the interim, I returned to the class/curriculum paper. Besides improving its readability, I wanted to weave three more threads into the argument. First, my attention had been drawn (by a postgraduate student, Allan Milligan) to the fact that John Calvin regularly preached that life on earth is an obstacle course which all true Calvinists should struggle to complete. Did Calvin use curriculum in these instances, or did he use other terms (for example, cursus)? Secondly, Keith Hoskin (University of Warwick) had directed my attention to the fact that, in the sixteenth century, the rise of the term 'method' had paralleled the emergence of the term 'curriculum'. That is, both came to denote a formalized set of operations: the 'method' of science provided a recipe for extracting knowledge from nature; while the 'curriculum' of schooling provided an analogous recipe for the promulgation of such knowledge. Could, therefore, the secondary literature on the history of 'method' throw a side-light on the history of curriculum? Finally, my failure to find any evidence of 'curriculum' in the manuscript records of the University of Geneva (which I visited in the summer of 1983) had left me with a stronger sense that Glasgow or Leiden (and not Geneva) had been its birthplace.

By the time I was ready to return to De la Salle, two options had presented themselves: either I could set the record straight on De la Salle's contribution to simultaneous instruction, or I could take on the more difficult task of locating his work in the wider context of seventeenth-century France.

In deciding upon the broader canvas, my task was to relate De la

Salle not only to simultaneous instruction but also to the history of charity schooling, and to the history of France. Already, of course, I had a general framework — charity schooling's association with the emergence of the able-bodied poor — but I knew very little about the particularity of De la Salle's contribution to schooling. Why De la Salle? Why France? Further, I had no real idea why so many historians — even those who played down his contribution to simultaneous instruction — were ready to claim that De la Salle's pedagogy had made a significant break with the past.

One popular explanation of De la Salle's originality derives from his decision to abandon latin as a teaching medium. It is claimed that, by differentiating latin from vernacular instruction, De la Salle fostered the creation (at least in France) of separate schools for the children of wage labourers. In these terms, De la Salle is regarded as an important pioneer in the history of European 'elementary' schooling.

This explanation has some force, but two items of data speak against it. First, De la Salle did, in fact, make provision for the teaching of latin (albeit only in the upper levels of his schools); and secondly, the schools of his Congregation seemed to have been particularly popular in medium-sized towns (i.e. those without a large population of wage labourers). Taken together, however, these data allow an alternative explanation: that De la Salle's formulations comprised a pedagogic amalgam that was ideally suited to towns that had neither enough 'poor' families for a separate charity school, nor enough wealthy families to sustain a local latin-based 'college'. From this perspective, then, De la Salle was more of a 'transitional' than a 'revolutionary' figure.

Despite my doubts about De la Salle's role in the emergence of a separate system of 'elementary' schooling, I still found originality in other aspects of his work. Following Michel Foucault (in *Discipline and Punish: The Birth of the Prison,* 1979)[73], I was drawn to the regulatory potential embedded in the fine detail of De la Salle's *The Conduct of Christian Schools.* I began to realize De la Salle's originality derived not from the specificity of his pedagogic recommendations, but from the way that, in combination, they created a new pedagogic 'order'. De la Salle, that is, projected a new over-arching rationality for schooling: pupils were expected to attend (both senses) all the time, and their every movement was to be accounted for in time and space.

But what organizing principles underpinned De la Salle's cosmology? And where had they come from? I floundered for two or three weeks but, as my general appreciation of French history grew, an explanation began to emerge — that De la Salle's work was part of the seventeenth-century intellectual revolution associated with the name of

René Descartes. If Descartes had made a break with the past — as most commentators suggest — then, by the same token, I could defensibly entertain a similar claim for De la Salle.

Accordingly, the detail in *The Conduct of Christian Schools* was more than mere decoration: it described how schooling could be coherently organized as a socially efficient and self-regulating educational 'machine'. From this perspective, De la Salle's detail was but one manifestation of a more general aspiration of the Scientific Revolution: the adoption of 'systematic' (or 'rational') approaches to the design and management of social institutions.

X

At the beginning of April 1985 I travelled to Sweden — Descartes' deathplace — having recently completed a reasonable draft of the De la Salle chapter. I had been drawn to Stockholm by the contents of *Between Hope and Happening: Text and Context in Curriculum*[74], a monograph written by Ulf Lundgren of the Stockholm Institute of Education. Like me, Ulf has a background in classroom research; and, like me too, he has subsequently nurtured an additional interest in the historical and social contexts that give meaning to schoolroom life. Our shared interest, however, had been pursued in different yet complementary ways. I had explored the educational record, while Ulf had conducted a series of theoretical modelling exercises — reported in *Between Hope and Happening* (and elsewhere). For such reasons, then, Stockholm seemed an ideal place to tease out the pivotal theoretical assumptions of my research programme and, in turn, use them as a basis for the introductory and concluding chapters of this book.

First I turned to the introductory chapter. I aimed to write for a wide educational audience, not just historians or classroom researchers. How could I provide access to the ideas and themes of my research programme? Should I, for instance, adopt an analytic approach and lay out my organizing principles as a series of premises, definitions, diagrams and theorems? Or would such an abstract style serve merely to exclude the general educational reader? Equally, was my working title — *Studies in the Development of Schooling* — an adequate signpost to the intentions as well as the contents of the case studies?

Both these difficulties were overcome while I was in Sweden. An alternative format for the opening chapter came quickly to hand. Within a few days of arriving in Stockholm, I was reminded by one of Ulf Lundgren's colleagues — Kerstin Mattsson — of an appendix I had written for the original open plan study. Entitled 'A methodological diary', it discussed the day-to-day dilemmas and decisions that had helped to flavour the final report.[75] And, as important, the diary had given outside readers a more open and informed basis for evaluating the report's findings and interpretations. For these reasons, then, I decided to write an equivalent introductory framework for this book. If successful, it would give access not only to the initial aims of my ten-year research programme but also to some of the intervening events that, for good or ill, had exerted a formative influence along the way.

This general problem of shaping a book for a specific audience also lay behind my search for a suitable title. I felt uneasy about *Studies in the Development of Schooling*. It over-emphasized the historical substance of the case studies, understating the wider theoretical issues that they illustrated and tested. Discussions in Stockholm deepened these doubts. My theoretical constructs (for example, 'state', 'labour market', 'social efficiency') received much more critical attention than the factual content of the supporting arguments. Seminar audiences validated my theoretical notions, not by reference to the data that I had adduced but, rather, against their own knowledge of the Swedish educational record. To them, the case studies were not so much repositories of historical data as vehicles for educational theory. Hence, they too believed that my original title was unnecessarily misleading.

Towards the end of my stay in Sweden I was able to overcome this difficulty. The opportunity arose when I came to think about the final chapter of this book. Initially, I had no real sense of what it might contain. Should it be a concluding statement? Or should it merely be a catalogue of unfinished business? In one sense, I had already addressed both these concerns: the introductory chapter was to embody an up-to-date statement of my thinking; and the case studies were to indicate where further research might be prosecuted. So what, then, remained to be said? Eventually, a workable solution came to mind. I began to assemble a set of propositions that could stand both as a condensed portrayal of my enquiries and as a set of generalizations (or hypotheses) that extended beyond the confines of the book. In recognition of these outcomes — the finished and unfinished attributes of my research programme — I lighted upon a new title for this book — *Towards a Theory of Schooling*.

Notes

1   Walker, R. (1971) *The social setting of the classroom: A review of observational studies and research,* MPhil. thesis, London, University of London, p.143.
2   Lundgren, U.P. (1979) *School Curricula: Content and Structure and their Effects on Educational and Occupational Careers,* Stockholm Institute of Education Department of Educational Research, Reports on Education and Psychology No.2, p.42.
3   Hall, S. (1981) 'Schooling, state and society', in Dale, R., Esland, G., Fergusson, R. and MacDonald, M. (Eds), *Education and the State: Volume 1: Schooling and the National Interest,* Lewes, p.13.
4   Hamilton, D. (1977) *In Search of Structure: A Case Study of a New Scottish Open Plan Primary School,* London.
5   A rigorous analysis of past pedagogies can be found in Broudy, H. and Palmer J.R. (1965) *Exemplars of teaching Method,* Chicago. The weakness of their account, however, is that it evaluates the past against a pedagogical model derived from twentieth-century circumstances. Other English-language secondary sources that I have consulted include Avery, G. (1967) *School Remembered: an Anthology,* London; Lass, A.H. and Tasman, N.L. (1981) *Going to school: An Anthology of Prose about Teachers and Students,* New York; Henderson, B.L.K. (n.d.) *Schoolboys of Other Days,* London; Brown, J.H. (1933) *Elizabethan Schooldays,* Oxford; (Anon.) (n.d.) *Schools and Scholars in History,* London; Rait, R.S. (1912) *Life in the Medieval University,* Cambridge; Watson, F. (1916) *The Old Grammar Schools,* Cambridge; and Timbs, J. (n.d.) *Schooldays of Eminent Men,* London. For collections of paintings and other artefacts of schooling, see Alt, R. (1960) *Bilderatlas zur Schul- und Erziehungs Geschichte* (Vol. 1), Berlin, and Broby-Johansen, R. (1974) *Skolen i Kunsten, Kunsten i Skolen,* Copenhagen (I am grateful to Kersti Hasselberg of the Stockholm Institute of Education for this last reference).
6   My systematic literature search was greatly assisted by Craigie, J. (1970) *A Bibliography of Scottish Education before 1872,* London, and (1974) *A Bibliography of Scottish Education 1872-1972,* London; Higson, C.W.J. (1967) *Sources for the History of Education,* London and (1976) *Supplement to Sources for the History of Education,* London.
7   Wilderspin, S. (1823) *On the Importance of Educating the Infant Children of the Poor,* London. This early use of class room is also noted in Seaborne, M. (1971) *The English School: Its Architecture and Organisation 1370-1870,* London, p.142.
8   The work of my fellowship year is reported in (1978) *Classroom Research and the Evolution of the Classroom System: Some Interim Papers,* Glasgow, University of Glasgow Department of Education (mimeo). Although the SSRC declined to accept my report, copies are available from the US Education Resources Information Center (ERIC), Document Number ED 168 139.
9   For cautionary comments on the secondary literature of British educational history see Silver, H. (1977) 'Aspects of neglect: The strange case of Victorian popular education', *Oxford Review of Education,* 3, pp.57-69; Simon, B. (1966) 'The history of education', in Tibble J.W. (Ed), *The*

       Study of Education, London, pp.91-131; and Withrington, D. (1970) 'What is and what might be: Some reflections on the writing of Scottish educational history', *Scottish Educational Studies,* 2, pp.110-8. See also, Bailyn, B. (1960) *Education in the Forming of American Society* (reprinted New York, 1972).

10   Dobb, M. (1946) *Studies in the Development of Capitalism,* London.

11   Unwin, G. (1904) *Industrial Organisation in the Sixteenth and Seventeenth Centuries,* Oxford.

12   Karier, C., Violas, P.C. and Spring, J. (1973) *Roots of Crisis: American Education in the Twentieth Century,* Chicago, IL.

13   Tyack, D. (1974) *The One Best System: A History of American Urban Education,* Cambridge, MA.

14   Pollard, S. (1965) *The Genesis of Modern Management: A Study of the Industrial Revolution in Great Britain,* London.

15   My own views on the connection between Robert Owen as a capitalist and Robert Owen as an educator are reported in Hamilton, D. (1983) 'Robert Owen and education: A reassessment' in Humes, W. and Paterson, H. (Eds) *Scottish Culture and Scottish Education 1800-1980,* Edinburgh, pp.9-24.

16   Stow, D. (1850) *The Training System,* London, pp.153-7. Eleven editions of David Stow's *The Training System* are believed to have been issued between the early 1830s and 1859 (see White, G.A. (1983) *Silks and saints: David Stow and infant education 1816-1836,* MEd thesis, University of Glasgow, pp.19-20).

17   See Hamilton, D. (1980) 'Adam Smith and the moral economy of the classroom system', *Journal of Curriculum Studies,* 12, pp.281-98.

18   Ariès, P. (1962) *Centuries of Childhood,* New York.

19   In the final section of *De Ratione Studii,* Woodward uses 'class' whereas the original uses 'pueri' (children/boys). See, respectively, Woodward, W.H. (1904) *Desiderius Erasmus Concerning the Aim and Method of Education,* Cambridge, p.177 and (1969) *Erasmi Opera Omnia,* Vol 2, Amsterdam. p.145.

20   Tawney, R. (1942) *Religion and the Rise of Capitalism,* Harmondsworth. Throughout these notes I have identified books according to the edition used in my investigations. To avoid apparent anachronisms in the text, however, I have sometimes substituted the date of earliest publication. In addition, all translations from foreign languages are my own.

21   Hamilton, D. and Gibbons, M. (1980) 'Notes on the origins of the educational terms class and curriculum', paper presented at the annual meeting of the American Educational Research Association (ERIC No. ED 183 453).

22   Selleck, R.J.W. (1968) *The New Education 1870-1914,* London.

23   Dunn, H. (c.1837) *Principles of Teaching,* London.

24   Findlay, J.J. (1902) *Principles of Class Teaching,* London. On the basis of my searches I produced a handlist of manuals of method that was published in the *Bulletin of the History of Education Society,* nos. 29 (1982) and 33 (1984).

25   Hamilton, D. (1981) 'On simultaneous instruction and the early evolution of class teaching', Glasgow, University of Glasgow Department of Education, mimeo.

26 My unease with 'social control' and 'internal momentum' theories of pedagogic change arose, in part, from reading such works as Sharp, R. and Green, A. (1975) *Education and Social Control,* London, Johnson, R. (1970) 'Educational policy and social control in early Victorian England', *Past & Present,* 49, pp.96-119; and Jones, K. and Williamson, K. (1979) 'The birth of the schoolroom', *Ideology and Consciousness,* 6, pp.59-110.

27 Bullough, D.A. (1972) 'The educational tradition in England from Alfred to Aelfric: teaching utrisque linguae', *La Scuola nell'Occidente Latino dell Alto Medioevo* (volume 19 of the Settimani di Studio del Centro Italiano di Studi sull'Alto Medioevo), Spoleto, p.491.

28 Leach, A.F. (1915) *The Schools of Medieval England,* London, p.111ff; and Parry, A.W. (1920) *Education in England in the Middle Ages,* London, p.82 ('The granting of licences was the first separate recognition of the teaching profession in England').

29 Parry, A.W. (1920) *op cit,* p.89. There is, it should be noted, an important difference between my conceptualization of 'school' and my conceptualization of 'schooling'. The latter is defined by reference to a particular pedagogic process, not by reference to its association with schoolrooms, classrooms etc. Thus, I accept that 'schooling' can take place without schools, just as schools can be sites of 'education', as well as 'schooling'.

30 To point to the twelfth century as the seedbed of 'schooling' is, I accept, likely to be a controversial claim. Other commentators, for instance, might want to draw attention to the 'schools' of Charlmagne or even to the 'schools' of ancient Greece and Rome. Certainly, these earlier 'schools' deserve further attention. Nevertheless, the period 1000-1200 remains historically significant. Cf. 'While between the seventh and the eleventh centuries, the conditions of education hardly changed, the crisis that agitated schooling in the middle of the eleventh century is a sign that another Middle Age is beginning' (Riché, P. (1979) *Les Ecoles et l'Enseignement dans l'Occident Chrétien de la fin du Ve au Milieu du XIe Siècle,* Paris, p.6).

31 Keen, M. (1969) *A History of Medieval Europe,* Harmondsworth, p.103.

32 Southern, R.W. (1970) *Western Society and Church in the Middle Ages,* Harmondsworth, p.106.

33 Clanchy, N.T. (1979) *From Memory to Written Record,* London, p.48.

34 Murray, A. (1978) *Reason and Society in the Middle Ages,* Oxford, pp.302-3 and 121.

35 For a wide-ranging discussion of the 'new state and the new church' see Heer, F. (1963) *The Medieval World,* New York, chapter 14.

36 Southern, R.W. (1970) *op cit,* pp.131-2 ('Every notable pope from 1159-1303 was a lawyer').

37 Duby, G. (1968) *Rural Economy and Country Life in the Medieval West,* London, pp.63-4 ('Without prolonged prosperity in the countryside the expansion of western civilization as a whole during the eleventh, twelfth and thirteenth centuries would be incomprehensible'). The impact of changing agrarian relationships upon the face of medieval Europe is discussed in great detail in Brenner, R. (1976) 'Agrarian class structure and economic development in pre-industrial Europe', *Past and Present,* 70,

pp.30-75 and *Past & Present* (1982) 97, pp.17-113. In particular, Brenner stresses the interplay between economic factors and political factors (i.e. 'extra-economic compulsion') in the shaping of social life.

38 Southern, R.W. (1970) *op cit,* pp.104-6 ('From about the middle of the twelfth century, the popes began for the first time to take the title "Vicar of Christ", and to claim it for themselves alone . . . Armed with this new title, precisely interpreted, the way was clear for the full exercise of power in the name of the "King of Kings and Lord of Lords to whom every knee shall bow, of things in heaven and things in (sic) earth"').

39 See the entry for 'celibacy' in Meagher, P.K., O'Brien, T.C. and Aherne, C.M. (1979) *Encyclopedic Dictionary of Religion,* Washington D.C. ('A decisive step was taken when Lateran Council II (1139) declared that marriages of sub-deacons, deacons and priests after ordination was not only unlawful but invalid. Thenceforth, for the latin Church, only those who freely accepted strict celibacy . . . were to be admitted to higher office . . . [These reforms] brought in a fairly high level of compliance by the mid-thirteenth century'). 'Lateran Council' was the name given to General Councils that met in the cathedral church of St John in Laterano, Rome.

40 Lynch, J.H. (1976) *Simoniacal Entry into Religious Life from 1000 to 1260: A Social, Economic and Legal Study,* Columbus, OH, p.39 ('Thus, in the mid-twelfth century child oblation was in decline, banished entirely in many of the new orders and regarded with ambivalence even within the older traditions').

41 *Ibid.,* chapters 7 and 8. The fourth Lateran Council also consolidated the authority of the church in other ways: it made 'auricular' confession a required sacrament; and gave particular emphasis to the elimination of internal heresy (see, respectively, Potter, G.R. and Greengrass, M. (Eds) (1983) *John Calvin,* London, p.40; and Heer, F. (1963) *op cit,* p.140).

42 See Leach, A.F. (1915) *op cit,* p.156. It should be noted, of course, that papal exhortation did not automatically have an impact upon ecclesiastical practice (see, for instance, Baldwin, J.W. (1982) 'Masters at Paris from 1179 to 1215: A social perspective' in Benson, R.L. and Constable, G. (Eds) *Renaissance and Renewal in the Twelfth Century,* Oxford, p.143).

43 Pre-twelfth century legislation on schools and schooling is summarized in Knowles, D. (1962) *The Evolution of Medieval Thought,* New York, pp.71-2.

44 See Duby, G. (1980) *The Three Orders: Feudal Society Imagined,* Chicago, IL, p.236. Cf. 'During the course of the twelfth century the parish in northern France became more and more the basic cell of the seigneurial organism . . . But the custodians of public power expected more from the bishops, canons and curates than just sermons, anathemas and instructions issued in the confessional. The clerks knew how to write, count and keep books. Everywhere available for service, they alone could effectively run the brand new administrative machinery, and appropriately channel into the coffers of the state the surplus produced not only by agriculture but also, in steadily increasing amounts, by vineyards, pastures and forests' (*Ibid,* pp.233-4); and 'the reformed church had more and more need for clerics instructed and capable of preaching to the people an orthodox doctrine' (Riché, P. (1979) *op cit,* p.342).

45 For alternative translations of 'discipulus' see Leach, A.F. (1911) *Educational Charters and Documents 598-1909,* Cambridge, pp.7 and 15. For an early discussion of the etymology of 'schola' see Paré, G., Brunet, A. and Tremblay, P. (1933) *La Renaissance du XIIᵉ Siècle: Les Écoles et l'Enseignement,* Paris, pp.59-60. For a more recent cognate discussion of schooling see various contributions to Benson, R.L. and Constable, G. (Eds) (1982) *Renaissance and Renewal in the Twelfth Century,* Oxford. Leclerq states that 'it is the meaning of "school" itself that is now in question' (p.72); Constable reports that an emphasis on 'preaching and teaching' became apparent in the new theological texts that accompanied the church's shift from apostolic (i.e. monastic) to evangelical (missionary) policies (p.55); Rouse and Rouse indicate that the formalization of a pedagogic 'apparatus' towards the end of the twelfth century was jointly linked to the 'attention paid to schools for the instruction of the clergy' and to 'an emphasis upon the instruction of the laity through preaching' (pp.224-5); and, finally, Southern speaks of the 'fairly rapid disengagement of "higher studies" from cathedrals', which, thereafter, 'existed primarily to provide education for a liturgical community or for a diocesan clergy' (p.118). The twelfth century also coincided with an associated change in the organization of cathedral chapters: 'Miniatures of the early twelfth century show that the bishop [at Chartres] still fulfilled the duty of chief teacher. But in 1115 a change of organization came about; the Chancellor whose function it had previously been to deputize for, and assist, the bishop withdrew altogether from taking any immediate part in the life of the school and confined himself to being its patron. These functions which the Chancellor had formerly fulfilled were now handed over in turn to the so-called *magister scholae,* the schoolmaster' (Klibansky, R. (1966) 'The school of Chartres' in Clagett, M., Post, G. and Reynolds, R. (Eds) *Twelfth Century Europe and the Foundations of Modern Society,* Madison, WI, p.4).

46 The existence of social efficiency thinking in the late Middle Ages is undisputed. The French aristocracy began to be 'won over by the idea of profit' in the twelfth century (Duby, G. (1968) *op cit,* p.72); the first accounts to calculate the profit and loss of an English feudal manor date from the fourteenth century (Clanchy, M.T. (1979) *op cit,* p.71); and the use of accounting as a 'tool of management and control' had been taken up by Italian merchants before 1400 (De Roover, R. (1956) 'The development of accounting prior to Luca Paciola according to the account books of medieval merchants' reprinted in Littleton, A.C. and Yamey, B.S. (Eds) *Studies in the History of Accounting,* London, p.118). Indeed, one commentator has claimed, in respect of the same period, that the 'criterion of utility . . . pervades the entire form of the family' (Teneti, A. (1977) 'Famille bourgeoise et idéologie au bas Moyen Age' in Duby, G. and le Goff, J. (Eds) *Famille et Parenté dans l'Occident Mediévale,* Rome, p.439).

47 For the early history of European arithmetic see Murray, A. (1978) *op cit,* chapters 6-8; and Irvine, T.A. (1982) *Number consciousness and the rise of capitalism: some preliminary considerations,* MEd thesis, Glasgow, University of Glasgow.

48 For an analysis of medieval and renaissance 'manners' see Elias, N. (1978) *The Civilising Process,* Oxford.

49   For the various educational options taken up by wealthy medieval parents
      see, variously, Gardiner, D. (1929) *English Girlhood at School,* Oxford,
      chapters 5 and 6; Goodrich, M. (1983) 'Encyclopedic literature:
      Childrearing in the Middle Ages', *History of Education,* 12, pp.1-8; Moran,
      J.H. (1979) *Education and Learning in the City of York 1300-1560,* York,
      University of York, Borthwick Institute of Historical Research; and
      Pirenne, H. (1929) 'L'instruction des marchands au Moyen Age', *Annales
      D'Histoire Économiques et Sociale,* 1, pp.13-28.

50   *Ibid.,* 20.

51   The general relationship between family structure and economic life needs
      further attention. Profitable starting points include Duby, G. and le Goff,
      J. (Eds) (1977) *op cit,* Hughes, D.O. (1975) 'Urban growth and family
      structure in Medieval Genoa', *Past & Present,* 66, pp.2-28; and Flandrin,
      J. (1979) *Families in Former Times,* Cambridge. Equally, attention might
      be given to the differences, if any, between the educational practices of the
      merchant and craft guilds.

52   Cf. 'We situate the origins of the modern catechism between 1541 and
      1660' and '[the catechism was] the hinge between the spiritual elites and
      the mass of the faithful, between the idea of reform indicated by the
      Council of Trent and its realization in the course of the [following
      century]' (Dhotel, J-C. (1967) *Les Origines du Catéchisme Moderne d'après les
      Premiers Manuels Imprimés en France,* Paris, pp.9 and 13).

53   For evidence of regulatory guild practices see Dunlop, O.J. and Denman,
      R.D. (1912) *English Apprenticeship and Child Labour: a History,* London,
      84ff; and McMahon, C.P. (1947) *Education in Fifteenth Century England,*
      Baltimore, MD, p.151 ('It was the craft guilds' rigid system of
      apprenticeship that gave them their power').

54   The economic categories 'skilled' and 'unskilled' were not, to my
      knowledge, widely used in the seventeenth century; and even in the
      Wealth of Nations (1776), Adam Smith chose to contrast 'skilled' with
      'common' labour. Accordingly, my use of the term 'unskilled' is intended
      primarily to indicate that, like schooling, the labour market has been
      partitioned (or 'segmented') according to a variety of historically-
      contingent criteria. For the economic concept of segmentation, see
      Carnoy, M. (1980) 'Segmented labour markets' in Carnoy, M., Levin,
      H.M. and King, K. (Eds) *Education, Work, Employment II,* Paris,
      UNESCO, pp.9-121.

55   For the transition from feudalism to capitalism see, among others, Hilton,
      R. (Ed) (1978) *The Transition from Feudalism to Capitalism,* London; Hill,
      C. (1969) *Society and Puritanism in Pre-Revolutionary England,* London;
      Hill, C. (1969b) *Reformation and Industrial Revolution,* Harmondsworth;
      Cohen, G.A. (1978) *Karl Marx's Theory of History: A Defence,* Oxford;
      Dobb, M. (1946) *op cit;* and Brenner, R. (1976) *op cit.*

56   The association between wage labour and the lack of property is indicated
      in the observation that by the third decade of the sixteenth century, 'no
      less than 1375 of the 2277 inhabitants recorded in the Hundred of
      Babergh in southern Suffolk [England], one of the most industrialized
      parts of the country, possessed neither land nor house' (Lis, C. and Joly,
      H. (1979) *Poverty and Capitalism in Pre-Industrial Europe,* Hassocks, p.71).

57 *Ibid.*
58 Jordan, W.K. (1959) *Philanthropy in England 1480-1660: A Study of the Changing Pattern of English Social Aspirations,* London.
59 The *Oxford English Dictionary* suggests that, in the sixteenth century, 'commonwealth' became the 'ordinary English term' for the 'whole body of people constituting a nation or state'.
60 See Vincent, W.A. (1950) *The State and School Education 1640-1660 in England and Wales,* London, p.33.
61 My interpretation of charity schooling derives, to a large degree, from Simon, J. (1968) 'Was there a charity school movement? The Leicestershire evidence' in Simon, B. (Ed) *Education in Leicestershire 1540-1940,* Leicester, pp.55-100 (cf. 'Shortage of labour had caused much of the interest in the way of the life of the poor', p.93); and from Clarke, W.K.L. (1959) *A History of the SPCK,* London (cf. 'Writing and arithmetic were of secondary importance . . . the scholars were to be "conditioned" for their walk in life', p.22). Complementary French and Scottish evidence for the diverse purposes served by charity schooling can be found in Poutet, Y. (1971) 'L'Enseignement des Pauvres dans la France du XVIIᵉ Siècle', *Dixseptième Siècle,* 90-91, pp.87-110; and Mason, J. (1954) 'Scottish charity schools of the eighteenth century', *Scottish Historical Review,* 33, pp.1-13. In an important sense, the history of charity schooling is the history of the penetration of the labour market into the organization of popular schooling.
62 See Hamilton, D. (1983) 'Schooling and capitalism 1100-1800: Some points of departure', paper presented at the annual meeting of the British Educational Research Association, London.
63 Callahan, R. (1962) *Education and the Cult of Efficiency: A study of the Social Forces that have Shaped the Administration of the Public Schools,* Chicago, IL.
64 Braverman, H. (1974) *Labor and Monopoly Capital: The Degradation of Work in the Twentieth Century,* New York.
65 In the preparation of this book I have consulted over 200 sources supplied through the British Library Loans Service.
66 Harris, W.T. (1891-2) *Annual Report* of the St Louis Superintendent of schools reprinted in the *Annual Report* of the U.S. Commissioner of Education, p.611.
67 Jordan, D.S. (1903) *The Care and Culture of Men,* San Francisco, CA, pp.70-1.
68 Butler, N.M. (1899-1900) 'Status of education at the close of the century' reprinted in the *Annual Report* of the U.S. Commissioner of Education, p.567.
69 See Richardson, J.G. (1980) 'Variation in date of enactment of compulsory school attendance laws: An empirical inquiry', *Sociology of Education,* 53, pp.153-63 ('Only four states enacted prior to 1870 . . . and all but two southern states had passed laws . . . [by] 1918', p.157).
70 'The work of the senior high school should be organized into differentiated curriculums' (*Cardinal Principles of Secondary Education,* Washington DC, 1918, p.22).
71 'Where there was but little differentiation in the work within the secondary school, and the pupils in attendance were less diversified as to

their heredity and social interests, social unification in the full sense of the term could not take place' (*ibid,* p.23).

72   My preliminary study of De la Salle is reported in Hamilton, D. (1981) 'Simultaneous instruction and the changing disciplines of eighteenth and nineteenth century schooling', paper presented at the annual meeting of the American History of Education Society, Pittsburgh. In choosing to study the educational work of the Brothers of the Christian Schools rather than, say, the pedagogical innovations of the Jesuits, I was following a particular interest in working class schooling. A different commentary would be required for middle- and upper-class schools.

73   Foucault, M. (1979) *Discipline and Punish: the Birth of the Prison,* Penguin, Harmondsworth.

74   Lundgren, U. (1983) *Between Hope and Happening: Text and Context in Curriculum,* Geelong.

75   Hamilton, D. (1977) 'A methodological diary' reprinted in Norris, N. (Ed) *Safari Papers II,* University of East Anglia Centre for Applied Research in Education, pp.136-46.

Chapter 2

On the Origins of the Educational Terms Class and Curriculum

The division of pupils into classes was to constitute one of the principal pedagogic innovations in the entire history of education. (Mir (1968) *Aux Sources de la Pédagogie des Jésuites*)[1]

It is hardly possible to exaggerate the importance of this innovation [the very idea of a 'curriculum'] in the history of education. (Rashdall (1936) *The Universities of Europe in the Middle Ages*)[2]

I

The discourse of schooling is an historical artefact. But its historical responsiveness is not always evident. Terms like 'kindergarten' and 'teaching machine' can be readily linked to particular periods of educational history; but other terms, like class and curriculum, have become universalized — their origins and evolution hidden from both educationists and historians alike.

Whenever, for example, historians refer to the 'curriculum' of the medieval university they unwittingly impose the language of the present onto the schooling of the past. As a result, the stability of educational practice is overstated; and educationists are left with the impression that teaching and learning are relatively sheltered from the turbulences of historical change.

But are historians solely to blame for this shortcoming? I think not. Responsibility also rests with the educational community at large — for neglecting to provide conceptual reference points against which the pedagogic past might be discerned. In short, historians have failed to discriminate chronologically where educationists have failed to discriminate conceptually. To break this impasse it is necessary, I believe, to bring the common-places of schooling much more to the foreground of educational analysis. They are not a backcloth to educational change: they are its warp and weft.

II

The most extensive discussion of the origins of classes in schooling can be found in Phillipe Ariès' *Centuries of Childhood* (original edition, 1960). Ariès noted that while 'class' is absent from medieval accounts of schooling, it had enjoyed a limited currency in classical times (for example, in Quintilian's *Institutes,* c.95AD).[3] Accordingly, Ariès claimed that the re-emergence of 'class' — in Erasmus' 1521 description of St Paul's School (London) — occurred because renaissance reformers were 'fond of borrowing from the ancients'.[4] From this perspective, then, Renaissance practice was continuous with its medieval predecessor: 'classes' already existed — they merely awaited a suitable label.[5]

There are, however, a number of problems with this argument. First, the renaissance reformers chose new labels, not only out of fondness for classical authors, but also because they wished to distance themselves from medieval practice. Secondly, a full version of Quintilian's *Institutes* had been rediscovered in 1416, so why did 'class' take over 100 years to enter the language of schooling? Thirdly, why did Erasmus — a leading humanist — fail to follow Quintilian's usage in his earlier educational works *De Copia* (1st ed, 1512) and *De Ratio Studii* (1st ed, 1511)? According to a recent translator, both were 'heavily indebted' to Quintilian for their 'content' and 'style'[6]; and, indeed, the full title of *De Copia* is, itself, 'after a phrase of Quintilian'.[7]

The earliest known use of class — in a source not reported by Ariés — appears in a condensed account of the University of Paris published in 1517 by Robert Goulet, a professor of theology. The last part of Goulet's *Compendium Universitatis Parisiensis* comprises a series of precepts that, Goulet believed, should be adopted by anyone wishing to found or reform a college. Besides exhorting his readers to follow the mode of living and teaching already practised in Paris, Goulet's first precept also described the layout of a suitable college: 'there should be at least twelve classes or small schools according to the exigency of place and auditors'.[8]

Goulet's juxtaposition of 'classes' and 'schools' reflects the coexistence of medieval and renaissance usages. In addition, his account also reflects the fact that, in medieval times, 'school' had a double meaning.

It could refer to a group of people or to the chamber in which instruction took place. What significance, therefore, should be attributed to the linking of class with 'small' school? Was Goulet commenting on the age (and size) of the students? Or were these new chambers (or groups) to be smaller than those used previously for teaching? Moreover, what were the existing college practices that Goulet referred to approvingly? To understand these developments it is necessary to take a closer look at the form taken by medieval schooling.

III

As noted in the previous chapter, a medieval school was primarily an educational relationship entered into by a private teacher and a group of individual scholars. Like guild masters and their apprentices, teachers took students at all levels of competence and, accordingly, organized their teaching largely on an individual basis. Such individualization fed back, in turn, upon the general organization of schooling. First, there

Figure 1

A sixteenth century schoolroom that illustrates the coexistence of classing and individualized instruction. Note, too, the possible assistant teacher at the back of the schoolroom. Taken from a German broadsheet, translated into English, and published in 1575. (Euing Broadside Ballad No. 1, copy in Glasgow University Library Department of Special Collections.)

was no presumption that every student was 'learning'[9] the same passage. Secondly, there was no pedagogical necessity that all students should remain in the teacher's presence throughout the hours of teaching — they could just as easily study (cf. memorize) their lessons elsewhere. And thirdly, there was no expectation that students would stay at school after their specific educational goals had been reached. Essentially, medieval schooling was a loose-textured organizational form which could easily encompass a large number of students. Its apparent laxity (for example, absenteeism, or the fact that enrollments did not match attendance) was not so much a failure (or breakdown) of school organization as a perfectly efficient response to the demands that were placed upon it.[10]

Gradually, however, these medieval practices underwent a process of reordering — a sequence of events that nurtured the term *class*. Three centres of innovation seem to have been important: the University of Bologna; the University of Paris; and the fifteenth-century schools associated with the Brethren of the Common Life, a devotional movement active in the Low Countries.

During the twelfth and thirteenth centuries, (mature) students converged on Bologna from all over Europe. They came to learn from an innovative group of jurists (legal theorists) whose revisions of the legal code eased, among other things, the problems faced by landholders wishing to transform their 'possession' (or stewardship) of land into a property-relationship of absolute (or free-hold) 'ownership'.[11] By comparison, then, with the cathedral schools, Bologna was a much more wordly (i.e. secular) educational setting. Likewise, the pedagogy of the jurists was comparable to that offered by other occupational groupings in the city. Knowledge, skills (etc.) were passed on to candidates who could meet the appropriate fees; and a small number of successful 'apprentices' were elevated to membership of the Bologna fraternity (or guild) of jurists.

In other respects, however, the Bologna students were unusual. As outsiders, they were denied the civil rights accorded to the citizens of Bologna. Yet, as senior and powerful figures in their own lands, many were well-equipped — financially, socially and intellectually — to overcome this difficulty. Together, the Bologna students formed their own guild and, through this agency, gradually formalized their relationship with the civic authorities. In turn, they also formalized their links with the jurists. According to one recent historian, this last connection prefigured a 'formidably rigorous' regime wherein the teaching was regulated by means of student-controlled appointment of teachers and student-imposed monetary fines for inefficient lecturing.[12]

Although the Bologna students controlled the organization of teaching, their masters retained the right to issue credentials. At the outset, these credentials merely admitted recognized students to the local guild. But after 1219 the masters obtained a papal privilege: the right to confer (with the local consent of the Archdeacon of Bologna) teaching licenses that had ecclesiastical and civic currency throughout the Papal domain. Licensed teachers armed with this privilege — the *jus ubique docendi* — were no longer subject to local restrictions upon tenure and practice. The net effect (if not also the intention) of this papal intervention was an increase in the production of civil and ecclesiastical administrators.[13] To increase its sphere of influence the Church of Rome transformed the Bologna guild of masters and apprentices into an international business school.

As far as the masters were concerned the *jus ubique docendi* gave a boost to the teaching side of their activities; and as far as the students were concerned it provided an incentive not merely to learn but also to acquire the social prestige that flowed from being a graduate (cf. the right to use the title 'Master' or 'Mr.'). Under the influence of such political and social pressures, educational institutions like Bologna began to grow in size, number and authority. In turn, certain of them, notably the University of Paris, yielded to new forms of discipline and management.

IV

The University of Paris was an outgrowth of the local cathedral or diocesan school, itself a product of an eleventh-century papal decree that the church should train up its own administrators rather than use lay persons. During the twelfth century certain important teachers — notably Peter Abelard (d. 1142) attracted (or brought) large numbers of students (and other teachers) to Paris where they lived and worked outside the direct control of the cathedral chancellor.[14] By 1215 these 'external' masters had acquired their own corporate (i.e. self-governing) status. The Chancellor still issued licences; but the masters controlled admission to their own 'consortium' of teachers.[15]

During the thirteenth century, however, the division of control between the masters and the Chancellor was cut across by a new organizational structure. Various benefactors — perhaps grateful for the legal counsel they had received from university-trained administrators and advisers — founded 'colleges' to provide accommodation for 'poor' scholars. Also known as 'hospices', 'pedagogies' and 'houses' (for example, the House of Sorbonne, founded in 1257), these residential (non-teaching) colleges were not attached to any particular religious grouping but, nevertheless, adopted a comparable discipline or rule.

Initially, the colleges were small. The earliest — founded 1180 — catered for only eighteen students. But, as time passed, the colleges changed in character. First, they took in fee-paying boarders; and, secondly, they began to offer teaching, not only to their own students but also to those from other residences. Although this gave certain colleges more money and a wider influence, their new clients were less bound by the discipline that, formally, applied only to the 'poor' scholars. This combination of a strong power base and a weak internal discipline provided the reason and the excuse for attacks on college autonomy. Critics maintained that the university was failing in its social mission and had become, as a consequence of college laxity, a breeding ground for anti-royalist and anti-state sentiment[16].

As various historians have indicated, these criticisms had a decisive impact. In the guise of replacing 'anarchy' with 'order'[17], the autonomy of the chancellor, teachers and colleges was subordinated to the control of lay and secular authorities. In 1446, for instance, the jurisdiction of Parliament was extended to all civil cases within the University — on the grounds that only the King and his court had the right to approve the creation of corporate bodies.[18] By this and other related interventions (for example, the 1453 reforms of Cardinal d'Estouteville), the University of Paris was deprived of both its 'chief privilege' and its 'independence'.[19] Its status changed from that of a 'mesmeric international university' to that of a 'circumscribed national institution'.[20] But this transition was not just a simple slide down the academic league table; rather, it was symptomatic of the fact that the University of Paris was moving out of the orbit of the Roman church and into the hands of national political interests. Local autonomy — allowed within guidelines supplied by a distant authority — was replaced by hierarchical forms of control designed to serve the needs of the national 'state'.[21]

The relocation of authority that accompanied these changes also penetrated the colleges. Power and privilege became concentrated in their upper echelons (i.e. among the doctors). And, in return, students were (supposedly) placed under constant surveillance. The colleges, that is, became subject to the 'same regularity' and the 'same order' as obtained in other French civic institutions.[22] In the late fifteenth century, this redistribution of power also showed itself through the internal division of colleges into different student cohorts. By this time, the rapid increase of (younger) day boys had, according to Ariès, 'completely swamped' the colleges — rendering them 'to all intents and purposes big day-schools'.[23] Control through residential requirements could not be applied in these circumstances. Instead, surveillance was to be exerted through closer regimentation of student attendance and student progress. According to Ariès, these reforms had a profound effect on University life. They transformed each 'collegiate administration' into an 'authoritarian system', and each 'community of masters and pupils' into a 'strict government of pupils by masters'.[24]

Moreover, it was at this time that, according to Mir, the modern sense of class was first used — but not named — in the statutes of the College of Montaigu:

> It is in the 1509 programme of Montaigu that one finds for the first time in Paris a precise and clear division of students into *classes* . . . That is, divisions graduated by stages or levels of increasing complexity according to the age and knowledge acquired by the students.[25]

But even if, as Mir goes on to argue, the College of Montaigu 'inaugurated'[26] such a class system in Paris, there is also other evidence that, by 1509, the division of large educational communities into (relatively) smaller cohorts already obtained in the schools of the Brethren of the Common Life.

V

The Brethren differed from monks and friars in their organization and origins. First, they shared a common life without taking a binding vow; and, secondly, they were 'essentially products of the medieval municipality'.[27] Further, they survived, not by begging, but on the basis of gifts from benefactors, fees from teaching, and income from book-copying. The attention of educational historians has been drawn to the Brethren largely because they are associated with certain important humanist educators. Besides Erasmus, for instance, the Brethren had a hand in the employment and/or schooling of John Standonck (Principal of Montaigu from 1483 to 1499) and John Sturm (founder of the Protestant Academy of Strasbourg in 1538).[28]

The early history of the Brethren is unclear.[29] But it seems that by the fifteenth century they had begun to take boys into their communities.[30] In some cases the boys were 'given' to the Brethren as candidates for future internal promotion; in other cases they were merely 'loaned' for the purpose of receiving a formal upbringing. Moreover, it also seems that the Brethren's schools also admitted 'poor' scholars who, presumably, could earn their keep by contributing to the book-copying side of the Brethren's activities.

Besides being part of a regional unit or 'colloquium' (for example, the Zwolle Colloquium), each 'local House or school'[31] of the Brethren was itself broken down into various internal divisions. It has been claimed, for instance, that during John Cele's tenure as schoolmaster of Zwolle between 1374 and 1417, the Brethren began dividing their (larger?) 'schools' into eight graduated groups.[32] Moreover, Cele is said to have attracted 'as many as 1200 pupils at a time' to Zwolle[33] — an enrolment figure which is comparable to those that have been reported for Alkmaar (900 students), Herzogenbusch (1200 students) and Deventer (2200 students).[34]

The Deventer figures — which are associated with Alexander Hegius' tenure between 1483 and 1498[35] — would suggest that each level of the Brethren's school had an average of 275 pupils. Such a 'class' size seems to have persisted into the 1520s since, at a later date, Sturm reported figures of 'up to 200 pupils' for each level of the Brethren's Liege school that he had attended between 1521 and 1524.[36] There is, however, a striking difference between these figures and the 'classes' of sixteen pupils reported in Erasmus' account of St Paul's School. Equally, the overall size of St Paul's differed from that of the Brethren's schools. Its foundation deed of 1509 merely envisaged a total enrolment of 153 'children'.[37]

For these reasons I think caution should be exercised before linking the classes of St Pauls with the earlier sub-divisions in either the colleges of Paris or the schools of the Brethren of the Common Life. In a sense, the earlier cohorts might best be seen as administrative rather than pedagogic units. Within them, pedagogic practices still echoed the medieval individualized methods described earlier. The later Renaissance educators, on the other hand, not only added more finely-tuned controls to the administrative procedures of their predecessors, they also made the resultant groupings (cf. 'small' schools) serve pedagogic as well as administrative goals. And it was this new state of affairs — which crystallized out in the second decade of the sixteenth century — that led Goulet and Erasmus to adopt a new language of schooling.

VI

If this is in fact the case, then Ariès' argument is in need of some revision. The word 'class' emerged not as a substitute for school, but, strictly speaking, to identify the subdivisions within 'schools'. That is, Renaissance thinkers believed that learning in general, and municipal schooling in particular, would be more efficiently promoted through smaller pedagogic units. In turn, these 'classes' became part of the 'minutely choreographed scripts' that, so one historian has claimed, were used in sixteenth-century French schools (and elsewhere in Europe) to 'control the teachers and the children' so that they might '[teach and] learn difficult subjects in record time'.[38]

Overall, then, I would suggest that three social developments came together to underwrite the emergence of the term 'class'. First, new patterns of organization and control emerged in response to a crisis of fifteenth-century administration and government. Secondly, Renaissance educationist-administrators extended these arguments to the close pedagogic supervision of students. And finally, an unidentified humanist recognized that Quintilian's earlier (but relatively vague) use of class could be readily adapted to these new circumstances.

All these events and outcomes, I believe, shaped the form of post-medieval schooling. They represented — at least in their conception — an important break with the past. Like contemporaneous proposals for the introduction of universal schooling (and universal taxation), they brought much sharper focus to the linkages between schooling and bureaucratic control, and to the relationship between schooling and the state.

But if the adoption of classes gave life to the idea — expressed in the 1544 prospectus of the College of Nimes — that 'every learning has its time and its place'[39], it also brought problems of internal articulation. How could these different fractions of a school be fitted together and managed as whole? The attempts made in the sixteenth century to answer this question form the basis of the second part of this chapter — the emergence of the term 'curriculum'.

VII

By comparison with class, there seems to be an absolute dearth of discussion on the origins of 'curriculum'.[40] A convenient starting point, however, is the *Oxford English Dictionary* which locates the earliest source of 'curriculum' in the records of the University of Glasgow for 1633. The word appears in the testimonial granted to a master on graduation; and is couched in a form that, so the nineteenth-century reprint claims, had been promulgated 'soon after'[41] the University was reformed by Protestants in 1577. Is this dictionary citation historically representative? Or does it derive from the fact that the original editor of the *OED* — James Murray — had been a teacher in Scotland? In fact, the reprinted material on other Scottish and North European universities yields no earlier uses of curriculum[42] — with the seemingly sole exception of the 1582 records of the University of Leiden.

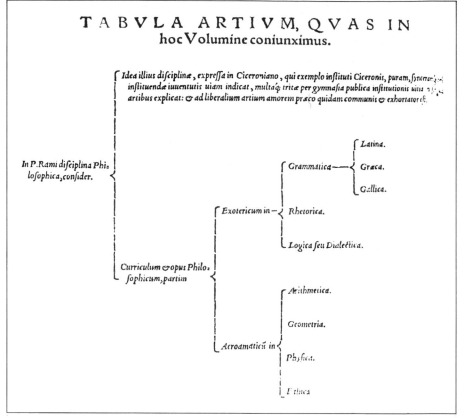

Figure 2

Earliest known appearance of the term 'curriculum', in a version of Peter Ramus'
Professio Regia, published posthumously by Thomas Fregius of Basle in 1576.
(Glasgow University Library Department of Special Collections)

Yet this answer only poses the historical question more sharply.
Why Leiden? Why Glasgow? The most obvious connection between
these two institutions is that, during the late sixteenth-century, both
were heavily influenced by Calvinist ideas. Indeed, Leiden was founded
in 1575 specifically for the purpose of training Protestant preachers, and
Glasgow's reconstitution in the same decade was to meet similar
purposes. What, then, might be the connection between protestantism,
Calvinism and curriculum?

As in the case of class, the answer seems to relate to the spread of
new assumptions about the efficiency of schooling in particular and the
efficiency of society in general. But why did Calvinist educational theory
adopt a latin word meaning a race or racetrack? More specifically, what
new educational aspirations were met by the adoption of the term
'curriculum'?

The answer to the last question is suggested by the original uses of curriculum. At Leiden and Glasgow, and in a subsequent reference in the 1643 records of Glasgow Grammar School (the University's feeder institution), 'curriculum' referred to the entire multi-year course followed by each student, not to any shorter pedagogic unit. In the Leiden case, for instance, it was used in the form 'having completed the curriculum of his studies'.[43]

To this extent, 'curriculum' seems to have confirmed the idea — already reflected in the adoption of 'class' — that the different elements of an educational course were to be treated as all-of-a-piece.[44] Any course worthy of the name was to embody both 'disciplina' (a sense of structural coherence), and 'ordo' (a sense of internal sequencing). Thus, to speak of a post-Reformation 'curriculum' is to point to an educational entity that exhibits both structural wholeness and sequential completeness. A 'curriculum' should not only be 'followed'; it should also be 'completed'. Whereas the sequence, length and completeness of medieval courses had been relatively open to student negotiation (for example, at Bologna) and/or teacher abuse (for example, in Paris), the emergence of 'curriculum' brought, I suggest, a greater sense of control to both teaching and learning.

VIII

But of the two tributaries of 'curriculum' — 'ordo' and 'disciplina' — it is the former that figured more strongly in sixteenth-century educational debates.[45] A crucial connection seems to have been the linking of ideas about order with a change in meaning of the term 'method'. In earlier times, 'methodus' had denoted procedures of investigation or analysis, but it had conveyed no sense of providing guidelines that could be rapidly assimilated and easily applied. 'Method', that is, existed as a leisurely intellectual art, not a purposive science of technique.

Nowhere was this distinction more evident than in 'dialectic' — the branch of philosophy used to analyze the structure of language. Late Renaissance dialecticians, unlike their predecessors, approached dialectic from a practical standpoint. Their dialectic handbooks replaced seemingly inexhaustible and hair-splitting rules with 'condensed and simplified'[46] precepts. They wrote for a general audience rather than for 'professional logicians'.[47] Dialectic was redesigned, therefore, to make it easier for students to extract and to apply the 'truths' embedded in the writings and speeches of great thinkers. Accordingly, techniques were reduced to a form that could be easily communicated. And it was this reformulation of dialectic — in the direction of concise sequencing and ease of communication — that, among other things, gave 'method' its new linearity.

Various teacher-dialecticians — of whom Sturm, Melanchthon and Ramus are the best remembered — played an important part in these developments. Sturm's earliest treatment of method appeared in 1539 — the year after he founded the Strasburg gymnasium. His reference to the practicalities of teaching was quite explicit:

> An art is an abundant collection of propositions. But in setting up the various arts a certain, short and direct way, a kind of short cut, has to be used. This the Greeks call method, such as may be used for teaching and communication.[48]

In emphasizing the relevance of presentation and communication (which originally belonged to the study of rhetoric), Sturm began the redefinition of dialectic. In the process, he also pushed back the boundaries of method. Dialectic ceased to apply solely to the study of written and spoken discourse. Instead, it began to denote a set of standard procedures relevant to the solution of all intellectual problems.[49]

This wider application of method was made explicit in the writings of Philip Melanchthon (1497-1560), founder of the Lutheran Gymnasium of Nuremburg (1526). In his *Questions in Dialectic* (1547), for instance, Melanchthon wrote: 'Method is a habit, that is, a science or an art which finds and opens a way through overgrown and impenetrable places and pulls out and ranges in order the things pertaining to the matter proposed'.[50]

These early suggestions for the realignment of dialectic were finally brought fully into the open through the writings of Peter Ramus (1515-1572), a teacher at the University of Paris and a former student of Sturm's. First, Ramus reaffirmed the sequential aspects of dialectical method:

> Method (he wrote in the 1569 edition of his *Dialectic*) is disposition by which that enunciation is placed first which is first in the absolute order of knowledge, that next which is next, and so on: and thus there is an unbroken progression.[51]

And secondly, Ramus consciously highlighted the intellectual generalizability and pedagogical relevance of the dialectical method — claiming that it was appropriate not merely to the philosophical arts but to 'every matter which we wish to teach easily and clearly'.[52]

Ramus' ideas were controversial, not least among those philosophers whose practices he sought to overturn. But there is little doubt — judging from the 150 editions/adaptations of his *Dialectic* published between 1555 and 1600[54] — that his ideas found a ready and accepting audience, particularly among teachers. By hybridizing the logical canons of dialectic with the communication and presentation rules of rhetoric, Ramist method brought an unprecedented 'orderliness' to teaching.[54] Further, it was claimed that, if formalized (or 'methodized')[55] in this way, teaching (or schooling) would be rendered more powerful (and/or more efficient). This connection between order, efficiency and improvement became fundamental to late sixteenth-century and early seventeenth-century school reform.[56] As Caspar Pfaffad restated the argument in his *De Studiis Rameis* (1597), reformed schooling (or 'formal education') provided the means by which human beings might be brought to their 'natural perfection'.[57]

IX

So much for 'method'; but when and where was it joined by 'curriculum'? Here the link with Calvinism can be discerned. After Ramus' death in Paris, his ideas on dialectic spread to Germany which, following the preparatory work of Sturm and Malanchthon, became the 'real seedbed of Ramism'.[58] Further, the influence of Ramist ideas within Germany was, according to the Jesuit scholar Walter Ong, 'most intense' in the areas 'tinged by Calvinism'.[59] And it was from these particular areas — the Rhineland and its environs — that Ramist ideas descended to the Calvinist sections of the Netherlands.

Ong makes no attempt to explain the mutual attraction of Ramism and Calvinism. But a likely explanation is that the all-encompassing character of Ramus' pedagogical notions resonated easily with Calvinist ideas about the general need for well-ordered forms of social organization. By the 1570s, Calvin's followers in Geneva and elsewhere (Calvin had died in 1564) were busy rearranging their own evangelical affairs along such structured lines. A well-ordered school, like a well-ordered church, was seen as essential to the maintenance of Calvin's ideas (as developed in successive editions of his *Institution of the Christian Religion;* viz. 1536, 1543, 1559). According to Tawney, for instance, a 'rule of life' was 'of the very essence of Calvinism'[60]; or, as Calvin put it in 1539, 'the body of the church, to cohere well, must be bound together by discipline as by sinews'.[61] From this perspective, then, the Ramist idea of method — with its overtones of 'orderliness'- could fill the same position of 'centrality'[62] in Calvinist educational proposals as the precept of discipline already held within Calvinist social practice.

This argument about the management and control of schooling may explain the link between Ramism and Calvinism, but where, in fact, did the word 'curriculum' appear? Here, unfortunately, the picture becomes a little muddied. While figurative descriptions of life as a 'race' or 'racecourse' were regular themes in Calvin's *Commentaries* (1540-1556)[63], the latin words consistently used for this purpose — in at least six different passages — were 'stadium' and 'cursus', not 'curriculum'.[64]

Nevertheless, by the final (i.e. 1559) edition of the *Institution* the phrase 'vitae curriculum' (or 'vitae curriculo') appears in Calvin's writings, though it is still outnumbered by the uses of 'vitae cursu' (or 'vitae cursum').[65] Nowhere, however, does curriculum appear in an educational sense. Neither does it take an educational form in any of the sixteenth-century records — published and manuscript — of the Academy of Geneva (founded 1559). This last state of affairs, which weakens Geneva's claim to be the ultimate source of curriculum, can be tied to the fact that, from the 1530s, Genevan documents appeared primarily in French, and were translated into latin only for the consumption of foreign Calvinist communities.[66]

For this reason, then, there exists the possibility that the educational term 'curriculum' originated, not in Geneva, but in the Latin discourse of its late sixteenth-century off-spring congregations. It is at this point that Leiden and Glasgow enter the story. One 'carrier' of the curriculum idea (if not the term) might have been the Scot, Andrew Melville, who spent five years teaching in the Genevan Academy (1569-1574) after earlier sojourns at the universities of St Andrews, Poitiers and Paris (where he came under the influence of Ramus). Following his departure from Geneva — at the request of influential friends in Scotland — Melville, then aged 29, took up the Principalship of the University of Glasgow where, according to a recent history, he assumed 'responsibility for introducing reforms on Ramist lines'.[67]

It was during Melville's time at Glasgow (1574-80) that the University underwent the major reorganization referred to earlier. Melville, like Calvin's successors in Geneva (for example, Theodore Beza), seemed to regard Calvinism in relatively tight organizational terms. For instance, residence in college was to be compulsory for the Principal; each teacher (or regent) was to be limited to particular areas of study (for example, Latin and Greek); student promotion was to be subject to satisfactory conduct and progress throughout the year; and, in return, the University was to vouch for the completeness of each student's course through the testimonial in which the word curriculum made its initial appearance in Glasgow.[68] As another historian of the

University of Glasgow has commented, these proposals not only meant that teaching was to follow a 'rigid plan', but also that the 'whole life' of each student was to be rendered open to teacher supervision.[69]

Much the same pattern seems to have been followed in Leiden. An early influx of teachers imbued with the 'spirit of Geneva', soon led to controversy (for example, over civic versus presbytery control of the University). But a compromise charter — still redolent of Calvinism — was eventually agreed in 1576, only six years before the word curriculum appeared in the University's records.[70]

X

Although there are still some loose ends in this story (Why did curriculum replace cursus? Was 'curriculum' adopted independently in Leiden and Glasgow?), the general outline seems clear. The educational term curriculum emerged at the confluence of various social and ideological movements. First, under the influence of Ramus' revisions, the teaching of dialectic offered a general pedagogy that could be applied to all areas of learning. Secondly, Ramus' views on the organization of teaching and learning became consonant with the disciplinary aspirations of Calvinism. And thirdly, Calvinist fondness for the figurative use of 'vitae curriculum' — a phrase that dates back to Cicero (died 43 BC)[71] — was extended to embrace the new ordered and sequential features of sixteenth-century schooling.

In conclusion, this chapter has argued that as part of the general political turmoil of the sixteenth century the adoption of curriculum and class was indicative of two separate waves of pedagogic reform. First came the introduction of class divisions and closer pupil surveillance; and second came the refinement of pedagogic content and methods. The net result, however, was cumulative: teaching and learning became, for good or ill, more open to external scrutiny and control. Moreover, curriculum and class came onto the pedagogical agenda at a time when schools were being opened up to a much wider section of society.[72] Municipal schooling — no longer under the jurisdiction of the church — gained in popularity; and, as important, protestant decrees (for example, the *Book of Discipline,* published in 1560 by Calvin's supporters in Scotland), voiced the belief that all children, irrespective of gender or rank, should be evangelized through the medium of schooling. As a result, the medieval educational agenda was not so much extended as substantially recast. And it is to a review of the pedagogic consequences of the new agenda that the remainder of this book is dedicated.[73]

Notes

1 Mir, G.C. (1968) *Aux Sources de la Pédagogie des Jésuites: Le Modus Parisiensis,* Rome, p.160.
2 Rashdall, H. (1936) *The Universities of Europe in the Middle Ages,* Vol 1, (edited by F.M. Powicke and A.B. Emden), Oxford, p.440.
3 Ariès, P. (1962) *Centuries of Childhood: A Social History of Family Life,* New York, p.176. Among other things, Ariès points out that 'classes' do not figure anywhere in Marrou, H. (1948) *Histoire de l'Education dans l'Antiquité,* Paris.
4 Ariès, P. (1962) *op cit,* p.180.
5 Ariès claims 'the idea (of classes) had preceded the word by a long margin, and it was already familiar when the terminology was established', *ibid,* p.177. For a detailed discussion of the etymology of 'class', see Clouatre, D.L. (1984) 'The concept of class in French culture prior to the revolution', *Journal of the History of Ideas,* 45, pp.219-44.
6 *Collected Works of Erasmus* (1978) (vol.24), Toronto, p.663. (In the matter of Erasmus' writings I would like to acknowledge the assistance of my Glasgow colleague, Betty Knott, whose translation of *De Copia* appears in the same series.)
7 Woodward, W.H. (1904) *Desiderius Erasmus Concerning the Aim and Method of Education,* Cambridge, p.20.
8 Goulet, R. (1928) *Compendium on the University of Paris,* Philadelphia, pp.100-1. (I am grateful to the Charles Patterson van Pelt Library of the University of Pennsylvania for providing a photocopy of the original passage.)
9 It should be noted, of course, that what passes for 'learning' is historically contingent. Indeed, a comprehensive discussion of this contingency would be a welcome addition to the literature on schooling.
10 Medieval schooling, or even the medieval conception of 'school' needs much more attention. It receives very little space, for instance, in Weijers, O. (1979) 'Terminologie des Universites Naissantes', *Miscellanea Mediaevalia,* 12, pp.258-80. One account, however, that recognizes the problem is Southern, R.W. (1982) 'The schools of Paris and the school of Chartres' in Benson, R.L. and Constable, G. (Eds) *Renaissance and Renewal in the Twelfth Century,* Oxford, pp.113-37. Southern writes: 'I hope to return to the stages and significance of the shift in meaning which brought the independent master and his group of pupils into strong relief in the twelfth century, and prepared the way for the new institutional *scholae* in the late middle ages' (p.115n).
11 Bologna's links with changing legal theory and changing patterns of possession/ownership are discussed in Anderson, P. (1979) *Lineages of the Absolutist State,* London, 24ff.
12 Cobban, A.B. (1975) *The Medieval Universities: Their Development and Organisation,* London, p.63.
13 For a general discussion of the links between schooling and administrative reform in the Middle Ages see Murray, A. (1978) *Reason and Society in the Middle Ages,* Oxford.
14 See, for instance Southern, R.W. (1982) *op cit.*

15 Bernstein, A. (1978) *Pierre D'Ailly and the Blanchard Affair: University and Chancellor of Paris at the Beginning of the Great Schism,* Leiden, p.6. The tension between licensing (by the chancellor) and inception (by the masters) is also discussed in Cobban, A.B. (1975) *op cit,* p.82ff.

16 See Verger, J. (1976) 'Les universités françaises au XVe siècle: Crise et tentatives de réforme', *Cahiers d'Histoire,* 21, pp.43-66; and Rashdall, H. (1936) *op cit,* Vol.1, p.515ff.

17 *Ibid,* p.526.

18 Cobban, A.B. (1975) *op cit,* p.95.

19 Verger, J. (1972) 'The University of Paris at the end of the Hundred Years War' in Baldwin J.W. and Goldthwaite, R.A. (Eds) *Universities in Politics: Case Studies from the Late Middle Ages and Early Modern Period,* Baltimore, MD, p.59.

20 Cobban, A.B. (1975) *op cit,* p.95. See also Le Goff, J. (1967) 'La conception Française de l'Université a l'époque de la Renaissance', in Commission Internationale pour l'Histoire des Universités, *Les Universités Européenes du XIVe au XVIIIe Siècle: Aspects et Problemes,* Geneve, p.95 ('The 1453 reform by Cardinal d'Estouteville in Paris is the last university reform of medieval date and character in France').

21 For a more extensive discussion of the growth of national forms of administration and control, see Anderson, P. (1979) *op cit,* pp.16-59 (for example, 'The absolutist monarchies of the West characteristically relied on a skilled stratum of legists to staff their administrative machines . . . These lawyer-bureaucrats were the zealous enforcers of royal centralism', p.28). The general relationship between renaissance educational institutions and the creation of the absolutist state merits further examination. A.T. Grafton and Lisa Jardine suggest, for instance, that humanist schooling had 'more to do with its appropriateness as a commodity than with its intrinisic intellectual merits', and that as 'potential servants of the state', fluent and docile young noblemen were a 'commodity of which the oligarchs and tyrants of late fifteenth century Italy could not fail to approve' (Grafton, A. T. and Jardine, L. (1982) 'Humanism and the school of Guarino: A problem of evaluation', *Past & Present,* 96, pp.76-7).

22 Verger, J. (1976) *op cit,* p.61. See also Brockliss, L.W.B. (1976) 'The University of Paris in the sixteenth and seventeenth centuries', PhD thesis, Cambridge, University of Cambridge, p.3 ('[In the colleges] good organization was above all considered to be the key to success. Traditional corporate ideas were rejected; instead ultimate control was to lie in the hands of one individual (the Rector or Principal) who was to provide for the necessary teaching and supervise the lives of the boarders').

23 Ariès, P. (1962) *op cit,* p.167.

24 *Ibid,* p.171.

25 Mir, G.C. (1968) *op cit,* p.101. See also Compère, M. M. and Julia, D. (1981) 'Les collèges sous l'ancien régime', *Histoire de l'Éducation,* 13, p.8 ('[At what moment did] the medieval school become a college in the modern sense of the word . . . It is surely the appearance of progressive classes set out hierarchically following the *modus parisiensis* with a teacher attached to each one'). For a supportive and more detailed discussion of the reform of the University of Paris, see Renaudet, A. (1916) *Preréforme et Humanisme à Paris (1496-1517),* Paris.

26 Mir, G.C. (1968) *op cit,* p.102.

27 Jacob, E.F. (1963) *Essays on the Conciliar Epoch,* Manchester, p.121.

28 Besides Erasmus, Standonck and Sturm, it has also been claimed that, as a boy in Magdeburg, Martin Luther attended a school run by the Brethren of the Common Life (see Dickens, A.G. (1976) *The German Nation and Martin Luther,* London, p.77).

29 Historiographic problems related to the Brethren of the Common Life are discussed in Post, R.R. (1968) *The Modern Devotion,* Leiden.

30 See, for instance, Hyma, A. (1950) *The Brethren of the Common Life,* Grand Rapids, MI, 1950, p.115ff. There was also a Sisters of the Common Life, who have received much less attention (but see Hyma, chapter 3).

31 Henkel, J. (1968) 'School organizational patterns of the Brethren of the Common Life' in Strand, K.A. (Ed) *Essays in the Northern Renaissance,* Ann Arbor, MI, p.37.

32 *Ibid,* p.43.

33 Jacob, E.F. (1963) *op cit,* p.124 (reporting Hyma).

34 See Janssen, J. (1887) *L'Allemagne et la Réforme* Vol. 1, Paris, p.19. More recently, Geoffrey Parker has claimed — without indicating his source — that the 'town school' of Zwolle had '2000 pupils by 1500' (1979 *The Dutch Revolt,* Harmondsworth, p.21). The ultimate source of twentieth century accounts of the Brethren's schools seems to be Schoengen, M. (1898) *Die Schule von Zwolle: von ihren Anfangen bis zu dem Auftreten des Humanismus,* Friburg. Despite Schoengen's painstaking research, reanalysis of the original sources is overdue.

35 See Hyma, A. (1950) *op cit,* pp.118-9.

36 Le Coultre, J. (1926) *Maturin Cordier et les Origines de la Pédagogie Protestante dans le Pays de langue Française (1530-1564),* Neuchatel, p.203.

37 See McDonnell, M. (1959) *The Annals of St Pauls,* privately printed, p.32. Erasmus' description appears in a letter to Justin Jonas, Ariès dates the letter from 1519, though Percy Allen (1922) *Letters of Erasmus,* Oxford, p.507) suggests that, from internal evidence, 1521 is a more likely year. (I am grateful to Keith Hoskin of the University of Warwick for drawing this detail to my attention, as well as for much other assistance with this chapter.)

38 Huppert, G. (1984) *Public Schools in Renaissance France,* Urbana, IL, pp.39, 40 and 45.

39 Gaufres, M.J. (1880) *Claude Baduel et la Réforme des Études au XVI Siècle,* Paris, p.47.

40 A search for the origins of 'curriculum' yielded nothing from the following works: Buisson, F. (1882) *Dictionnaire de Pédagogie,* Paris; Foulquie, P. (1971) *Dictionnaire de la Langue Pédagogique,* Paris; Monroe, P. (1911) *A Cyclopedia of Education,* New York; Rein, W. (1903) *Encyklopädisches Handbuch der Pädagogik,* Langensalzer; and Watson, F. (1921) *The Encyclopedia and Dictionary of Education,* London.

41 *Munimenta Alma Universitatus Glasguensis* (Records of the University of Glasgow from its Foundation till 1727), vol.2 (1854), Glasgow, p.X.

42 Sources consulted in search of early uses of curriculum include le Coultre, J. (1926) *op cit;* Junod L. and Meylan, H. (1947) *L'Académie de Lausanne aux XVIe Siècle,* Lausanne; Massebieau, L. (1886) *Schola Aquitana:*

Programme d'Études de Collège de Guyenne au XVIe Siècle, Paris; Mellon, P. (1913) *L'Académie de Sedan*, Paris; and Reusen, E.H.J. (1867) 'Statuts primitifs de la Faculté des Arts de Louvain', *Comptes Rendue des Séances de la Commission Royale d'Histoire*, 9, pp.147-206.

43 Molhuysen, P.C. (1913-24) *Bronnen tot de Geschiedenis der Leidsche Universiteit 1574-1871)*, vol 2, The Hague, p.96. (This source was located by Maria Gibbons, with whom I wrote an earlier version of this chapter for the annual meeting of the American Educational Research Association in Boston, 1980.) The notion that a 'curriculum' relates to teaching that takes place over more than one year seems to have survived until the twentieth century: for example, 'The term "curriculum" is used by this commission to designate a systematic arrangement of subjects . . . extending through two or more years' ((1918) *Cardinal Principles of Secondary Education*, Washington, p.18n).

44 Strictly speaking, this chapter's epigraph on 'curriculum' is misplaced. Rashdall's comment related, in fact, to a 'complete account' of a master's studies dating from 1215. Indeed, to make matters worse, Rashdall's editors suggest an even earlier provenance for 'comprehensive yet definite programmes of study' (*The Universities of Europe in the Middle Ages* vol.1, pp.439-40). In response, however, I would argue that, compared with those of the sixteenth century, the thirteenth-century regulations had a much weaker sense of sequence and closure. Support for the notion that 'curriculum' implies coherence is provided in Gilbert, N. (1960) *Renaissance Concepts of Method*, New York. Gilbert suggests that Erasmus' late-renaissance study of theology — *Ratio seu Methodus Compendio Parviendi ut Veram Theologiam* (1520) — is a typical humanist text insofar as it examines courses of instruction 'as a whole' (p.108).

45 For a discussion of the educational use of 'ordo' see Mir, G.C. (1968) *op cit*, p.160ff; and for a discussion of 'disciplina' see Durig, W. (1952) 'Disciplina: Eine Studie zum Bedeutungsumfang des Wortes in der Sprache der Liturgie und des Vater', *Sacris Erudiri*, 4, pp.245-279.

46 Jardine, L. (1974) *Francis Bacon: Discovery and the Art of Discourse*, Cambridge, pp.5 and 17 ('The development of dialectic in the sixteenth century is essentially a development within a textbook tradition'). See also Mahoney, M.S. (1980) 'The beginnings of algebraic thought in the seventeenth century' in Gaukroger, S. (Ed) *Descartes: Philosophy, Mathematics and Physics*, Hassocks, Harvester Press, p.149 ('[Ramus] represents the beginning of the writing of textbooks').

47 Jardine, F. (1974) *op cit*, 5.

48 See Ong, W.J. (1958) *Ramus, Method and the Decay of Dialogue: from the Art of Discourse to the Art of Reason*, Cambridge, MA, pp.232-3 (quotation abridged).

49 Cf. Jardine, L. (1974) *op cit*, 26 ('[The reformers] identified dialectic . . . with the whole of logic . . . on the grounds that the study of techniques of argument does not depend on the status . . . of the material to which they are applied').

50 Ong, W.J. (1958) *op cit*, p.237 (quotation abridged).

51 *Ibid*, p.249 (quotation abridged).

52 *Ibid*, p.250.

53   *Ibid,* p.296.
54   *Ibid,* p.297.
55   *Ibid.*
56   Links between method and efficiency are noted by both Gilbert and Ong: 'The emphasis on speed and efficiency sets apart the renaissance notion of method . . . The notion that method can provide a short cut to learning an art did not seem crucial to medical students or educational reformers. Only when the milieu had become more time-conscious did method become the slogan of those who wished to speed up the processes of learning' (Gilbert, N. 1960, p.66); 'Ramus lived in an age where there was no word in ordinary usage which clearly expressed what we mean today by "method", a series of ordered steps gone through to produce with certain efficacy a desired effect — a routine of *efficiency*' (Ong, W.J. (1958) *op cit,* p.225).
57   *Ibid,* p.149. Despite Pfaffad's judgement, Ong offers a rather different evaluation of Ramism — that it brought forth a 'pedagogical juggernaut' that ran unhalted through the 'western intellectual world' (*ibid,* p.167). For an exploration of the links between Calvin, Ramus, Bacon and Comenius, see Hamilton, D. (1987) 'The pedagogical juggernaut', *British Journal of Educational Studies,* 25, pp.18-29.
58   Ong. W.J. (1958) *op cit.* p.298.
59   *Ibid.*
60   Tawney, R. (1942) *Religion and the Rise of Capitalism,* Harmondsworth, Penguin, p.98.
61   See Hopfl, H. (1982) *The Christian Polity of John Calvin,* Cambridge, p.100.
62   *Ibid,* p.104. Hopfl also claims that the 'first instance' of Calvin's wider use of discipline (i.e. outside references to excommunication) occurred in 1537 (p.73).
63   Parker, T.H.L. (1971) *Calvin's New Testament Commentaries,* London, chapter 1.
64   *John Calvin's Commentaries* (in Latin), Berlin, 1833-34, vol.5, 320. See also, Acts 13.25; Acts 20.24; I Corinthians 9.24; 2 Timothy 4.7 and 2 Thessalonians 3.1. (I am grateful to Allan Milligan for drawing this source to my attention.)
65   See Battles, F.L. and Miller, C. (1972) *A Computerised Concordance to Institutio Christianae Religionis (1559) of Ionnes Calvinus,* Pittsburg, PA. 'Vitae curriculum (or curriculo)' appears six times; 'vitae cursus (or curso)' appears twelve times.
66   The founding ceremony of the Genevan Academy was conducted in both French and Latin, and a dual-language version of the regulations was published in the same year. By contrast, the 1578 revision of the regulations does not seem to have appeared in Latin until 1593 — a document, incidentally, that cannot be traced in the manuscripts department of the (joint) Public and University Library of Geneva. For data on the Genevan ceremonies and regulations see Bourgeaud, C. (1900) *Histoire de l'Universite de Geneve: l'Academie de Calvin,* Geneva, pp.48, 49 and 626.
67   Durkan, J. and Kirk, I. (1977) *The University of Glasgow 1451-1577,* Glasgow, p.276.

68 One datum which suggests that 'curriculum' might not have been used in Glasgow until some time after 1577 is the presence of the phrase 'vite disciplina' (rather than 'vitae curriculum') in the university's refounding constitution of that year — the *Novum Erectio (ibid,* p.433).

69 Mackie, J.D. (1954) *The University of Glasgow 1451-1951,* Glasgow, p.76.

70 Jurriaanse, M.W. (1965) *The Founding of Leyden University,* Leiden, 13.

71 Cicero's use of 'vitae curriculum' is recorded, for instance, in the entry for 'curriculum' in *Cassell's Latin Dictionary,* London, 1893.

72 Extended discussion of the expansion of schooling in the sixteenth century can be found, for instance, in Simon, J. (1966) *Education and Society in Tudor England,* Cambridge, and Strauss, G. (1978) *Luther's House of Learning: the Indoctrination of the Young in the German Reformation,* Baltimore, MD. For a valuable commentary on the political and religious background to sixteenth- and seventeenth-century views on the role of the state see Oestreich, G. (1982) *Neostoicism and the Early Modern State,* Cambridge.

73 Since completing this chapter I have located a use of 'curriculum' in the *Professio Regia* (1576), a text usually attributed to Ramus but, in fact, published after his death by Thomas Fregius of Basel. In effect, this source provides the missing link between Ramus, Calvin and latter educational innovators — notably Comenius (see, variously, Hamilton, D. (1987) *op cit;* Hooykaas, R. (1958) *Humanisme, Science et Reforme: Pierre de la Ramée,* Leiden; Moltmann, V.J. (1957) 'Zur Bedeutung des Petrus Ramus für Philosophie und Theologie im Calvinismus', *Zeitschrift für Kirchengeschichte,* 68, pp.295-318; Beitenholz, P.G. (1971) *Basle and France in the Sixteenth Century: the Basle Humanists and Printers in their Contacts with Francophone Culture,* Geneva, chapter 8; and the entry for 'Disciplina/ discipline' in the *Enciclopedia Einaudi,* Turin, 1977-84). [I am grateful to Norberto Bottani for the last of these sources.]

Chapter 3

Schooling to Order: Jean Baptist de la Salle and the Pedagogy of Elementary Education

In the course of the period 1660-1720, and as a result of the reforming zeal of the Bishops, the great majority of charity schools developed in French towns. This immense campaign which aimed to reduce the 'prodigious ignorance' of the poor (as well as police them) jointly embraced both a public (notably the poorer people) and a corpus of knowledge appropriate to their upbringing. In excluding the learning of the rudiments of latin from his schools Jean Baptist de la Salle created a boundary that did not exist in J. de Batencourt's *The Parochial School* (1654). He combined a pedagogic programme with a socially determined clientele.   (Compère, M-M. and Julia, D. (1981)
'Les collèges sous l'ancien régime')[1]

Most of the various aspects of [De la Salle's] system may be found among the methods of his predecessors. It must be admitted, however, that no method before this was so thoroughly regulated. Although he used the works of others extensively, his method is so analytic and precise that it would be useless seeking an exact model of this type of presentation anterior to him.
(Moran, W. (1966)
*Development and Evolution of the Educational
Theory and Practice of Jean Baptist de la Salle)*[2]

I

Three features recur in the history of schooling. New pedagogic forms come into being; they persist; and they fade away. To account for these changes, educationists have a two-fold task. First, to identify the circumstances that 'call forth' the new pedagogies; and, secondly, to chart the cultural and material realignments that give the new pedagogies their innovative character.

These two aspects of change are relatively independent. New circumstances, that is, do not necessarily evoke a new pedagogy. Outdated remedies may simply be applied with renewed vigour. Sometimes, however, new practices are invented to bring schooling more into line with new social priorities. But such 'solutions' don't just happen. Nor are they simply 'read off' from the 'problem'. Rather, their emergence is contingent upon a reappraisal both of the problem itself and of the resources that might be applied to its resolution. Thus, among other things, new pedagogic practices embrace new visions of society, new images of teaching and learning, and — a recurrent theme of this book — new conceptions of educational management. Not surprisingly, the full cycle of renewal — from 'problem' to 'solution' — provides plenty of scope for shortfall and failure. Success is as remarkable as it is unusual.

II

One success story in the history of education is that of the elementary school — a form of schooling that, for a century or more, served a socially-distinct population — the children of wage labourers. The full story of the elementary school — particularly its early history — has still to be written. Yet, most commentators agree that its roots are to be found in the 'charity schools' of the seventeenth and eighteenth centuries.

One innovator regularly associated with the charity schools of that period is Jean Baptist de la Salle (1651-1719). Born in Rheims of an aristocratic but pious family, De la Salle's claim to fame is that he devoted much of his life and personal fortune to the establishment, organization and management of a network of 'free' schools run by local communities of 'Brothers of the Christian Schools'.[3] What, then, was original about these schools? And what part did De la Salle play in their emergence?

As noted, De la Salle came from a comfortable background. His family was well connected to both the nobility and bourgeoisie of Rheims. His father's family included lawyers and cloth merchants. And his mother came from a noble family that included royal service among its privileges. Further, when De la Salle was installed as a canon of Rheims cathedral in 1667 the position was vacated in his favour by an uncle — Pierre Dozet — who was also the then Chancellor of the University of Rheims. Entering the local Collège des Bons Enfants in his ninth year, De la Salle completed the full programme of studies, receiving a Master of Arts degree in 1669. Thereafter, he spent two years in Paris, taking classes at the Sorbonne and extending his theological training at the Seminary of St Sulpice.

Following the deaths of his mother and father, De la Salle returned to Rheims in 1672 to take responsibility for his two sisters and four younger brothers. Back in his home town, he assisted an older Canon — Nicholas Roland (also a distant relation) — in various pastoral and evangelical endeavours. De la Salle's training at St Sulpice had emphasized the importance of rescuing and catechizing the poor — a policy that also fitted well with the changing social composition of Rheims. In the preceding two decades the city had been burdened by a considerable migration of peasants from the countryside, only some of whom had found work in the various departments (for example, spinning, weaving) of the woollen industry.[4]

The main thrust of Roland's early work was to establish free schools for 'poor' girls. In common with similar initiatives elsewhere in France, Roland had two related difficulties to overcome. First, he needed to create a cadre of reliable teachers for these schools; and, secondly, he needed to generate funds to ensure their survival. Using various one-off donations, Roland created residential communities of devout women who could take responsibility for the day to day running of the schools. Collectively, these communities — with Roland as their spiritual director — became known as the Sisters of the Holy Child Jesus. After Roland's death in 1678, De la Salle worked to ensure the survival of the Sisters. In the following year, and with the support of the Archbishop of Rheims, he obtained 'lettres patentes' from the state. These documents, which enabled the Sisters to be the legal object of donations and legacies, also indicated the form and goals of their communities:

> Some women, widows, and young women of piety would join together and live in the same house . . . in order to make themselves capable and subsequently to apply themselves to the instruction of young persons of their sex.[5]

In 1678 De la Salle gave up the canonry and was ordained as a priest — a move that symbolized his wish to move out of the cathedral and take up parish work. Over the years that followed — and through the great famines of 1693-94 and 1709-10 — De la Salle followed Roland's example. He created lay communities of male teachers — two was the minimum size — who established houses and boys' schools wherever they received assurances of financial assistance (i.e. contracts from town councils and/or donations from wealthy citizens). But difficulties still arose. Without the legitimacy conferred by lettres patentes, funding was always liable to be withdrawn; and, even when schools were established, the Brothers regularly met opposition from fee-charging teachers who felt their livelihoods were under threat.[6]

It was not until after De la Salle's death that the full corporate status of the Congregation was recognized — by the Crown in 1724 and the Pope in 1725. Nevertheless, at that time the Brothers had already established schools in more than twenty-two locations throughout France (for example, Calais, Rouen, Dijon, Marseilles and Chartres). And, by 1790, this figure had risen to 108 locations, the majority of which (55 per cent) were medium-sized towns of from 2000-5000 inhabitants.[7]

Towards the end of the seventeenth century De la Salle had begun to codify his social, theological and educational views for dissemination among the growing Congregation (or Institute) of Brothers. Included among his writings was the *Conduct of Christian Schools,* a 220-page school manual written in French. Begun in 1695, and initially circulated in manuscript form, the *Conduct* was finally published in the year after De la Salle's death.[8]

As described in its preface, *The Conduct of Christian Schools* was divided into three parts. The first part (114 pages) detailed 'all the exercises and everything else' that was to be done 'from the opening to the closing hour'. The second part (104 pages) set out the 'necessary and useful means' by which the teachers should 'maintain order in the school'.[9] And the final part — not included in the printed edition — related to the inspection of schools and the training of teachers.

As far as can be discerned, the average size of the Brothers' schools was somewhere between 100 and 300 pupils[10], with the larger ones divided into two (or perhaps three) rooms or 'classes'.[11] The schools were furnished with moveable benches; a storage chest or cupboard; seating for the teacher(s); religious artifacts; a set of the five school rules; and, where required by the programme of studies, a chalk board (for arithmetic); tables for (ink) writing; and charts of the alphabet, syllables and numerals (arabic and roman).

Within each school the basic programme of studies (i.e. reading) was divided into a sequence of nine 'lessons', each of which was further sub-divided into three 'orders' (i.e. for beginners, intermediate and advanced scholars). Consecutively, the reading 'lessons' comprised (i) the alphabet, (ii) the syllables; (iii) the primer; (iv) the second book (for spelling and syllabic reading); (v) the second book repeated (for more advanced, fluent reading); (vi) the third book (for eloquent reading); (vii) the Psalter; (viii) De la Salle's tract on Christian civility; and (ix) reading from hand-written documents.[12] In addition, the Brothers offered instruction in writing (six orders) to those who were well-versed in reading, and arithmetic (an unspecified number of lessons) to those who had reached the fourth order of writing.[13]

Each pupil moved up through the orders before being examined — by a director of the school(s) or a school inspector — for promotion to the next lesson. The results of these examinations, together with the teacher's recommendation and the inspector's ultimate decision, were recorded in the school 'catalogue'. All told, it was anticipated that a full reading programme would take a minimum of three-four years.[14] In these terms, then, De la Salle's pedagogy still followed the individualized approach of previous centuries. Neither 'class' nor 'lesson' referred to the grouping of pupils.[15] Rather, the first was a place where individuals assembled; and the second was a course unit which pupils followed at their own pace (albeit under the supervision of a teacher). Similarly, there was no expectation that all pupils would complete the course; nor that there was any particular age at which a child should start at school.

There was, however, one important respect in which De la Salle's pedagogy offered an amended form of individualization. Although children were examined 'one after another according to their position on the benches'[16], all the children of a given lesson were expected to follow these proceedings. Each child was to be ready to answer if the examinee faltered. Likewise, each teacher was required, 'from time to time', to call upon ill-attending pupils to read 'a few words'.[17]

A final noteworthy feature of De la Salle's pedagogy was that, having established an initial sense of order, the subsequent regulation of a school was to be achieved non-verbally. For instance, prayers were to be initiated by the teacher clasping his hands; recitation of the catechism was to be commenced after the teacher had made the sign of the cross; and organization of lessons was to be orchestrated by means of a sonorous iron instrument known as a 'signal'.[18]

III

Since it first took shape, De la Salle's pedagogy has received considerable attention. In the middle of the nineteenth century it was claimed as the ultimate source of the newly-popular 'simultaneous' or 'class' methods of teaching.[19] As already indicated, this attribution should be treated cautiously. Nevertheless, those early discussions brought De la Salle's work to a wider audience — a process that, for subsequent generations, was repeated by John Adamson's (1905) *Pioneers of Modern Education in the Seventeenth Century*[20] and W.J. Battersby's (1949) *De la Salle: Pioneer of Modern Education.*[21] Presumably, this general cross-national interest in French education also helped towards De la Salle's canonization in 1900 and towards his being declared Patron Saint of All Teachers of Children and Youth by Pope Pius XII in 1950. Certainly, this last designation was celebrated in A. Fitzpatrick (1951) *La Salle: Patron of All Teachers* (1951), a volume which also includes 'a study of the treatment of La Salle in all the histories of education'.[22]

More recently, De la Salle has received a new wave of attention — one that attempts to place his work in a wider context. Two studies, both written by members of De la Salle's own congregation — William Moran and Yves Poutet — are particularly important in this respect. The first, a University of London doctoral thesis completed in 1966, explicitly offers a 'new assessment'[23] of De la Salle, linking his contributions to the common stock of seventeenth-century French educational change. The second study — a two-volume, 1100-page analysis of the origins of the Brothers of the Christian Schools (published in 1970) goes even further, recognizing that De la Salle's work was also tied up with a fundamental change of international proportions — the seventeenth-century 'Crisis of the European Conscience'.[24]

Finally, English-speaking readers have been given more direct access to De la Salle in Michel Foucault's *Discipline and Punish* (original edition, 1975). In a section entitled 'docile bodies', Foucault claims not only that De la Salle's plans brought an unprecedented 'technical rationality' to schooling but also that, in their attention to detail, they provided a model for eighteenth-century economics, medicine and military theory.[25]

The general view — shared by De la Salle's critics and admirers alike — seems to be that his work undoubtedly took place at a time of general pedagogic innovation. Low cost, semi-custodial, 'charity' schooling — financed by municipalities and/or wealthy citizens — had become a 'solution' to the 'problem' of larger and larger numbers of able-bodied poor. Yet, in its precision and rationality, De la Salle's model of the charity school appears to stand out from earlier efforts. Three questions, therefore, present themselves: (i) 'what were the new social circumstances of late seventeenth-century France?'; (ii) 'where did De la Salle draw the inspiration for his seemingly major break with the past?'; and (iii) 'how does De la Salle's work stand in relation to earlier "charity" schooling and to later "elementary" schooling?'.

IV

As noted in the previous chapter, much sixteenth-century innovation — educational or otherwise — was linked to the restructuring of management and administration. At the national level, for instance, governmental agencies were given (or took) responsibility for issues that cut across the boundaries of local control. Indeed, this realignment of authority was an integral part of the nation-building process.

One new phenomenon that figured in post-Renaissance local and national politics was the large scale migration of work-seeking poor. To understand this problem it is necessary to examine both the demographic and economic circumstances of sixteenth and seventeenth-century Europe.

During the sixteenth century Europe's population rose from 82 million to around 105 million, reaching an eventual peak in the early seventeenth century.[26] This increase put a general pressure on landholdings. Insofar as farming methods remained unchanged, and no new land was brought under cultivation, population pressure pushed up the prices of agricultural produce.[27] A so-called 'price revolution' ensued, marked by a doubling or even trebling of prices between 1500 and 1650.[28] Accordingly, persons whose income was fixed in monetary terms (for example, landlords who had granted long leases in exchange for money rents) were subject to a gradual decline in their standards of living. On the other hand, those able to sell their agricultural produce in the market place (for example, tenant farmers) could draw repeated cash benefits from rising prices.[29]

Over time, then, changing economic circumstances drew different responses from the various sections of society. The smallest landholders suffered a crisis of subsistence; more substantial farmer-tenants increased their wealth; and the largest (absentee) landlords received a reduced return on their assets. Within this framework, the middle strata were best equipped to withstand the inclement economic weather. To survive, the smallest peasants sought additional income; and the landlords switched to short-term leases or to the direct cultivation of their own land. Given access to markets, a suitable supply of labour and adequate legal (or other) regulation of wage levels, the switch to commercial, cash-crop, market-oriented farming was an attractive option in many parts of Western Europe.[30].

The general outcome of this trend was the gradual breakup of feudal-type patterns of landholding. Peasants became less likely to live solely from the working of their own land. Instead, they worked on a more regular basis (for example, as day labourers) for their landlords and/or for peasant neighbours with larger landholdings. In certain parts of Europe, however, they also had another economic option: to take up the spinning and weaving of wool and flax, using yarns and looms provided by cloth merchants.[31]

In these latter areas (for example, Northern France) day- or wage-labourers were subject to the vagaries of both agricultural and commercial economics. Poor harvests could cause famine; but they could also release labour to work in the weaving industry. Economic and geographic mobility, therefore, became an integral part of the way of life of the wage-labourer.[32] At times, the agricultural and industrial spheres buffered each other. But if stagnation hit both spheres simultaneously, the effect could be disastrous. Typically, these crises were localized, but the possibility of being swamped by an influx of landless, mobile, and work-seeking poor aroused widespread concern in municipal circles.[33]

Within France, this general pattern was exacerbated by an economic recession which, it is claimed, 'dragged on' from about 1630 to 1700.[34] Throughout, France sought to solve her economic problems militarily — a policy which left her with only forty-seven full years of peace in the seventeenth century.[35] But with a standing army and a fleet of warships to maintain, the French fiscal system was placed under great pressure.[36]

The middle and poorer sections of French society seem to have shouldered a considerable financial burden. Taxation doubled between 1600 and 1641; and nearly doubled again between 1661 and 1715.[37] In turn, small-scale popular protests and uprising became endemic. For instance, it is reported that the 600,000 people of Provence organized 374 revolts between 1596 and 1715.[38] Although local in extent and character, these uprisings — of a type which occurred throughout France[39] — were directed against state officials (for example, tax collectors) and the policies and demands that they symbolized.

Besides specific fiscal difficulties, seventeenth-century France also confronted two religious problems: the relationship between church and state, and the relationship between Catholics and Protestants. In both cases, the possible emergence of a 'state within a state' gave cause for concern. In the late sixteenth-century, for instance, there was royal suspicion of Catholic plotting against the king — a fact reflected in the expulsion of the Jesuits in 1594. Gradually, however, the state became ascendent, coopting major church notables to its own vision of the divine right of Kings.[40]

The same period also witnessed attempts to tackle Catholic-Protestant strife. In 1598 the Calvinist-educated, Catholic convert, Henry IV, tried to settle decades of civil/religious war by using the Edict of Nantes. The Edict permitted armed garrisons in 100 named Protestant towns and endorsed the survival of the Protestant universities and the national synods of the Reformed Church.[41]

The Edict, however, was never accepted by the Pope; and was only registered by the Parisian courts (in 1599) after repeated threats of sanctions by the King. In return, the Catholic authorities abandoned the hope of eliminating Protestantism by force. With the King's encouragement — illustrated by the recall of the Jesuits in 1603 — an extensive programme was mounted to convert the French protestants (the so-called Huguenots). One reflection of this initiative was the foundation of twelve missionary orders — each offering 'elementary education' — in the years between 1592 and 1684 (for example, the Sisters of Notre Dame, 1598; the Piarists, 1621; and the Sisters of Charity of St Vincent de Paul, 1633).[42]

V

Initially, such missionary work was heavily influenced by 'fideism' — a standpoint which held that belief in God was demonstrated through faith, not reason. Further, fideists assumed, like Duns Scotus (c.1265-1308) and William of Ockham (1270-1347), that theological belief could not be scrutinized by the same rational procedures as philosophical knowledge. In turn, fideist theology had three practical consequences. First, that a person's faith could be gauged against their willingness to accept, without question, the teachings of the church and the authority of the clergy.[43] Secondly, that piety, personal asceiticism and self-denial were taken as the outward manifestations of a person's inward faith. And thirdly, that church leaders like François de Sales (1567-1622) and Vincent de Paul (1581-1660) could, through an appeal to the self-denial of others, attract recruits to the church's missionary campaigns.[44]

There was, however, another theological current in Catholic France — one that aspired to put the church's work on a stronger intellectual footing. This movement — part of the 'Catholic Renaissance' — identified reason as a complement to fideism. Faith was to be a matter of proof, not acceptance. Taking their cue from the synthesis of faith and reason attempted by the medieval scholastic Thomas Aquinas (1225-1274), these 'neo-scholastics' aimed to provide a justification of faith that was (a) sufficiently powerful that it could overcome the resistance of religious scepticism; and (b) sufficiently logical that it could be communicated in the form of a scientific proof.

The neo-scholastics' interest in communication also took the form of an interest in pedagogy. In this respect, for instance, the Jesuits were typical neo-scholastics. Their major educational treatise — the *Ratio Studiorum* — took up its public form in 1599, serving to keep the Jesuits in the pedagogic vanguard after their return to France. But the blending of theology and intellectualism was not restricted to the Jesuits. In the later years of the seventeenth century, other groupings also combined attention to Catholic rationalism with the management of schools, seminaries and colleges (for example, the French Oratorians, originally founded by Pierre de Bérulle in 1611; and the St Sulpicians, originally founded in 1642 by a pupil of Vincent de Paul — Jean Jacques Olier). Indeed, this period also coincided with a major strengthening of organized training for the priesthood. Ninety-two seminaries were founded between 1642 and 1682 — in marked contrast to the 'six or eight', of 'mediocre quality', that existed in 1614.[45]

Overall, the rise of new religious orders coincided with both the extension of the church's missionary work and the re-evaluation of the church's theological precepts. In one sense, these ecclesiastical tasks fell to different orders. Missionary work occupied the church's foot-soldiers, while theological labour engaged its think-tanks and staff colleges. But in another sense, these movements worked in tandem. The missionary orders furnished intelligence from the front lines which, in turn, was embodied in the strategic 'solutions' devised by the church's leaders.

One such 'solution' to the scale of seventeenth-century social disaffection was the replacement of voluntary alms-giving with more organized methods of social relief. To this end, the reforming organization known as the Company of the Holy Sacrament was founded, in the late 1620s, by followers of François de Sales and Pierre de Bérulle.[46] A powerful secret group of lay persons and clerics, the Company drew its 'main inspiration' from the 'ascetic spirituality' (cf. fideism) of the French counter-reformation.[47] Yet, as the influence of Pierre de Bérulle, and the membership of Jean Jacques Olier might suggest, the Company was also touched by early neo-scholasticism. Poverty, like theology, began to be opened up to the influence of logic, rationality and systematization.

The Company took a broad approach to reform. It promoted missions; it mounted campaigns of religious observance; and, most tangibly, it sought to control begging and vagabondage. In large towns (for example, Paris, Lyons, Toulouse and Marseilles) its local branches — some sixty in all — worked to regularize, unify and centralize the relatively disorganized forms of voluntary relief. Where successful, the Company was instrumental in the erection of 'General Hospitals' for the confinement of all categories of poor persons. These institutions — also known as 'Maisons de Charité' — operated as combined workhouses, asylums and medical institutions. In Paris the crowning achievement of the Company was the opening, in 1657, of the Hôpital General des Pauvres. During its first year, the Hospital harboured around 6000 persons — some of whom (for example, the aged, infirm and orphaned) entered voluntarily; while others (for example, 'sturdy beggars') were held, for a few weeks at a time, under forced confinement.

The internal regime of each hospital was governed by rules of 'rigorous and dour precision'.[48] Every aspect, from hours of rising, through modes of dress, to forms of punishment was prescribed.[49] Thus, in one important respect — its attention to detail — the Company adopted a rational, ordered approach to social administration. But its rationality was ill-developed. The Company of the Holy Sacrament still saw poverty in terms of a debased human 'nature'[50], rather than as the outcome of important structural changes in society. And its response to poverty hinged more upon self-denying devotion by the missionary orders' members, than around any attempt to refashion the poor to meet the changing structure of the labour market.[51] The application of faith to the elimination of disorder was not enough. In the 1660s the Company went into decline. New methods of social administration, themselves based on new concepts of rationality, came into prominence.

VI

To recap: the first half of the seventeenth century was marked by various new and intersecting movements in French life. In the absence of significant surpluses for economic redistribution, social stability was threatened by political and religious unrest. The scale of this disorder cast into doubt the piecemeal 'solutions' borrowed from previous centuries (for example, alms-giving). Order was to be restored through the concentration of power at the centre (i.e. in the 'state') and through the dissemination (by the church) of an accepting piety among those deprived of power. Finally, new institutions designed to strengthen rural and urban piety were caught up in wider discussions about the relationship between theology, politics and social administration.

By the second half of the century many of these ideas about the elimination of disorder had become harnessed to the intellectual synthesis proposed by René Descartes (1596-1650). Descartes' personal contribution related primarily to the field of natural philosophy (cf. the related works of Copernicus, 1472-1543; Galileo, 1564-1642; and Kepler, 1571-1630). But the implications of his proposals (for example, the differential importance they gave to God, nature, and human beings) readily made them a focus of debate in other spheres.

Born in Rennes of monied parents, Descartes received his early schooling at a Jesuit seminary. At the age of 22 he left France and spent much of his remaining life in Holland, Germany and Sweden (where he died). Like the neo-scholastics, he sought to place human thought (and theology) on a more logical or rational basis. At the risk of oversimplification, his contribution to this aspiration was three-fold. First, he offered an account of the material world that was much more susceptible to mathematical analysis (i.e. he gave 'quantities' priority over Aristotelian 'qualities'). Secondly, his contribution to mathematics — a fusion of algebra and geometry — was claimed as a model both of the internal world of thought and of the external world of 'nature' (i.e. Descartes professed the unity of natural philosophy, mental philosophy and mathematics). And finally, Descartes' quantitative/geometric approach underwrote an atomistic and mechanistic model of nature (i.e. he believed in the law-like interaction of both material and mental phenomena). In short, Descartes assumed that there was a rational and harmonious 'order of things' — like the movement of the planets around the sun — to which nature complied and to which human society (ethics, government etc.) could also be adjusted.[52]

Descartes' claims for a 'universal science' that could 'perfect the human situation' were made public in his *Discours de la Méthode* (1637).[53] Despite certain potentially-controversial features (for example, his 'evasion'[54] of theological issues pertinent to the neo-scholastics), Descartes' vision of an accessible, comprehensible and (ultimately) controllable world had a wide appeal among philosophers, scientists and politicians.[55] Within fifty years Descartes' ideas had come of age. By the end of the seventeenth century, it is claimed that Cartesianism had 'infiltrated everywhere'[56], even into the seminaries of those orders, like the St Sulpicians, Oratorians and Jesuits, who had opposed (and sometimes banned) Descartes' works in earlier years.[57]

VII

By the time, then, that Jean Baptist De la Salle began his educational works (i.e. in the 1680s) it would seem that Cartesianism (and its derivatives) had begun to shape the mainstream of French intellectual life. Yet few, if any, subsequent commentators point to the influence of Cartesianism on De la Salle's work. Is this because he remained outside the sphere of cartesian influence? Or is it because Cartesianism was, by then, so all-pervasive as to be invisible? Poutet, for instance, seems to prefer the former explanation. He claims that the theological training of St Sulpice and Sorbonne (1670-72) had left De la Salle with a lasting preference for the 'assurances of faith' over the 'arguments of reason'.[58]

Certainly, De la Salle's attention to detail can be explained in fideistic terms: a life ruled by constant attention to minutiae was held to be a better demonstration of faith than a life punctuated by occasional acts of heroism.[59] But there are also other features of the *Conduct of Christian Schools* which seem more cartesian in origin. For instance, De la Salle's model for school organization pays particular attention to the dispositions of time and space. Taken together with a pedagogy which also tried to account for all pupils at all times, the *Conduct of Christian Schools* is strongly evocative of the Cartesian cosmology.[60]

Further, there is more than a whiff or Cartesianism in De la Salle's practice not only of giving reasons for his methods but also of trying to show how they, in turn, might serve a range of educational purposes. That is, the 'detail' provided by De la Salle related both to the elements of his system and to the ways in which the elements fitted together. For instance, in requiring pupils to bring breakfast and lunch to school, the Brothers were to create a context whereby their charges could (a) nourish themselves; (b) donate any surplus to the 'poor'; (c) learn table manners; and (d) rehearse the religious rituals associated with eating.[61]

Finally, De la Salle's decision to abandon latin as a teaching medium would also have had the support of the Cartesians of the day. For them, French was preferable to latin on the grounds that its structure (for example, word sequence) was more in tune with the 'natural order of thought'.[62] In fact, De la Salle did not omit latin from the *Conduct of Christian Schools*. Rather, he moved it to the psalter stage of the reading programme where it became, in effect, a second language taken only by senior students.

Overall, De la Salle and the Cartesians had much in common. For both, questions of order were paramount. An ordered world was both an end in itself — a faithful reflection of God's design for nature; and a means to an end — a framework for disciplining the minds and bodies of each new generation of God's children. Of course, in constructing his system De la Salle drew upon theological and educational practices that pre-date Cartesianism (for example, the attention to detail, the importance of silence and the adoption of vernacular instruction). Yet, to seek De la Salle's originality in individual practices is to look in the wrong place. To define a system is to identify more than its constituent parts; it is also to identify the relationships that hold the parts together. If De la Salle did, indeed, make a break with the past then it is these ordering principles — cartesian or otherwise — that, I believe, hold the key to his originality.

68

VIII

By addressing the form of schooling detailed by Jean Baptist De la Salle, this chapter has tried to throw some further light on the links between schooling and social structure in seventeenth-century France. In particular, an attempt has been made to identify the intellectual matrix from which new pedagogic practices were cast. It seems defensible, therefore, to claim that despite his close connection with earlier forms of charity schooling De la Salle made an important educational intervention in seventeenth-century French life. In drawing upon the managerial/control assumptions, of the Scientific Revolution, he brought a new maturity to the standardization of schooling. Yet, just as I believe it is unwise to attribute 'simultaneous' instruction to De la Salle, so I also feel that a degree of caution should be exerted before claiming him — at least on the basis of the *Conduct of Christian Schools* — as a founder of 'elementary' schooling.[63] De la Salle certainly established 'free' schools, but these were not necessarily restricted to the registered poor. In the provision of writing and arithmetic, for instance, the Brothers' schools were well-positioned to take over the child-rearing responsibilities of self-employed artisans and small merchants. Indeed, to this end, the *Conduct of Christian Schools* makes reference to the fact that 'rich' parents were to supply their children's books, paper, and (ink) writing implements.[64]

This general attention to a broad curriculum and a heterogeneous clientele may also account for the particular success of the Brothers in the smaller towns. As such, the *Conduct* was compiled neither for 'charity' (i.e. poor) nor for 'elementary' (i.e. working class) schools. Rather, its intentions resonated most successfully with the educational interests of families who, socially, economically and geographically, lay outside the network of latin-centred 'colleges' founded in the previous century.[65] In turn, however, the *Conduct* also served another purpose: insofar as it fostered a homogeneous and nationwide system of schools — albeit in parallel with the 'colleges' — it further strengthened the connections between local municipalities and the national state. Nevertheless, before a full-blown, state-regulated and socially-distinct elementary school system could emerge, a further set of educational and economic transformations had to occur. For these, it is necessary to move on and examine the impact upon schooling of the Industrial Revolution and the European Enlightenment.

Notes

1 Compère, M-M. and Julia, D. (1983) 'Les collèges sous l'ancien régime', *Histoire de l'Education,* 13, p.16 (quotation abridged).

2 Moran, W. (1966) 'Development and evolution of the educational theory and practice of John Baptist De la Salle in the congregation of the Brothers of the Christian schools in France in the eighteenth and nineteenth centuries', PhD thesis, London, University of London, p.48 (quotation abridged).

3 The following sources provide information on De la Salle's early life: Fitzpatrick, E.A. (1951) *La Salle: Patron of All Teachers,* Milwaukee; and Poutet, Y. (1970) *Le XVIIe Siècle et les Origines Lasalliens,* Rennes. (I am grateful to Marie Claire Jacquié and Robert Jacquié for obtaining this last work for me, together with the facsimile edition of the *Conduct of Christian Schools.*)

4 For details of the economic circumstances that prevailed in Rheims during the 1660s see Poutet, Y. (1970) *op cit,* Vol 1, pp.103-5.

5 Quoted in Fitzpatrick, E.A. (1951) *op cit,* p.75. The priority that seems to have been given to girls' education in seventeenth century France deserves further attention. More than forty years ago W. Kane (1938) wrote 'No adequate account of the rise and development of religious congregations of women devoted to teaching has been written' (*An Essay Toward a History of Education,* Chicago, IL, p.279n) — a state of affairs only partially rectified by H.C. Barnard's (1954) *Girls at School Under the Ancien Régime,* London.

6 For the difficulties encountered by De la Salle's early schools see Fitzpatrick, E.A. (1951) *op cit,* Chapter 3.

7 Chartier, R., Julia, D. and Compère, M-M. (1976) *L'Éducation en France du XVIe au XVIIIe Siècle,* Paris, pp.80-1.

8 A facsimile of the 1720 edition of the *Conduite des Ecoles Chrétiennes,* together with the third (unpublished) section, and together with comparative notes on the 1706 manuscript, was pulished in Rome as volume 24 of *Cahiers Lasalliens* (1965). An uneven English translation, by F. de la Fontainerie, was published by McGraw-Hill (New York) in 1935. Page references in this chapter, unless otherwise indicated, relate to the facsimile edition.

9 *Conduct,* preface.

10 This estimate for the size of the Brothers' schools is derived from figures reported in Fitzpatrick, E.A. (1951) *op cit,* (for example, 96, 98 and 102). These, in turn, are consonant with the 1790 figure of 34,964 pupils spread across 108 locations, some of which had more than one school (see Chartier, R. *et al* (1976) *op cit,* p.80).

11 Two schools are described briefly in the introduction to Fontainerie's translation of the *Conduct of Christian Schools.* One had 300 pupils, four classes (i.e. rooms) and three teachers; and the other had 120 pupils and two teachers (p.38n). Other circumstantial evidence concerning the size and architecture of the schools can be gleaned from the room dimensions recommended in the *Conduct:* 324-625 square feet (30-58 m.sq.) for the larger school rooms and 225-324 square feet (20-30 m.sq.) for the 'small and middle classes'. Assuming six square feet (0.55 m.sq.) per child (a

figure recommended by the English Privy Council in 1840), a one-room school could hold up to 104 pupils and, depending on the combination of rooms, a three-room school could accommodate from 162 312 pupils.

12 *Conduct,* p.16ff.

13 *Ibid,* pp.49-70.

14 *Ibid,* p.275 (i.e. in section three)

15 It is in respect of the word 'class' that Fontainerie's translation is weakest. He appears to confuse groups of students with the rooms in which they were taught. For instance, he offers 'if he is in charge of a class of writers' (p.146) for 's'il est dans la classe (i.e. room) des Ecrivains' (*Conduct,* p.120). Indeed, Fontainerie further compounds these problems of interpretation when he translates the French word 'catalogue' (p.21) as 'class list' (p.67).

16 *Conduct,* p.4; see also pp.10 and 99.

17 *Ibid,* p.20; see also p.120.

18 *Ibid,* p.124ff.

19 The earliest English reference to De la Salle as the originator of simultaneous instruction appears to be in Robinson, R. (1869) *Teachers Manual of Method and School Organisation,* London, p.283 where the author quotes from the earlier 1856 Commissioners Report on National Education in Ireland. Jan Amos Comenius (1592-1670) has also been claimed as an early advocate of 'class teaching' (see, for instance, Montmorency, J.E.G. (1902) *State Intervention in English Education: A Short History from the Earliest Times Down to 1833,* Cambridge, p.100). In fact, it seems that the caution required in the interpretation of De la Salle's 'class teaching' is also needed in the interpretation of Comenius' proposals (for example, '(The master) shall then bid the boys read in turn and while one reads in a clear voice the rest should attend and follow in their books' (Comenius, J.A. (1896) *The Great Didactic,* London, p.424). In chronological and conceptual terms, Comenius' ideas came midway between those of Ramus and those of De la Salle.

20 Adamson, J.W. (1971) *Pioneers of Modern Education in the Seventeenth Century,* New York (reprint of 1905 edition).

21 Battersby, W.J. (1949) *De la Salle: A Pioneer of Modern Education,* London.

22 Fitzpatrick, E.A. (1951) *op cit,* p.vii.

23 Moran, W. (1966) *op cit,* preface.

24 Poutet, Y. (1970) *op cit,* vol.1, p.11. Poutet's reference is to Paul Hazard's *La Crise de la Conscience Européene* (1935), translated into English as *The European Mind 1680-1715* (1953). Hazard's theme, that there was an abrupt and decisive social change at the end of the seventeenth century, has certain affinities with Hobsbawm's claims concerning 'The (general) crisis of the seventeenth century' (1954). Both works receive attention in Rabb, T.K. (1975) *The Struggle for Stability in Early Modern Europe,* New York.

25 Foucault, M. (1979) *Discipline and Punish: The Birth of the Prison,* Harmondsworth, Penguin, p.140. For cognate and complementary account of De la Salle's historical importance, see Ariès, P. (1962) *Centuries of Childhood,* New York; Elias, N. (1978) *The Civilising Process,* Oxford; and Snyders, G. (1965) *La Pédagogie en France aux XVIIe et XVIIIe Siècles,* Paris.

26 Minchington, W. (1973) 'Pattern and structure of demand 1550-1750' in Cipolla, C.M. (Ed) *The Fontana Economic History of Europe,* vol 3, London, p.100.

27 *Ibid,* pp.90, 91 and 95.

28 Dunn, R.S. (1970) *The Age of Religious Wars 1559-1689,* London, p.112. One factor in the price revolution was the circulation of silver coin made from raw materials imported from South America.

29 Kiernan, V.G. (1980) *State and Society in Europe 1550-1650,* Oxford, pp.80-9.

30 See, for instance, Minchington, W. (1973) *op cit,* pp.98-9.

31 For discussion of cottage industries based on wool- and flax-processing see, variously, Mousnier, R. (1979) *The Institutions of France Under the Absolute Monarch 1598-1789,* Chicago, IL, pp.265-6; and Goubert, P. (1965) 'The French peasantry of the seventeenth century: a regional example' in Aston, T. (Ed), *Crisis in Europe 1500-1660,* London, pp.148-9.

32 Despite its title, an extended discussion of the subsistence culture of the seventeenth century can be found in Hufton, O. (1974), *The Poor of Eighteenth Century France 1750-1789,* Oxford.

33 For municipal responses to problems caused by high prices and food shortages see, variously, Mousnier, R. (1971) *Peasant Uprisings in Seventeenth Century France, Russia and China,* London, pp.40-1; and Poutet, Y. (1970) *op cit,* vol 1, p.103ff.

34 Lis, C. and Joly, H. (1979) *Poverty and Capitalism in Pre-Industrial Europe,* Hassocks, Harvester Press, p.122. See also Kiernan, V.G. (1980) *op cit,* pp.90-1; ('Cottage industry was spreading quite widely, chiefly in textiles, and industrial capital sprouting, most quickly in northern areas whose development had most in common with the Netherlands and England. France as a whole lagged well behind those countries'); and Minchington, W. (1973) *op cit,* p.98. Further, Roland Mousnier has used the phrase 'permanent crisis' to describe the workings of sixteenth-eighteenth century France (see Church, W.F. (Ed) (1969) *The Impact of Absolutism in France,* London, p.17ff).

35 Parker, G. (1979) *Europe in Crisis 1598-1648,* London, p.73.

36 See also Church, W.F. (Ed) (1969) *op cit,* p.5 ('In foreign affairs, the French kings adopted an anti-Hapsburg stance that combined defense of the realm and strengthening of her frontiers with outright aggression in its later phases. To support the resulting wars, which were increasingly frequent, the burden on the lower classes steadily grew to the point of massive exploitation through expenditure of life and goods').

37 See, respectively, Lis, C. and Joly, H. (1979) *op cit,* p.99; and Dunn, R.S. (1970) *op cit,* p.158.

38 Parker, G. and Smith, L.M. (Eds) (1978) *The General Crisis of the Seventeenth Century,* London, p.12.

39 For a wide-ranging discussion of popular resistance see Kierstead, R.F. (Ed) (1975) *State and Society in Seventeenth Century France,* New York, part 2.

40 See Mousnier, R. (1979) *op cit,* p.653ff.

41 For information on the Edict of Nantes, see Parker, G. (1979) *op cit,* pp.116-9. The Huguenots were forbidden to seek new converts after

1598; they lost their political privileges in 1629; and they were expelled from France in 1685 (*ibid*, p.50).

42 Parker claims, without giving actual figures, that 'the total number of religious establishments in France doubled between 1600 and 1650' (*ibid*, p.118). For a list of the orders devoted to 'elementary education' see Fitzpatrick, E.A. (1951) *op cit*, p.220. It should be noted, however, that Fitzpatrick probably used a generous definition of 'elementary'.

43 For the philosophical background to the catholic renaissance see Kearns, E.J. (1979) *Ideas in Seventeenth Century France*, Manchester, chapter 1.

44 For information on François de Sales and Vincent de Paul, see Dickens, A.G. (1968) *The Counter Reformation*, London, p.172ff.

45 Mousnier, R. (1979) *op cit*, pp.347 and 342.

46 This account of the Company of the Holy Sacrament draws heavily upon Chill, E. (1962) 'Religion and mendicity in seventeenth century France', *International Review of Social History*, 7, pp.400-25.

47 *Ibid*, p.400.

48 *Ibid*, p.415.

49 For details of one seventeenth-century General Hospital see Hufton, O. (1974) *op cit*, pp.140-1.

50 Chill, E. (1962) *op cit*, p.421.

51 Cf. 'The Company's bureacratic, disciplinarian tendency, its passion for religious decorum, its flair for systematic and rational means derived, not from new needs or from a rational program or conception of society, but rather from ascetic impulses turned in a socially repressive direction and colored by a profound conformism to the existing order' (*ibid*, p.423).

52 For accounts of Descartes' philosophy see, variously, Kearns, E.J. (1979) *op cit*, Gaukroger, S. (Ed) (1980) *Descartes: Philosophy, Mathematics and Physics*, Hassocks, Harvester Press; Anscome, E. and Geach, P.T. (Eds) (1970) *Descartes' Philosophical Writings*, London; and Collins, J. (1971) *Descartes' Philosophy of Nature*, Oxford. For associated background material see Maland, D. (1970) *Culture and Society in Seventeenth Century France*, London; and Wade, I.O. (1971) *The Intellectual Origins of the French Enlightenment*, Princeton.

53 According to Kearns, Descartes' original title for the *Discours* was 'A Universal Science which will Raise Human Nature to the Highest Degree of Perfection' (*Ideas in Seventeenth Century France*, p.42).

54 *Ibid*, p.32.

55 One of the earliest patrons of Descartes had been Pierre de Bérulle who, besides being a cardinal, was also a minister of Louis XIII. Bérulle met Descartes in 1627 and encouraged him to commit his philosophical ideas to print. Bérulle, it is claimed, believed that Descartes might serve the revival of catholic rationalism (*ibid*, p.40).

56 Mousnier, R. (1979) *op cit*, p.715.

57 For the responses of the religious orders to cartesianism see *ibid*, pp.349 and 354; Kearns, E.J. (1979) *op cit*, p.76; and Chartier, R. *et al* (1976) *op cit*, pp.201-2.

58 Poutet, Y. (1970) *op cit*, vol. 1, pp.312 and 109 ('Deliberately [De la Salle] set aside the ways of nature and rationalism, conducting himself only by faith').

59 *Ibid,* p.337. See also Chill, E. (1962) *op cit,* p.422.
60 The structuring of time and space in De la Salle's pedagogy is discussed, variously, in Chartier, R. *et al* (1976) *op cit,* p.116; and Foucault, M. (1979) *op cit,* p.141ff. See also Newton's statement in the *Principia* (1687) that 'all things are placed in time according to succession and in space as to order of situation' (quoted in Alexander, H.G. (1945) *Time as Dimension and History,* Albuquerque, NM, p.74). Some pregnant observations on 'the spacial model as key to the mental world' can also be found in Ong, W.G. (1958) *Ramus, Method and the Decay of Dialogue,* Cambridge, MA, pp.314-8.
61 *Conduct,* 7-8. An additional feature of the Cartesian view of reason was the idea that all persons possess a 'good sense' that enables them to make up their own minds. There is a cartesian flavour, then, in the way in which the Brothers — who took no life-long vows — were admitted to the Congregation on the basis not only of faith but of choice. This rationalist tone is also reflected in the fact that the *Conduct* explicitly hoped that the Brothers would be 'persuaded' (rather than instructed?) as to the efficacy of De la Salle's methods (see preface).
62 Tocanne, B. (1978) *L'Idée de Nature en France dans la Seconde Moitié du XVIIe Siècle,* Paris, p.384.
63 Any evaluation of De la Salle's contribution to elementary schooling depends, of course, upon the criteria used to define 'elementary'. It should be noted, too, that this problem is further compounded by the different connotations that 'elementary' has in the French and English languages.
64 *Conduct,* p.259.
65 For discussions of seventeenth century charity schooling in England that overlap with my own see Vincent, W.A.L. (1950) *The State and School Education (1640-1660) in England and Wales,* London, SPCK, and Simon, J. (1968) 'Was there a charity school movement?' in Simon, B. (Ed) *Education in Leicestershire 1540-1940,* Leicester, pp.55-100.

Chapter 4

Adam Smith and the Moral Economy of the Classroom System

If the number of boys studying the same lesson . . . should amount to six, their proficiency will be nearly doubled by being classed.   (Lancaster (1806) *Improvements in Education*)[1]

In general, the larger the classes the greater the improvement.
(Bell (1823)
Brief Manual of Mutual Instruction and Moral Discipline)[2]

Three children . . . cannot by any possibility make the same progress as if there were thirty, and the reason is obvious, each one of the thirty sympathizes with those of the same age and the example operates mutually.   (Stow (1822) *Infant Training*)[3]

The recent history of schooling is, among other things, the history of attempts by teachers and others to reconcile the educational interests of the individual with those of the social group. Pedagogically, these reconciliations have been sought in two ways: (i) by revising the conventions used to group (or 'class'-ify) learners; and (ii) by changing the criteria used for allocation of educational resources (teaching time, paper, texts etc.) within each group of learners.

These distributive rationales, however, are not prominent in the educational record. It is not sufficient to know that a school was divided into 'classes'; or that 'class teaching' was a teacher's preferred mode of instruction. Finer-grained forms of investigation are called for. In particular, closer scrutiny needs to be given to the material artefacts of schooling — the textbooks, school logbooks, desks etc. that, in the best archaeological traditions, are now held in the safe keeping of museums and archives. But even the contribution of these artefacts is limited. Displaced from their original settings, they can only give a partial sense of the cultural webs that they served to sustain. Overall, then, there is much to be gained from revisiting the classical sites of educational innovation.

II

On 11 May 1762 a meeting of the Faculty of the University of Glasgow decided to convert a College 'chamber' (living room) into a 'class room' for civil law. The appearance of the term classroom is historically noteworthy: indeed, its use is perhaps unprecedented in English language sources. The term does not reappear in the Faculty *minutes* until 1774 yet, by the time the University opened a new suite of teaching rooms in 1813, the comparable medieval and Renaissance labels — 'school' and 'class' — had virtually disappeared.[4]

In 1762 Glasgow was a centre of educational and intellectual innovation. The eleven members of the Faculty meeting included Joseph Black, whose discovery of latent heat enabled James Watt to revolutionize the steam engine; John Anderson, whose educational and social ideas helped to shape popular adult education in the nineteenth century; and, not least, Adam Smith, whose writings did much to establish the science of political economy.

Although Black, Anderson and Smith achieved fame well beyond the boundaries of the University of Glasgow, their work also had an important local impact. Anderson's use of practical demonstrations in physics was sufficiently notorious to earn him the nickname 'Jolly Jack Phosphorus'. Smith's service as College quaestor (bookkeeper) in the late 1750s coincided with a rapid growth of the University library. And Black's earliest communications on latent heat were given, a month before the Faculty meeting, to a College gathering of the Glasgow Literary Society.[5]

The presence of 'several gentlemen of the city' at the Literary Society's meeting and its subsequent change of name to the 'Literary and Commercial Society of Glasgow' underlines the fact that the local trade in philosophic, economic and social ideas embraced both town and gown.[6] Further, the same 'commerce intellectuel' continued through time — linking members of the 1762 Faculty with influential nineteenth-century figures such as Robert Owen of New Lanark (who helped to introduce Enlightenment ideas into British elementary schooling); William Hamilton of Edinburgh (who encouraged public support for a state-run system of education along Prussian lines); and David Stow of Glasgow (who founded a 'normal seminary' which served as a prototype for teacher training in England and elsewhere).

This chapter examines the general ferment of educational and social ideas that, in Glasgow and beyond, was associated with the work of reformers like Smith, Owen and Stow. Specifically, it is activated by two related assumptions. First, that the educational practices of the University of Glasgow had a direct influence upon those adopted in the elementary schools of the nineteenth century. And secondly, that the change from 'class' to 'classroom' symbolized a more general upheaval in schooling — the ultimate victory of group-based pedagogies over the more individualized forms of teaching and learning that had been dominant in earlier times.

The political and industrial upheavals of the late eighteenth and early nineteenth centuries (viz. the American Revolution, the French Revolution and the Industrial Revolution) provided the context for these changes. In pedagogic terms, the net result of these revolutions was a major revision in the ethical and economic criteria used to organize the internal workings of schools. In effect, a new 'moral economy'[7] of schooling came into being — one that, for most of the nineteenth century, served to give the 'classroom system'[8] its overall coherence.

Moreover, the fact that such practices were envisaged as a 'system' is, itself, historically significant. The term 'system' had come into use in the seventeenth century alongside the spread of mechanical accounts of the workings of nature.[9] A major figure in this respect was Isaac Newton (1642-1727) whose success in explaining the law-like workings of planetary and terrestrial motion (for example, in the *Principia*, 1687), served both as a model and a motivation for thinkers in other fields.[10]

Against the background of Newton's achievements, various attempts were made to apply the principles of 'natural' philosophy to the workings of the 'moral' (i.e. social) sphere. The overriding intention was to identify those principles which not only held together civil society but which also regulated the movement of its component parts. Whereas Newton had pivoted his natural universe around the unifying concept of gravity, Smith and his Enlightenment contemporaries set out to identify the invariant relationships (or 'general rules')[11] of social life. Smith's own historical importance derives largely from the fact that he was outstandingly successful at this task. *The Theory of Moral Sentiments* (1st ed, 1759) built upon the 'natural principle' of 'sympathy'; while *The Wealth of Nations* (1st ed, 1776) paid particular attention to the human 'propensity' to 'truck, barter and exchange'.[12]

With these conceptual cornerstones in place, Smith was able to construct a sophisticated and coherent philosophical system. From his assumption that human action is the result of 'natural' forces, he was able to deduce that the moral world was driven without reference to the will of individuals. Further, Smith went on to deduce that God's ultimate design for humankind was best served if such forces were allowed to operate freely (i.e. without human interference). If such conditions could be created Smith believed that, by the 'natural course of things', the overall 'progress of society' would be maintained.[13]

Smith's arguments in favour of natural liberty and against artificial restraint were, of course, the answer to every entrepreneur's prayer. In particular, they gave legitimacy to the (then) marginal members of society who, outside the restrictive practices of the established merchant and craft guilds, were actively developing new forms of industrial production around, for instance, the factory spinning of cotton fibre.[14]

III

One of the most successful Glasgow entrepreneurs was David Dale who, in 1786, entered into partnership with Richard Arkwright (inventor of the water frame). Together, they built a water-powered cotton mill on a fast-flowing stretch of the river Clyde about 40 kilometres upstream from Glasgow. Dale provided the appropriate finance and Arkwright supplied the relevant technical support. By 1800, the New Lanark mill was one of the largest in Britain.[15]

Early cotton mills such as New Lanark were a mechanical embodiment of the systematic ideas of the seventeenth-century scientific revolution. Production was organized around a series of discrete processes, powered by a single energy source, and harmonized by a disciplined army of drive shafts, pulleys, gears and 'hands'. Under optimum conditions — a surplus of water, raw materials and labour — the production of cotton yarn was to be administered, quite literally, like clockwork.

But the rhetoric and practices of systematization were not restricted to social philosophy or to industrial production. Their impact was much wider. Within education, for instance, some of the consequences of this general social transformation can be traced out in the single-volume *Complete Works* of Andrew Bell (1753-1832), a Scots-born Church of England minister and self-styled 'discoverer' of the monitorial system. Bell's earliest involvement with the organization of schooling came in 1789 when he was appointed superintendent of the East India Company's orphanage (or 'military male asylum') at Egmore, near Madras. The asylum was funded jointly by the Company and by public subscription; and was one of several whose prime purpose seems to have been to cater for the illegitimate (i.e. mixed-race) off-spring of military personnel. As

Chaplain as well as Superintendent, Bell's mission was not only to manage the asylum but also, more generally, to instil the principles of 'religion and morality'[16] into the minds of the Company's charges.

To achieve these goals more efficiently, Bell made two initial interventions in the affairs of the Madras asylum. First, he organized the educational activities of the two-room school around the idea of having *'a teacher and an assistant for every class'*; and, secondly, he further divided every class into pairs of *'teachers and scholars'*.[17] In combination, these innovations account for the contrasting labels — 'monitorial' and 'mutual' — that, in later years, Bell gave to his instructional methods. If 'mutual' drew attention to the peer-teaching aspects of Bell's proposals, then 'monitorial' pointed to the youth of the supervisory teachers and assistants. In 1796, for instance, the 186 pupils of the Madras school received most of their instruction from 'nine assistants' and 'five teachers' whose ages ranged from 8 years 9 months, to 14 years 3 months.[18] Such a wide age range among the teaching personnel was not, however, a matter of chance. Rather, it was part of Bell's overall design. To ensure that his teachers would not 'lose' time in teaching 'beyond the comprehension of their scholars'[19], Bell chose them from among the immediate graduates of each class. After a year (or two), the teachers and assistants were returned to their original places in the school, and replacements were

Figure 3
A version of mutual instruction derived from Bell's monitorial system. Taken from J. Stoat, *A Description of the System of Inquiry; or Examination by the Scholars Themselves,* London, 1826 (Glasgow University Library)

drawn from the remaining personnel. Besides these temporary staff, Bell also retained three permanent adult 'schoolmasters' whose collective responsibility was to ensure the (day to day?) maintenance of the asylum's 'general order and harmony'.[20]

These, then, were the educational/managerial principles which Bell used to regulate the general 'economy' of the Madras School, and to ensure the 'constant and perpetual attention' of the learners. By such means, as he put it, 'THE SCHOOL TEACHES ITSELF (sic)'.[21] Such a statement, of course, was not merely a claim about the mechanical effectiveness of Bell's proposals, it was also a reminder to his patrons of the financial savings that could be accumulated. By using juvenile teachers instead of 'ushers', Bell noted that the asylum's overall expenses were reduced by more than 60 per cent.[22]

In recent times, educationists have widely identified the employment of cheap pupil labour as Bell's most significant innovation. Certainly, one of the consequences of this practice — the fact that pupil teachers were intellectually ill-equipped for their task — was the main criticism of those innovators (for example, Owen) who eventually broke with the monitorial system. Nevertheless, in the longer term (for example, the timescale of this book), the most noteworthy pedagogical feature of Bell's work was, I believe, unrelated to the employment of pupils: it was, instead, his instence that every class should come under the constant supervision of its own teacher.

While in India, Bell laid down the basic principles of his system — that each level of teaching personnel was responsible for the immediately lower rank, and that at the lowest levels, each class had a permanent teacher. The source of this rationale is not particularly evident from Bell's writings. However, given the context of the Madras asylum, it is probable that Bell drew upon military rather than manufacturing precendent.[23]

On the basis of a favourable reception of his 'Experiment in education' at Egmore, Bell was encouraged to prepare his ideas for the home market. By the end of the eighteenth century British charity schools (of the kind originally developed in the seventeenth century) were in a state of crisis. They could not cope, educationally or financially, with the increasing numbers of indigent poor children who populated areas of urbanization and industrialization. In extending his Madras experiences to meet these new circumstances, Bell also began to assimilate the language and ideologies of the Industrial Revolution.

In 1815, for instance, he wrote of confronting a need to 'diminish the labour, multiply the work, and perfect the manufacture . . . of our schools'.[24] And by this time, too, he had given much more attention to the streamlining of his teaching practices. He eased the promotion of pupils from class to class by providing a course of studies arranged in a 'methodical series, gradually and almost imperceptibly progressive'.[25] He smoothed the workings of each class by introducing 'equalized' classification (i.e. classes formed from scholars of presumed 'equal proficiency').[26] And finally, he harnessed the workings of his system to the 'spirit of imitation and competition'[27] that already existed, so he believed, among his pupils. Overall, by combining the fine-tuning possibilities of the 'new'[28] classification with the idea that 'every lesson' is 'intimately connected' with 'that which went before'[29], Bell believed that he had devised a pedagogical mechanism that would automatically 'accelerate' the progress of 'each and every scholar'[30].

Having oiled his system, and promoted its dissemination throughout Britain (aided by the National Society for the Education of the Poor in the Principles of the Established Church, founded in 1811), Bell seems to have spent the last phase of his life formalizing the 'natural laws'[31] that would turn his pedagogic techniques into an educational science. These writings add little to the practices Bell had discussed earlier, but they are valuable for the clues they give about the broader canvas of his thinking. A single page of *Mutual Tuition and Moral Discipline* (7th ed, 1832) provides some clear examples. Bell echoed eighteenth-century psychology when he described the Madras system as stemming from an 'innate' faculty that has its 'seat' in the 'infant mind'. Similarly, he highlighted the technocratic views of Francis Bacon (1561-1627) when he described the Madras system as an 'organ' (Bacon's term) for the 'multiplication of power and the division of labour in the moral and intellectual world'. And finally, he acknowledged a debt to Newton when he noted that, 'like the principle of gravitation', the Madras system 'pervades, actuates, invigorates, and sustains' the entire scholastic enterprise.[32]

IV

Twentieth-century historians often link the educational work of Andrew Bell with the efforts of his non-conformist counterpart, Joseph Lancaster (1778-1838). Like Bell, Lancaster started his educational experiments before the end of the eighteenth century. As a young man in Southwark (London), he set up a small school in his father's house, later receiving financial support from a network of local Quakers. Although Lancaster's major work, *Improvements in Education* (1st ed, 1803) gives little indication of the source of his ideas, the influence of Bell's earliest writings can be detected.[33] In its 'mechanical part'[34], Lancaster's system was, broadly speaking, the same as Bell's. Both innovators believed that every 'class' should have its own teacher; that every teacher should be subject to the inspection of a superior; and that every pupil should pass, in turn, through a graduated series of lessons in reading, writing and arithmetic.

Nevertheless, there is at least one striking pedagogic difference in the writings of Bell and Lancaster: the latter gave much more attention to prize-giving. Lancaster, that is, regarded tickets, pictures, pens and medals as necessary incentives[35], whereas Bell made only 'extraordinary' use of such 'expedients'[36]. Instead, Bell's system was motivated by 'preferment' and 'forfeiture of rank'[37], procedures that were, he claimed, already 'intrinsic' to 'improved classification'[38].

The reasons for these Bell/Lancaster differences are not altogether clear. They may be merely cosmetic. Or they may reflect an important discontinuity in the social philosophies of Bell and Lancaster. Bell's system, supported predominantly by the established church and the landed classes, was designed to retain the status quo. Its functioning and rhetoric were dedicated more to the efficient operation of the social machine (viz. its 'distributive justice')[39], than to the improvement of its human product. From this view, Bell's relative neglect of extrinsic rewards was deliberate. He regarded them as superfluous to his overall design. On the other hand, Lancaster's system, supported by the dissenting churches (and the British and Foreign Society, founded 1814), gave proportionately more attention to the individual achievements of 'deserving youth'.[40] 'Whenever superior merit shows itself', Lancaster wrote in *Improvements in Education,* 'it should always be honoured, rewarded and distinguished'[41]. Indeed, Lancaster's meritocratic vision soon drew the rebuff of Sarah Trimmer — an educational writer and 'devoted defender'[42] of the Church of England:

> When one considers [she wrote in 1805] the *humble rank* of the boys of which common *Day Schools* and *Charity Schools* are composed, one is naturally led to reflect whether there is any occasion to put notions concerning the 'origin of nobility' into their heads . . . Boys, accustomed to consider themselves as the *nobles of a school,* may in their future lives, form a conceit of their own *trivial merits . . .* [and] aspire to be *nobles of the land,* and to take place of the *hereditary nobility*.[43]

If Bell's ideas hinged on a vision of an ordered, static, agricultural society, Lancaster's system was, by comparison, built around a future-oriented technological and Utopian vision of the new moral world. Bell and his supporters sought to stem the flow of history; Lancaster and his colleagues struggled to channel its social energies along more efficient and profitable lines. For Bell, schooling was a static steam engine; for Lancaster, it was a locomotive. Yet, if Lancaster's automotive principles differed from Bell's, how did they in turn relate to the sources of action proposed earlier by Adam Smith?

V

In 1751 Adam Smith had become Professor of Logic at the University of Glasgow. His appointment was a direct reflection of a modernizing climate in Scottish life. To secure the services of this already-noted scholar, the Glasgow Faculty suspended the regular logic syllabus and allowed Smith to repeat a series of lectures on literature and economics given in Edinburgh between 1748 and 1751. Although Smith's modern notions were not to the liking of all Faculty members, it was generally agreed that this appointment would revive the flagging fortunes of the university by attracting students from 'industry and commerce'[44] — a relatively new and untapped constituency.

Smith spent only one year as Professor of Logic. In 1752 he was translated, following the death of the incumbent, to the Chair of Moral Philosophy, a position that accorded more reasonably with the content of his Edinburgh lectures. Gradually, Smith's moral philosophy course took shape in four parts: natural theology, ethics, jurisprudence (legal theory) and political economy, with the second and fourth of these providing the basis for *The Theory of Moral Sentiments* and *The Wealth of Nations*.

Both these works started with a discussion of the origin of the 'distinction of ranks'. But their subsequent analyses differed in an important respect. The former work built upon static images of a multi-layered society, using such terms as 'rank' and 'station' to describe an individual's place in the social structure.[45] *The Wealth of Nations,* however, operated with a different set of premises. First, Smith's attention to the 'division of labour' arose from the idea that the supposed multitude of social ranks could, in fact, be divided into a much smaller number of groupings (viz. social 'divisions' or, as they later came to be known, 'classes').[46] Secondly, Smith held that the distinction of ranks was due not to nature but, rather, to acquired differences in 'habit, custom and education'.[47] And thirdly, Smith argued that, unlike other animal species, human beings could, by 'barter and exchange', draw upon a 'common stock' of 'talents' available to all members of society.[48] Overall, then, *The Wealth of Nations* regarded the ideal civil society as a bustling market-place of social transactions from which everyone could reap a positive benefit.

Smith's economic theorizing was also important from two other standpoints. His identification of landlords, capitalists and wage labourers as the three major economic units in society helped to make 'division' a much more significant social category than 'rank'. Similarly, Smith's arguments about the social benefits that accrue from the free exercise of human propensities, made economic liberty a more popular social policy than the pursuit of artificial restraint (for example, the granting of monopolies). Indeed, Smith's rhetoric of 'talents', together with his predictions about the social benefits of redistributing the 'common stock', were just as easily applied to the microeconomics of the schoolroom as they were to the macroeconomics of the market place.

Although *The Wealth of Nations* marked, in certain respects, a break with *The Theory of Moral Sentiments,* there is another sense in which these works remained in harmony. *The Wealth of Nations* focused upon social exchange, yet it gave no reason why people should be drawn to recognize the value, to them, of such activity. For this part of his argument, Smith relied upon the social-psychological theories of *The Theory of Moral Sentiments.* Specifically, he believed that the 'continual motion' of the 'industry of mankind'[49] was, itself, powered by a more fundamental source — the moral faculties of 'sympathy' and 'emulation'[50].

As noted earlier, 'sympathy' was a pivotal concept in *The Theory of Moral Sentiments.* Smith believed it to be an ethical relationship that exists among all members of society, irrespective of their wealth or rank. Previously, sympathy had been regarded by moral philosophers as a kind of spiritual essence that was distributed, like alms, by the well-endowed to the less fortunate (cf. sympathy 'for'). In Smith's revised usage, sympathy became something that is shared, like common property (cf. sympathy 'with'). To the extent, therefore, that individuals were in sympathy with each other, they could be regarded as morally equal (cf. the presumed economic equality of buyer and seller under conditions of free trade).

If the concept of sympathy accorded all human beings the same initial natural or moral status, Smith adopted the concept of emulation to account for any subsequent differentiation. He argued that, through an appreciation of (or sympathy 'with') the achievements of the successful, the poor would be motivated to further their own self-improvement. Smith and his supporters believed, therefore, that sympathy and emulation were inseparable sentiments: sympathy promoted society's social cohesion; while emulation underpinned society's continuous progress.[51]

Smith's analysis differed markedly from that of Bell and Lancaster. He connected emulation to sympathy, whereas Bell and Lancaster looked to a supposed connection between emulation and competition.[52] For them, the key to educational (and social) progress was 'pedagogic rivalry' not 'mutual sympathy'. Place-taking 'contests'[53] were to be fought out among 'combatants'[54] carefully matched through the 'new' methods of equalized classification. In fact, Bell and Lancaster's views on rivalry were part of an older educational lineage, one that stemmed from the classical writings of Quintilian[55] and that had been subsequently reaffirmed by, among others, Erasmus[56] and the Jesuits.[57]

Against these criteria, Smith's social philosophy represented a clear break with the past. As noted, he believed that sympathy was the ultimate moral sentiment since, without it, there could be neither emulation nor progress. Moreover, emulation was held to be about self-esteem and self-improvement, not about conflict and rivalry. Finally, Smith's recasting of these sentiments was consistent with the early optimistic days of the Industrial Revolution. Sympathy and emulation were to be regarded as devices for the levelling-up of human beings, not as instruments for the further differentiation of an already divided society.

Disentangling Smith's ideas about progress, sympathy and emulation also makes it possible to distinguish the pedagogic practices of Bell and Lancaster from those of Owen and Stow. The two later innovators — Owen and Stow — not only rejected the monitorial system, they espoused a pedagogy that was markedly collectivist in its assumptions. By the 1820s, Owen's teaching was designed around 'friendly emulation' that enabled learners to 'go . . . forward with their companions'[58]; and by the 1830s, Stow could claim that the 'sympathy of numbers' afforded a 'better and more favourable opportunity of training . . . than possibly can be accomplished singly and alone'.[59]

If these quotations are representative, they support the view that the collectivist (or batch) methods of class teaching did not evolve from within the monitorial methods of Bell and Lancaster but grew, instead, from the kind of social psychological assumptions promulgated by Adam Smith. Nevertheless, equivalence of terminology does not prove linearity of descent. To strengthen this hypothesis, it is necessary to fill the chronological gaps between Smith, Owen and Stow. Insofar as Smith wrote little about pedagogy, and insofar as he died ten years before Owen moved from Manchester to become David Dale's successor at the New Lanark Mill in 1800, it is probable that other persons acted as exponents, popularizers and couriers of his ideas. Again, there are good grounds for looking towards events at the Scottish universities.

VI

The eighteenth century was a major period of change for the University of Glasgow. The early decades were marked by the replacement of generalist 'regents' with specialist 'Professors' and by the spread of English rather than Latin as the main medium of instruction. The most significant pedagogic changes, however, came at the end of the century and were, it seems, initiated by pupils and successors of Adam Smith — John Millar (Professor of Law, 1761-1801); James Mylne (Professor of Moral Philosophy, 1797-1839); and, most notably, George Jardine (Lecturer and Professor of Logic, 1774-1827). Jardine's particular contribution — besides reporting these changes in *Outlines of Philosophical Education* (1st ed, 1818) — was to complete the transformation of the logic class set in train by Adam Smith.

In his own words, Jardine sought to shift the substance of the logic class away from the 'mere communication of knowledge' (cf. the influence of Ramus) towards the more general enhancement of 'intellectual powers', those 'habits of thinking, judging, reasoning, and communication, upon which the farther prosecution of science, and the business of active life, almost entirely depend'.[60] Drawing upon the Enlightenment ideas and direct influence of Smith, Hume and Helvetius (whom he had met briefly through an introduction from Hume), Jardine's revision of the logic class was two-fold. First, he replaced a curriculum based on Aristotelian logic with a set of notions drawn from the nascent field of Faculty psychology. And secondly, he built his teaching methods around the self-same psychology.

The first part (or 'division') of Jardine's lectures was devoted to the 'study of mind' — the *'mother science . . .* from which all others derive at once their origin and nourishment'.[61] Within this framework, Jardine chose the 'powers of the understanding' as his initial topic, giving priority to the contributing 'faculties' of 'perception' and 'attention'.[62] Jardine's decision to begin with these two concepts was probably not accidental: he held that perception was the 'first and wonderful communication between mind and matter'[63]; and that, in turn, attention was the instrument by which the 'intensity'[64] of a perception could be increased. Despite these major revisions, Jardine remained true to the traditional (i.e. post-renaissance) purposes that lay behind the teaching of 'logic' to undergraduates. His intention, like Ramus', was to give students access to the 'tools and engines of the intellect — study techniques that would be useful not only in the remainder of their student days but also in the remainder of their lives.[65]

Nonetheless, Jardine's espousal of (a variant of) Faculty psychology also prompted a major reorganization of the conduct of the logic lectures. Jardine recognized that if a student's faculties were to operate at full power, they also needed regular exercise. Accordingly, Jardine began to incorporate a system of extempore questioning into (and alongside) his lectures. Moreover, such questioning was carefully designed both to control the group and to meet the intellectual needs (as defined by Jardine) of its individual members. Questions were not 'put indiscriminately'[66] but, rather, tailored to the 'particular circumstances of each individual'.[67] Nevertheless, as Jardine recognized, the 'active discipline'[68] of the logic class placed 'constant demands' upon the 'attention' of all students.[69] 'In [such] a class-room', he wrote, 'a sympathetic animation pervades the whole'.[70]

Corroborating evidence for such attention to collectivist processes can be gleaned from the gradual extension of University prize-giving after 1776.[71] Prizes given solely for achievement had been known since the Reformation (if not earlier), but Jardine and his colleagues pioneered a broader approach, seeking to ensure that 'none must have reason to consider themselves excluded'.[72] By opening prize-winning to 'every degree of talent and industry'[73], and by rewarding effort (viz. 'regular and spirited exertion')[74] as well as achievement (viz. 'genius or proficiency')[75], it was hoped that the 'spirit of emulation'[76] would remain buoyant in the classes of the University.

Overall, then, Jardine and his colleagues proposed a major revision of the University lecture. In its new form it was to be construed not as a 'dictate' (as it had been known earlier) but as a vernacular discourse — an 'easy dialogue'[77] between a teacher and a group of 'not more than thirty or forty' students.[78] Jardine retained the label 'lecture' for these teaching methods yet, as he clearly recognized, they also included important elements of the 'tutorial system'[79].

> Everyone knows that the method of teaching philosophy which is pursued in the Scottish colleges, differs considerably from that which has been long acted upon in the universities of England. In the former, a series of written lectures, composed or compiled by the professors, are annually delivered from their respective chairs; whereas, in the latter, the business of education is carried on almost entirely by means of private reading, and a species of colloquial examinations. In the prosecution of this last method, the college tutor, instead of lecturing peruses certain authors along with his pupils, explaining particular passages as he goes along, and conversing with them on the doctrines or facts to which their attention has been directed.[80]

VII

To anyone schooled within the classroom system, Jardine's writings seem long-winded and unoriginal. Yet, the fact that his *Outlines of Philosophical Education* covered more than 500 pages and ran to two editions, suggests that its contents were both new and acceptable. Jardine's blending of Faculty psychology and moral philosophy was a powerful argument for the superior social efficiency of class-based teaching methods. Through the agency of colleagues (like John Millar), fellow members of the Glasgow Literary and Commercial Society (like Robert Owen), and pupils (like William Hamilton), Jardine's ideas took on a life of their own and successfully penetrated into the wider educational debates of the early nineteenth century (for example, reform of the universities, schooling for the working classes, state control of education).[81]

Their penetration, however, was far from inevitable. There was still a large gulf, socially and ideologically, between the 'classes' of the University of Glasgow and the 'classrooms' of a model nineteenth-century elementary school.[82] In particular, why would a form of instruction directed to the promotion of 'understanding' have any relevance to elementary schooling — an institution built around Reformation notions about rote learning and catechesis? What, therefore, were the changes in educational thinking that allowed such a connection to be made? And who, once again, were the educational entrepreneurs that brought them to life?

At first glance, George Jardine seems to have had very little involvement in the schooling of the urban proletariat. Most of his energies were directed towards the reform of the University of Glasgow and its preparatory institution, Glasgow Grammar School. Nevertheless, there is evidence that, if Jardine did not so much give his ideas to elementary schooling, others were ready to take them. A key figure in this respect seems to have been Robert Owen. Besides their concurrent membership of the Glasgow Literary and Commercial Society, Jardine was also present in 1812 when Owen made his first major pronouncements on education (at a banquet held to honour a visit to Glasgow by Joseph Lancaster).

Since taking over the management of the New Lanark Mill, Owen had gradually become more active in reorganizing its day-to-day affairs. In addition, the years between 1810 and 1814 seem to have been particularly profitable, enabling Owen to invest in major managerial reforms (including alterations to the factory school founded by David Dale). The culmination of these moves came in 1816 when Owen entered into a new partnership with a small group of London-based financier-

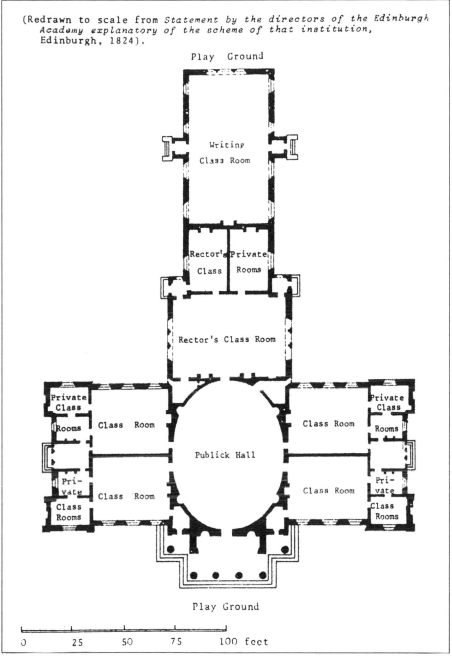

(Redrawn to scale from *Statement by the directors of the Edinburgh Academy explanatory of the scheme of that institution*, Edinburgh, 1824).

Play Ground

Writing Class Room

Rector's Class   Private Rooms

Rector's Class Room

Private Class   Class Room   Class Room   Private Class

Rooms   Rooms

Publick Hall

Pri-vate   Class Room   Class Room   Pri-vate

Class   Class

Rooms   Rooms

Play Ground

0   25   50   75   100 feet

Figure 4

Early appearance of the term classroom in school architecture. Taken from one of the founding documents of Edinburgh Academy: *Statement by the Directors of the Edinburgh Academy Explanatory of the Scheme of that Institution.* Edinburgh, 1824 (Glasgow University Library)

philanthropists. Henceforth, having paid a four percent dividend to his partners, Owen was permitted to reinvest the remainder of the mill's profits as he saw fit.

The influence of Enlightenment (as opposed to charity school) ideas at New Lanark is most evident in the eventual layout, pedagogy and rationale of the 'New Institution for the Formation of Character' (designed and built between 1809 and 1816). The institution — a kind of educational and community centre — was intended as a means by which Owen could extend his influence over the New Lanark workers and their children. Owen's son, writing in 1824, reported not only that the institution contained a 'lecture room' and various schoolrooms, but also that older children were taught advanced subjects (for example, natural history) through 'sensible signs and conversation' in 'familiar lectures' that were delivered 'extempore' to 'classes of from forty to fifty'.[84] This parallelism between Owen's and Jardine's ideas seems to have arisen from the fact that both men were particularly interested in promoting a mental rather than a corporal discipline among their students, albeit for different reasons.

For his part, Owen believed that the disruptions caused by the Industrial Revolution — Scotland had undergone a twelve week national weavers strike in late 1812 — would be better contained if levels of schooling could be raised. If children could be taught to understand the 'inseparable connection' between their own interests and 'the interests and happiness of every other individual'[85] then, so Owen believed, the harmony of society would be restored.

This realignment within Owen's social philosophy was part of a wider educational groundswell.[86] With others, Owen argued that rationality (the promotion of understanding) was as appropriate to the 'character' of the lower classes as it was to the 'active life' of the upper strata. Unlike the conservatives of the day — who assumed that the virtue (and docility) of the working class could be assured merely through the inculcation of habits — Owen claimed that, for all people, a more 'durable' character would be formed if 'the mind fully understands that which is true'.[87]

For such reasons, then, a range of 'intellectual' (or 'rational') systems of working class schooling began to appear in the early nineteenth century.[88] Whereas urban elementary schooling in Britain before 1815 was structured around a presumed linkage between virtue and piety, subsequent initiatives paid much more tribute to beliefs about the connection between virtue and rationality. Thus, it was from theorists like Jardine and Owen that post-1815 educators took their pedagogical models. There was a new-found pedagogic potency in the claim that young people could acquire moral and intellectual rationality through the medium of class-based instruction. But this was not the end of the matter. Insofar as class-based 'instruction' required the orchestrating presence of a teacher, its adoption could also serve as a basis for pupil surveillance. Indeed, this dual appeal — managerial and pedagogic — attracted much of the ideological capital that eventually brought the 'classroom system' into being.

VIII

This chapter has identified some of the ideological tenets that enabled 'simultaneous' methods to appear more socially meaningful than individualized instruction. For the sake of coherence, the ideas of Adam Smith, Andrew Bell, Joseph Lancaster, George Jardine and Robert Owen have received particular attention. No claim is made, however, that these theorists fully comprehended the range of ideas circulating in the early nineteenth century.[89]

At one level, then, this chapter can be regarded as a case study of a more general phenomenon — the extension of mass schooling. Within such a framework, the choice of Glasgow is purely arbitrary: Manchester, London, Amsterdam or Paris would have served the same purpose. At another level, however, the choice of Glasgow is less than arbitrary. The early appearance of the word classroom in that city allows an alternative reading — that Glasgow's importance as an intellectual and economic centre enabled it not only to invent a solution to the problem of urban schooling but, more important, to export such ideas to all parts of the (English-speaking) world. In these terms, then, the ideas of Jardine and Owen had an initial trading advantage over equivalent notions (for example, those of Pestalozzi) that, elsewhere, were also emerging from the common European heritage of charity schooling and Enlightenment philosophy.

By the 1840s, however, such a free market in ideas increasingly became the subject of state intervention. Thereafter, pedagogic practices were regulated more along national than international lines — albeit against a common background of the spread of capitalist forms of factory production. Indeed, as suggested in the following chapters, a full account of the classroom system must accommodate these later developments just as much as it should pay attention to the nurturing conditions of the Enlightenment and the Industrial Revolution.

Notes

1   Lancaster, J. (1806) *Improvements in Education,* London, p.40.
2   Bell, A. (1831) *Brief Manual of Mutual Instruction and Moral Discipline,* Edinburgh, p.71n. Throughout this chapter, page numbers are taken from Bell's *Complete Works* (Edinburgh, 1832).
3   Stow, D. (1833) *Infant Training,* Glasgow, p.11.
4   The earliest printed reference to 'classroom' known to me occurs in Gibson, J. (1777) *The History of Glasgow,* Glasgow, p.143. Use of 'class room' outside Glasgow presumably followed its popularization in Wilderspin, S. (1823) *On the Importance of Educating the Infant Children of the Poor,* London, pp.18 and 26. See, for instance, McCann, P. and Young, F.A. (1982) *Samuel Wilderspin and the Infant School Movement,* London.
5   See Scott, W.R. (1937) *Adam Smith as Student and Professor,* Glasgow; and Read, J. (1950) 'Joseph Black M.D.: The teacher and the man', in Kent, A. (Ed) *An Eighteenth Century Lectureship in Chemistry,* Glasgow, pp.78-98.
6   The emergence of the term classroom may, itself, have been a product of town and gown links in Glasgow. During the late eighteenth-century, Glasgow usage of 'ware room' (not recorded in the *Oxford English Dictionary)* followed an analogous form: 'the premises . . . could be divided into several ware rooms' (*The Glasgow Advertiser and Evening Intelligencer,* 24 January 1794).
7   For the term 'moral economy' see Stow, D. (1850) *The Training System,* London, p.22. Stow presumably took the term from Thomas Chalmers who, besides being his Glasgow patron, was also noted as an evangelical churchman and writer on social and economic affairs.
8   The term 'classroom system' was used, for instance, in a leading article in *The Builder* (July 1868), quoted in Seaborne, M. (1971) *The English School: Its Architecture and Organisation 1370-1870,* London, p.268.
9   The earliest recorded use of 'system' in the *Oxford English Dictionary* dates from 1638. For an early educational use of 'system' see Comenius, J.A. (1969) *A Reformation of Schools* (translated by Hartlib, S., 1642), Menston, p.81. Comenius' opus and/or Hartlib's translation are noteworthy insofar as they lie on the chronological boundary between sixteenth-century 'ordered' conceptions of the world and seventeenth-century 'systematic' (i.e. mechanical) views of nature.
10 Newton, himself, had made the argument that the 'experimental [i.e. empirical] method' could be applied to moral philosophy (see Skinner, A.S. (1974) 'Introduction' to Adam Smith's *The Wealth of Nations,* Harmondsworth, Penguin, p.15). For a discussion of Newton's wider influence on human thought see Buchdahl, G. (1961) *The Image of Newton and Locke in the Age of Reason,* London.
11 Campbell, R.H. and Skinner, A.S. (1982) *Adam Smith,* London, p.105 (quoting from Smith's *Lectures on Jurisprudence,* 1763-1764).
12 'Sympathy' and the 'propensity to truck, barter and exchange' are discussed, respectively, in the first chapter of *The Theory of Moral Sentiments* and the second chapter of *The Wealth of Nations.*
13 Smith, A. (1755) Lecture, quoted in Campbell, R.H. and Skinner, A.S. (1982) *op cit,* p.34.

14 Skinner comments on the political significance of *The Wealth of Nations* in the following terms: '[Its arguments] seemed to lend a certain sanctity to the self-interested pursuit of gain, by showing that such activity was productive of benefit to society at large . . . Smith seemed to have provided a great "masked battery", whose fire could be used to support the pretensions of the emergent mercantile or manufacturing interests (whose motives Smith often doubted)' ('Introduction' to *The Wealth of Nations*, pp.11-12).

15 For David Dale's educational initiatives at New Lanark and elsewhere see McLaren, D.J. (1983) *David Dale of New Lanark*, Milngavie.

16 Bell, A. (1797) *An Experiment in Education Made at the Male Asylum of Madras*, London, p.12. Bell's mission at Egmore was strengthened by his belief that the teaching of the orphans by their own [Indian] mothers was 'the source of every corrupt practice, and an infallible mode of forming a degenerate race' (13).

17 *Ibid*, p.20.

18 *Ibid*, p.17.

19 *Ibid*, p.20.

20 *Ibid*.

21 *Ibid*, pp.11, 19 and 20.

22 *Ibid*, p.51.

23 Although Bell makes no military references in *An Experiment in Education*, it should be noted that military metaphors appear in *Elements of Tuition* (Part III), a work first published in 1815 (viz. 'In a school, as in an army, *discipline* is the first, second, and third essential', p.49; '[the master] is the general of an army . . . with his non-commissioned and petty officers, acting voluntarily and gratuitously, and multiplied at pleasure as occasion requires', p.53).

24 *Ibid*, p.20.

25 *Ibid*, p.37.

26 *Ibid*, p.36. The earliest reference to 'equalized classification' that I have located is Haig, T. (n.d.) *Advantages to be Derived from Equalized Classification*, London.

27 *Elements of Tuition* (Part III) p.45. Elsewhere Bell also writes of 'imitation and emulation' (*Mutual Tuition and Moral Discipline*, p.52).

28 Bell, *Elements of Tuition* (Part III) p.45.

29 *Ibid*, p.37.

30 *Ibid*, p.45.

31 Bell, *Mutual Tuition and Moral Discipline*, p.55 and elsewhere.

32 *Ibid*, p.15.

33 Lancaster acknowledges his debt to Bell in *Improvements in Education*, p.60. For a general account of Lancaster's educational work see Kaestle, C. (Ed) (1973) *Joseph Lancaster and the Monitorial School Movement*, New York.

34 Trimmer, S. (1973) 'A comparative view of the new plan of education promulgated by Mr Joseph Lancaster' in Kaestle, C. (Ed) *op cit*, p.101.

35 For Lancaster's views on prizes and punishments see *Improvements in Education*, p.89ff.

36 Bell, *Mutual Tuition and Moral Discipline*, p.56.

37 Bell, *Elements of Tuition* (Part III) p.51.

38 Bell, *Mutual Tuition and Moral Discipline*, p.56.

39   Bell, *Elements of Tuition* (Part III) p.51.
40   Lancaster, J. (1806) *op cit,* p.94.
41   *Ibid.*
42   Kaestle, C. (Ed) (1973) *op cit,* p.100.
43   Trimmer, S. (1973) *op cit,* pp.105-6,
44   It has been reported that between 1740-49 and 1790-99 the proportion of matriculated students at the University of Glasgow with fathers in 'industry and commerce' rose from 26 per cent to 50 per cent (see Mathew, W.M. (1966) 'The origins and occupations of Glasgow students 1740-1839', *Past and Present,* 33, p.78).
45   The use of 'rank' and 'station' to describe the 'order of society' occurs in Smith, A. (1976) *The Theory of Moral Sentiments* (edited by Raphael, D.D. and McFie, A.L.) Oxford, pp.51-2.
46   One of the first persons to use the word class in its modern sense was John Millar — a former student of Adam Smith (see Morris, R.J. (1979) *Class and Class Consciousness in the Industrial Revolution 1780-1850,* London, p.9).
47   Smith, A. (1776) *op cit,* p.120.
48   *Ibid,* p.121.
49   *Ibid,* quoted in Skinner, A.S. 'Introduction' to the same work, p.23.
50   For Smith's discussions of sympathy and emulation see *The Theory of Moral Sentiments,* pp.62-3; and Campbell, T.D. (1971) *Adam Smith's Science of Morals,* London.
51   For discussion of the harmony between Smith's notions of sympathy and his ideas about enlightened self-interest see Lamb, R.B. (1974) 'Adam Smith's system: Sympathy not self-interest', *Journal of the History of Ideas,* 5, pp.671-82; and Wills, G. (1976) 'Benevolent Adam Smith', *New York Review of Books,* 9 February (I am grateful to Tom Popkewitz of the University of Wisconsin — Madison for this last reference.)
52   For Lancaster's views on 'emulation and rewards' see (1806) *op cit,* p.89; for Bell's interest in the 'principle of emulation' see *Elements of Tuition* (Part III) p.46.
53   Lancaster, J. (1806) *op cit,* p.98.
54   Bell, *Mutual Tuition and Moral Discipline,* p.56. Bell's account of place-taking exemplifies the individualized basis of his system: 'When, in learning, or saying, or rehearsing a lesson on the floor, a boy fails or errs, the next below, or, after a few seconds, any other in succession who prompts him takes of his own accord the place above him, and all between; and if he does not then repeat what he has been told, he is in like manner again corrected. If all below fail, the head boy is referred to; but if he also fails, any one who now prompts takes the head of the class. The next to the defaulter, and one only in his turn, must speak at a time. The scholar who prompts before his turn, or, if above the reader, till the head boy has been appealed to, forfeits a place. These simple laws keep every one on the alert, as well above as below the speaker, all being liable on every mistake to take a place' (*ibid,* p.53).
55   Bell's fondness for long quotations from Quintilian is demonstrated in *Elements of Tuition* (Part III).
56   Erasmus' attention to emulation is evident, for instance, in *De Ratione*

Studii (1512): 'the teacher should stimulate the pupils' spirits by starting with comparisons among them, thereby arousing a state of mutual rivalry' ((1978) *Collected Works,* Vol. 24, Toronto, p.682).

57   Jesuit interest in the methods of 'combat', 'emulation' and 'holy rivalry' is indicated, variously, in Charmot, F. (1943) *La Pédagogie des Jésuites,* Paris, pp.537-8; and Ganss, G.E. (1956) *Saint Ignatius's Idea of a Jesuit University,* Milwaukee, WI, p.315. Other influential writers who also commented favourably upon emulation include John Locke, Francis Bacon and Jan Comenius (see, respectively, Locke, J. (n.d.) *Some thoughts Concerning Education* (1693), section 7; Bacon, F. (1623) *De Augmentis,* quoted in Armytage, W.H.G. (1970) *400 Years of English Education,* Cambridge, p.13; and Comenius, J.A. (1896) *The Great Didactic* (1632), London, p.317). For a general review of emulation in educational theory see Queyrat, F. (1919) *L'Emulation et son Rôle dans l'Éducation,* Paris.

58   Owen, R.D. (1972) 'An outline of the system of education at New Lanark (1824)' in Simon, B. (Ed) *The Radical Tradition in Education in Britain,* London, p.175.

59   Stow, D. (1836) *The Training System,* Glasgow, p.22.

60   Jardine, G. (1825) *Outlines of Philosophical Education Illustrated by the Method of Teaching the Logic Class in the University of Glasgow,* Glasgow, p.v-vi.

61   *Ibid,* p.45.

62   *Ibid,* p.47.

63   *Ibid,* p.51.

64   *Ibid,* p.100.

65   Jardine described the relevance of the logic class to the general preparation of University students in the following terms: 'Those who are masters of it may extend their conquests. The faculties of the understanding are the tools and engines to be used in every inquiry and disquisition. Knowledge of them promotes their activity and gives them new force' (Jardine, G. (1797) *Synopsis of the Lectures on Logic and Belles Lettres Read in the University of Glasgow,* Glasgow, p.7).

66   Jardine, G. (1825) *op cit,* p.282.

67   *Ibid,* p.284.

68   *Ibid,* p.290.

69   *Ibid,* p.284.

70   *Ibid,* p.435.

71   Information on the University of Glasgow prizes can be found in *Deeds Instituting Bursaries, Scholarships and Other Foundations in the College and University of Glasgow,* Glasgow, 1850; and Anderson, W.I. (1902) *Prize Lists of the University of Glasgow from session 1777-8 to session 1832-3,* Glasgow.

72   Jardine, G. (1825) *op cit,* p.378.

73   *Ibid.*

74   *Ibid.*

75   *Ibid,* p.377.

76   *Ibid.*

77   *Ibid,* p.464 (describing the teaching of John Millar).

78   *Ibid,* p.426.

79   *Ibid,* p.425.
80   *Ibid,* It should be noted, however, that Jardine's hopes for class teaching were gradually overtaken. By the early years of the nineteenth century the expansion of the University of Glasgow meant that the size of the logic class was measured in hundreds rather than tens of students (see, variously, a series of letters (1765-1810) from Jardine to Robert Hunter (Glasgow University Special Collections); Jardine, G. (1825) *op cit,* p.426; and a review of Jardine's *Outlines* published in *Blackwood's Edinburgh Magazine,* 1818, July, pp.420-4).
81   English educationists who became aware of Jardine's ideas include Henry Dunn, Secretary of the British and Foreign School Society (see (n.d.) *Principles of Teaching,* London, pp.16-17); and James Butler of Handsworth, Birmingham (see *Outlines of Practical Education,* London, 1828). Indeed, Butler's title was probably chosen to complement Jardine's *Outlines of Philosophical Education.*
82   Although socially separate, the distance between the University of Glasgow lecture rooms and the teaching rooms of elementary schools was, nonetheless, diminished by the fact that students in Jardine's logic class were below the age of '17 or 18' (Jardine, G. (1825) *op cit,* p.426). Elsewhere in the same volume, Jardine also refers to his students as 'pupils' (for example, p.284).
83   For further information on Robert Owen and New Lanark, see Hamilton, D. (1983) 'Robert Owen and education: A reassessment' in Humes, W. and Paterson, H. (Eds) *Scottish Education and Scottish Culture 1800-1980,* Edinburgh, pp.9-24.
84   Owen, R.D. (1972) 'An outline of the system of education at New Lanark' in Simon, B. (Ed) *op cit,* pp.153-60.
85   Owen, R. (1972), 'A new view of society (1814)' in *ibid,* p.75.
86   For a brief account of the change in Robert Owen's thinking during the years 'between 1812 and 1814', see Stewart, W.A.C. and McCann, W.P. (1967) *The Educational Innovators 1750-1880,* London, pp.59-60. Owen's arguments against the monitorial system appear in the evidence of the *Report of the Select Committee on the Education of the Lower Orders in the Metropolis,* 1816, p.241.
87   Owen, R. (1972) 'A new view of society', in Simon, B. (Ed) *op cit,* p.67.
88   Besides the schemes developed by Owen and Stow, other Scottish 'intellectual' school programmes include John Wood's 'explanatory system' (*Account of the Edinburgh Sessional School,* Edinburgh, 1828) and James Gall's 'lesson system' — where pupils were expected to use 'intellectual' processes in the 'concoction' of their answers (*The Effects of the Lesson System of Teaching on Criminals, General Society, and the Lowest Orders of the Human Intellect,* Edinburgh, n.d. p.58). For further discussion of this rationalist movement in early nineteenth-century elementary education see Silver, H. (1965) *The Concept of Popular Education: a Study of Ideas and Social Movements in the Early Nineteenth Century,* London; and McCann, P. & Young, F.A. (1982) *op cit,* chapter 4.
89   Additional writers whose pedagogic impact deserves further attention include Thomas Malthus and Jeremy Bentham.

Chapter 5

On Simultaneous Instruction and the Emergence of Class Teaching

We are taught almost exclusively how to operate on the *individual*. The great question, however, in the management of *schools* is how you can classify *numbers* so as to carry them forward effectually together. (Abbott (1833) *The Teacher*)[1]

In fitting up the principal apartment of the school, it may be expedient that the seats be moveable, in order that they may be occasionally arranged, so that the children may sit in one compact body, with their faces towards their instructor.

(Dick (1836)
On the Mental Illumination and Moral Improvement of Mankind)[2]

[The teacher] economizes the expenditure of his labour by constantly keeping in view the principle of acting with the greatest efficiency on the greatest possible number. Like the machine which drives a hundred spindles, he never departs from the great end of his labour, nor, for one moment, relaxes his directing and all controlling power.

(Tate (1854) *The Philosophy of Education*)[3]

I

Periodization of the past is a troublesome feature of all historical writing. Yet, in the fullness of time, 'new' teaching methods are deemed to have supplanted 'traditional' practices just as surely as the Renaissance replaced the Middle Ages. Such theoretical categorizations are certainly valuable. They draw attention to qualitative changes in the order of things. In another sense, however, chronological boundaries have a limiting effect. Taken at face value, they make the dynamic of change appear to be fitful rather than continuous. Every discontinuity becomes a hiatus, every revolution more of an event than a process. In return, there is a tendency to smooth out the intervening periods of restlessness.

One such period of quiescence (or, more accurately, pseudo-quiescence) occupies the years between the emergence of 'equalized' (cf. homogeneous) class-ification at the beginning of the nineteenth century and the rebirth of pedagogic individualism nearly 100 years later. In Britain (and elsewhere), however, these decades of presumed pedagogic stability also coincided with a major administrative upheaval — the creation of a unified state apparatus of schooling. Was there, then, a major disjunction between the pedagogic and administrative levels of schooling? Did the latter have no influence upon the former? Or was the apparent lack of pedagogic change simply a function of the modest attention that historians have given to this topic?

II

At the start of the nineteenth century, the boys at Glasgow Grammar School were regularly examined and allocated class positions on the basis of their attendance and achievement.[4] Such a 'place-taking' pedagogy fitted comfortably with the (then) dominant view that every person occupied a different 'rank' on the social 'ladder'. Similar pedagogic procedures were also used in less populous areas; though, in these cases, the practice of teaching pupils 'in turn' was as likely to be shaped by irregular pupil attendance as it was by any particular social philosophy. Whatever the reasons, pupils at eighteenth-century schools spent most of their time beyond the immediate supervision of their teacher(s). Moreover, the intermittence of individualized teaching increased in proportion to class enrolments. Confronted by an expanding intake, Schools like Glasgow Grammar School could use their augmented fee income to employ teaching assistants alongside the permanent staff. But this solution was not available to the managers of schools for the poor. Fee revenue was a much smaller part of their budgets. School expansion, therefore, could not be self-financing. Unless new measures were adopted, it could only be achieved through a proportionate decline in teacher surveillance.

By the nineteenth century, critics began to recognize that conventional arrangements were out of date. A pedagogic discipline adequate to the eighteenth century had become unable to counteract the popular appeal of industrial unrest, political sedition and religious dissent. Two related proposals arose from such critiques. First, that children should be brought more easily within the orbit of schooling; and, secondly, that pupils reached by such policies should be kept constantly employed for the duration of the school day.[5]

The 'monitorial' system stands out among early attempts to meet these specifications, if only for the publicity that its protagonists attracted. The individualized instruction of the old system was retained, but the use of (low paid) monitors meant that more children could be 'heard' for more of the time. Pedagogically, therefore, the monitorial system was an important bridge between the old and the new. The 'mighty power' in the 'machinery of the new school' could, so Andrew Bell claimed in 1829, 'keep every child busily, earnestly, profitably, uninterruptedly, and happily employed'.[6]

Despite these powerful, economic-related arguments, the monitorial system began, in its turn, to lose influential support. By the 1830s various new factors had intervened to transform thinking about the education of the labouring classes. First, the main publicists for monitorial instruction — Andrew Bell and Joseph Lancaster — had ceased to campaign actively (Bell died in 1832, and Lancaster had emigrated to the Americas in 1818). Secondly, the 'oral' place-taking methods of the monitorial system were confounded by the fixed seats and writing surfaces that accompanied the entry of writing into the core of the elementary school curriculum. Finally, and most importantly, the fate of the monitorial system was sealed by the argument that the civilizing goals of elementary education would be realized more successfully if pupils could be taught not merely to memorize their 'lessons', but also to understand them. In 1814, for instance, Robert Owen had claimed following an upsurge of industrial unrest — that the 'inconsistencies and follies' of adults were traceable to two features of popular schooling: the practice of teaching children to 'believe without reasoning' and the fact that children were 'never taught to understand what they read'. In turn, Owen argued that the school system should be reconstructed. All children — including those from the 'poor and labouring classes' — should be equipped to make 'rational judgment[s]'. To this end, their reasoning faculties were to be exercised, and their minds were to be furnished with 'all the facts'.[7]

The criticisms and proposals voiced by Owen (and others) became increasingly accepted among educationists. In 1832, James Kay-Shuttleworth (a Manchester physician and philanthropist) pointed out that a 'little knowledge' (of the kind provided by the monitorial system) was indeed 'a dangerous thing'. To him, the connection between schooling and adult behaviour was undeniable. The 'disturbances of social order' that marked the Parliamentary and economic upheavals of the 1830s were attributable to *'a people only partially instructed'*.[8] Kay-Shuttleworth's solution to this problem was the same as Robert Owen's. On the one hand, the elementary school curriculum was to be extended to include secular subjects (viz. those that provided information about the world and its workings); and on the other hand, pedagogic methods were to be amended to ensure that children could understand the teachings of the new curriculum. Overall, Kay-Shuttleworth believed that pupils would be more ready to accept the inequalities of society if their schooling had previously demonstrated that such social facts had a natural and/or providential origin.

Kay-Shuttleworth (1839) made the clearest statement of this view in *Recent Measures for the Promotion of Education in England:*

> The sole effectual means of preventing [anarchy] . . . is, by giving the working people a good secular education, to enable them to understand the true causes which determine their physical condition and regulate the distribution of wealth among the several classes of society. Sufficient intelligence and information to appreciate these causes might be diffused by an education which could easily be brought within the reach of the entire population, though it would necessarily comprehend more than the mere mechanical rudiments of knowledge.[9]

In the same year, Kay-Shuttleworth was made Secretary to the newly-created Committee of the Privy Council on Education. As senior civil servant in education, he was in a strong position to promote the realization of social ideas in the realm of educational practice. The immediate need (as he saw it) was to match high mental activity on the part of pupils with high levels of pedagogic control on the part of teachers. Yet, as Kay-Shuttleworth recognized, few teachers retained the teaching skills required by such schoolroom practices. In the event, the Committee seems to have arrived at a compromise: they proposed that the 'simultaneous method' was to be introduced (i.e. to check for pupil understanding), but they also accepted that it would be used alongside pre-existing forms of monitorial instruction.[10]

Even so, the design and accomplishment of this mild reform was not without its problems. Neither 'simultaneous' instruction nor its ultimate successor 'class' teaching sprang fully formed from the minds of Robert Owen or James Kay-Shuttleworth. What, for instance, was the optimum size of a teaching group? And how were school designs to accommodate interrogatory methods?

Figure 5
Representation of schoolroom prepared by Samuel Wilderspin for *A System for the Education of the Young,* London, 1840. Note the coexistence of lesson poles and a gallery. (Glasgow University Library)

Figure 6
Wilderspin's Gallery lesson. Note the children putting their hands 'out' (S. Wilderspin, *A System for the Education of the Young,* London, 1840; Glasgow University Library)

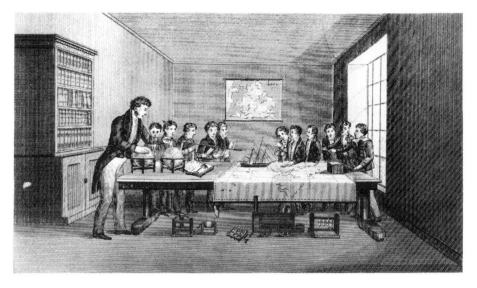

Figure 7
The classroom in Wilderspin's model school (S. Wilderspin, *A System for the Education of the Young,* London, 1840; Glasgow University Library)

III

To answer these questions, it is useful to examine the terms 'class' and 'simultaneous instruction'. As noted in the previous chapter, the classing of early nineteenth century students came under the influence of ideas about homogeneous (or 'equalized') grouping. Classes ceased to be relatively arbitrary cohorts (for example, all pupils working through the same reading book) and, instead, became clusters built around criteria of member-similarity (for example, age and proficiency). As in biological and social theory, equalized classes were regarded, therefore, as natural taxonomic units whose members could be readily distinguished from those in other classes.[11]

Just as the word 'class' took on a new connotation, so 'simultaneous' also underwent pedagogically-significant revisions in the 1820s and 1830s. Initially, it seems to have had a two-fold meaning: it could refer to the 'simultaneous' (i.e. combined) teaching of reading and writing; or it could refer to teaching which required class-members to repeat their reading lessons simultaneously (i.e. in unison). The former usage is demonstrated, for instance, in a reference to 'simultaneous spelling, reading and writing' in Andrew Bell's *Elements of Tuition* (1815), and in the chapter title 'Simultaneous instruction in reading and writing' in the same author's *Mutual Tuition* (original edn, 1823).[12] Bell's proposals were relatively novel since, as noted, writing had not previously been part of the accepted charity school curriculum.

The alternative usage of 'simultaneous' appears, for instance, in the *Glasgow Herald* of 26 February 1819: 'the method adopted by this teacher, making his scholars read simultaneously and separately by turns, is well calculated to command their attention to the business of their several classes'. Again, this practice seems to have been relatively novel, being described at the time as 'newly-adopted'. Nine months later, the same journal reported a similar innovation — a 'plan of making scholars read together' that had been attempted for 'four years past'. The virtue of such a system, so the report claimed, was not only that it made children 'more practised in reading', but also that it avoided the 'confusion of voices' present in schools 'run on the Lancasterian plan'. [13]

By the end of the 1830s, a third meaning of 'simultaneous' had appeared. It described a pedagogic method whereby teachers were to command the simultaneous attention of all their pupils. Thus, when the 1840 *Minutes* of the Committee of Council projected the 'simultaneous method' as an improvement upon 'individual and successive' instruction, they stressed the requirement that 'the mind of each child' should be 'at all times under the influence of the master'. [14] The *Minutes,* however, contain no further elaboration of this idea — a sign, perhaps, that their readers were already cognizant with the issues at stake. Certainly, the most extensive early discussion of this new meaning of 'simultaneous' had occurred four years previously — in the 1836 edition of David Stow's *The Training System.*

Despite its use of the term 'simultaneous answers', Stow's account had nothing, in fact, to do with unison answering. Indeed, it not only embraced answers provided by 'single' pupils; it also proclaimed the benefits that 'simultaneous' answers might bestow upon 'silent' children:

> The girls or boys may answer, or a single class may be named, or a single individual may be called upon; all, however, listen and all learn. Perhaps the one-half of the children only may answer; but if the teacher so commands their attention as to keep their eyes upon himself, then he is quite sure they are receiving the instruction; and we must revert to the fact that during *simultaneous* answers it is found that the silent children very often acquire the greatest amount of knowledge and are most communicative on the subject of their lessons to their parents at home. [15]

Stow's main concern was that the teacher should command the simultaneous attention of all the learners; and that the learners

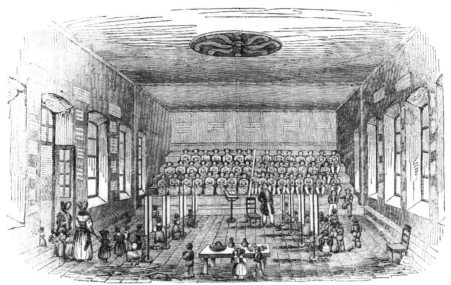

[Interior of an Infant School.]

COVERED SCHOOL ROOM.

Figures 8 and 9
Different representations of schoolrooms in the 1836 and 1850 editions of David
Stow's *The Training System* (Glasgow and London). Note the blackboards in the later
edition. (A copy of the 1836 edition is held in Glasgow University Library)

themselves should experience the simultaneous effect of mutual sympathy. Unison answers might arise in the course of such lessons but they were not, it seems, an essential part of 'simultaneous' answers.

Clearly, Stow's use of 'simultaneous answers' was potentially (if not actually) confusing to his audience. His preference for this term over, say, 'simultaneous instruction' remains difficult to understand.[16] Nevertheless, Stow's ideas became very popular. They offered a pedagogic solution to a cluster of social/educational problems that exercised the school organizers of the 1830s and 1840s. The equalized classification of the simultaneous method resonated with new class-based ideas about the social structure of society; its 'familiar' (or 'conversational') style met growing calls for 'understanding' as well as 'memorization'; and, above all, its 'interrogative' discipline satisfied those whose concern was to ensure the 'perpetual employment' of the children of the labouring classes.

But enthusiasm for an idea is not always a good index of its implementation. New methods (and new teachers) could not be summoned up overnight. Small groups of pupils — 'drafts' or 'classes' — were still taught by monitors using individual methods; but pupil groups were also amalgamated into 'sections' or 'divisions' for the purpose of simultaneous gallery instruction. 'Classes' were not, therefore, usually the organizational units regarded as most appropriate to simultaneous instruction. Nor, indeed, was there any direct connection, at that time, between simultaneous instruction and the use of classrooms. As befits a form of large-group instruction, the simultaneous method was conducted in schoolrooms not classrooms. The latter were small anterooms used merely for small-group (i.e. 'class') instruction.[17] For instance, the Scottish writer and former schoolmaster, Thomas Dick, used this distinction when he reviewed educational provision in Britain and elsewhere in 1836:

> the best dimensions for the schoolroom are found to be 80 feet long by 22 or 24 wide, with seats all round and a rising platform or gallery at one end. Connected with this should be a room from 14 to 18 feet square, for the purpose of teaching the children in classes.[18]

Nevertheless, such a strong architectural separation between small group individualized instruction (in classrooms) and large-group simultaneous instruction (in schoolroom galleries) did not survive the 1830s. In an 1839 *Supplement* to *The Training System*, Stow himself indicated that galleries might also be erected in classrooms. Indeed, he specifically referred to the teaching of 'divisions' in a 'class-room gallery'.[19]

IV

In addition to the support it received from Stow's writings and from the *Minutes* of 1840, simultaneous instruction must also have been powerfully promulgated through the teacher training schools that had been set up in Glasgow and London by, respectively, Stow (in 1837) and Kay-Shuttleworth (in 1840). But the transmission of Stow and Kay-Shuttleworth's message was not always free from distortion. In *School Economy* (1852), for instance, Jelinger Symons (a schools' inspector and barrister) picked up only part of their reasoning. He recognized that 'gallery lessons' heralded a 'new era' in education; and, like Stow, he endorsed the flexible use of school space: 'Questioning and answering should be both individual and simultaneous. Neither of these is necessarily confined either to the gallery or the class, as is often supposed, but both are applicable to each'.[20]

But that was about all. Symons spoke positively about 'Mr Stowe' (sic)[21], while failing to appreciate the pedagogic importance of Stow's conception of the 'sympathy of numbers'. This neglect led Symons to regard individual and simultaneous questioning as different 'modes', rather than (in Stow's terms) as different aspects of the same mode. Without the incorporation of individual questioning, Symons' portrayal of the simultaneous mode could easily be conflated with unison answering. Certainly, this was true in Symons' own case:

> To use the simultaneous mode alone [Symons claimed], is almost inevitably to neglect the bulk of the children, who readily catch and repeat the answers of the few most forward ones . . . The only way to prevent this is to question individually.[22]

Insofar as Symons' comments are typical, it seems likely that mid-nineteenth century practitioners had difficulty in coming to terms with the notion that simultaneous instruction could, without contradiction, be conducted through the questioning of individuals. Nevertheless, Symons' characterization of simultaneous and individual instruction as different 'modes' should not be seen as a reversion to the pedagogic practices of the pre-1830s. Under the influence of Stow and Kay-Shuttleworth, he construed them less as separate options, more as complementary procedures. As already noted, both were regarded as appropriate to the instruction of gallery groups.

Gallery groups were also associated with other new pedagogic practices. For instance, their relatively large size had an impact upon patterns of teacher questioning. Conventionally, drafts and classes had been questioned in the rank order of the pupils; but, for some years, this seriatem method had been recognized as an inefficient mechanism for maintaining attention among large groups of pupils. As early as 1823, for instance, William Meston's *Practical Essay on the Manner of Studying and Teaching in Scotland* proposed, following Jardine (see chapter 4), that school questioning 'should be so frequent and so promiscuous as never to allow any one to conjecture when his turn will come'. Meston, who was Headmaster of the Protestant Academy at Caen (France), also went on to offer an alternative technique. Whenever randomized questioning proved too cumbersome (for example, with larger groups), he suggested that teachers should, instead, direct their questions to 'the whole school'. But since 'confusion . . . might arise from a number presenting themselves', Meston also recommended that 'each one who thinks himself able to answer' should 'rise or give some signal'.[23]

The ultimate origins of this signalling procedure are not clear. Meston made no claim to be its originator. Yet, whatever its source, the organization and management of pupil signalling went on to become a key element in nineteenth-century pedagogy. In 1840, for instance, Samuel Wilderspin linked it directly to the conduct of gallery lessons. 'Any child who thinks he can answer' was to 'stand up' and 'hold out (sic) the arm'. Wilderspin then went further than Meston to indicate how teachers were to select respondents: the children in the 'bottom row' of the gallery were to be allowed to answer first but, if they failed, children in the higher rows were to be 'successively' called upon.[24]

By Symon's time — the 1850s — this gallery technique had become even more elaborate. First, teachers were to ask all potential respondents 'silently' to hold 'out' their hands; secondly, teachers were to initiate the questioning by naming children who were 'least' likely to answer correctly; thirdly, they were to point out all errors during the course of the lesson; and finally, they were to rephrase the 'cream' of the responses and make the pupils repeat them 'simultaneously'.[25]

Two years later, Thomas Tate —of Kneller Training College, Twickenham — described essentially the same procedures in *The Philosophy of Education* (1854). He did, however, make one small but significant amendment: children were to put their hands 'up' rather than 'out'.[26] Although semantically trivial, this change gives support to the view, hinted at by Symons, that simultaneous instruction had begun to be conducted on the 'floor' of the schoolroom as well as in specialized galleries. Certainly, Tate downplayed the pedagogic significance of the gallery. He felt, for instance, that the 'triple-division' of schoolrooms into standing areas (for reading), sitting areas (for writing at desks) and galleries (for simultaneous instruction) interfered with the 'order, quiet and discipline' of the school. Instead, Tate felt that these different activities could be served equally well by a 'series of parallel desks', arranged in a gently-rising 'gallery form', and 'sub-divided for the accommodation of the different classes'.[27]

In advocating a new schoolroom design, Tate (a former teacher at Kay-Shuttleworth's Battersea Training School)[28] was only following, it seems, a lead taken earlier by the Committee of Council. In a *Memorandum Respecting the Organization of Schools in Parallel Groups of Benches and Desks* (1851), the Committee had given their reasons for this architectural realignment. Its 'main end', so they claimed, was the 'concentration' of the teacher upon 'his own separate class'.[29] No longer, therefore, could the elementary school be automatically regarded as a one-teacher school. In part, this change in educational thinking arose from improvements in teacher supply. Five years earlier a state-financed pupil-teacher system had been introduced — an arrangement whereby (from a minimum age of 13 years) ex-pupils could serve a five-year, school-based apprenticeship. Further, *Minutes* of 1851 and 1852 had also made it possible for ex-pupil-teachers to be appointed as adult 'assistants' to certificated teachers.

With these developments, a division of labour began to emerge between a school's 'head master' and his adult (and increasingly female[30]) assistants. Moreover, this division of labour was also configured as a hierarchy of labour. According to the 1851 *Memorandum,* 'Each teacher and his class' was to be isolated from 'distracting sounds and objects', but not to the extent of obstructing 'the headmaster's power of superintending the whole of the classes and their teachers'. In fact, the *Memorandum* was ambivalent on this organizational issue. It conceded that the concentration of teachers would be 'effected the most completely' if each one 'held his class in a separate room', but it hesitated to endorse such a practice on the grounds, among other things, that separation was 'inconsistent with a proper superintendence'.[31]

In practice, however, neither the use of adult assistants, nor the construction of multi-room schools figured prominently in the educational manuals of the 1850s. That is, despite the upgrading of monitors to pupil teachers and (sometimes) to assistant teachers; and despite alterations to the layout of new schools, established practice seems to have been dominated by the one-room school and by derivatives of simultaneous instruction. Unison answering remained in existence too; but, as in Stow's day, it survived only as an adjunct to more 'rational' teaching methods. Thus, John Gill — sometime Master of Method at Cheltenham Normal College — noted in his *Introductory Textbook to Method and School Management* (1858) that unison answering could help to 'gather' what was already known; or to 'fix more deeply' what had previously been taught.[32] Likewise, 'uniform promiscuous answering' was deprecated by James Currie, Principal of the Church of Scotland Training College (Edinburgh), in his *Principles and Practice of Early and Infant-School Education* (1857). Nevertheless, Currie also accepted that 'repeated answers' might be used for the purpose of 'having [them] impressed upon the minds of all'.[33]

V

By the beginning of the 1860s, however, the cumulative effect of these small-scale changes resulted in the irrevocable breaching of a long-standing category distinction. The old monitorial and individualized sense of 'class' teaching began to fade away. But the term 'class' did not, itself, suffer the same fate. Quite the reverse. It took on a new lease of life. Henceforth, 'simultaneous' instruction and 'class' teaching began to be used as synonyms. An early example of this tendency occurs in *A Handbook of School Management and Method of Teaching* (1864) written by Patrick Joyce, Headmaster of the Central Model Schools, Dublin:

> When a teacher gives instruction to a number of pupils together, either standing in a draft before him, or sitting in a gallery, this is what is called simultaneous or collective teaching. Some of the more common faults in connection with simultaneous or class teaching . . .[34]

Blurring of pedagogic boundaries also seems to have infected the labels used to distinguish the size of teaching groups (for example, 'draft', 'class', 'section' and 'division'). Again, 'class' became ascendant, with the remaining terms gradually falling into abeyance. Indeed, this important change of nomenclature seems to have taken little more than a decade to become established. In 1854, The British and Foreign School Society's *Handbook to the Borough Road Schools* confidently advocated that 'a large school' should be 'divided into sections'; and that each section should be divided into 'drafts containing from ten to fifteen pupils'.[35] Four years later, John Gill's *Introductory Textbook* was equally crisp in its categorizations:

> Class instruction should devolve principally on the pupil-teacher who has charge of the section to which the class belongs. When thus engaged with one class, the other children belonging to his section should be working in 'drafts', under monitors, preparing lessons for subsequent examination in class.[36]

By the early 1860s, however, such assuredness had literally become less categorical. In 1862, *The Primary School,* by William Unwin of Homerton College (London), used 'classes' and 'sections' interchangeably (viz. a school 'should generally be divided into at least four classes or sections'[37]); and in the same year George Collins, one time Lecturer on school management and method at Borough Road Training College (London) accepted a large measure of terminological disarray in his *Notes on School Management* (1862): 'the term class is variously employed by different teachers. What one would term a class would by others be called a draft, a section, or a division'[38].

Seven years later, the rout was all but complete. Robert Robinson, Inspector of National Schools (Ireland), felt no need to hide his preference for 'class' in *The Teacher's Manual of Method and Organisation* (1869): 'the word class is to be taken as applying to any collection of children under one teacher receiving instruction in the same subject'[39]. And within another decade, the National Society's *The Teacher's Manual of the Science and Art of Teaching* (1879) could devote an entire section of thirty-five pages to a discussion of 'class teaching' without mentioning any other form of grouping.[40]

Although 'class' consolidated its position over this period, its adoption did not mark the onset of a period of pedagogical stability. There was, for instance, still plenty of scope for debate about where these 'classes' should be taught (in the common schoolroom or in separate classrooms?) and about who should teach them (pupil-teachers, assistant teachers or certificated teachers?). Moreover, by the 1870s these debates were more than merely academic. They also shaped the policy decisions of the newly-founded School Boards. Established by national legislation in the early part of the decade, School Boards were empowered to remedy local deficiencies in the provision of schooling. One urban response, pioneered by the London School Board, was the creation of large, multi-room schools.

But multi-room schools, built on more than one level, did not just happen. They, too, figured in the educational debate. The London School Board's 1872 recommendation that schools should house up to 1000 pupils was opposed by a school's inspector (M. Mitchell) who believed that the 'civilizing influence' of schooling was weakened if more than 250 pupils occupied the same institution.[41] Similarly, John Currie's *Principles and Practices of Common-School Education* (1874) showed more than a hint of uncertainty in its statement that 'the fullest development of [teaching power] is when each class has a teacher — and it may be a classroom — exclusively for itself'[42]. And even the construction of large classroom schools did not halt the debate. It was still an 'open decision', wrote the Secretary of the Glasgow School Board (W. Kennedy) in 1879, 'whether a single building should constitute one school, or three or four schools meeting under one roof'[43].

Besides bringing new distinctions into school discussions (for example, large vs small, urban vs rural), the appearance of multi-room schools had one further terminological consequence. It led to the *de facto* (if not *de jure*) relabelling of assistant teachers as 'class' teachers. Overall, the wave of school building initiated in the 1870s brought teachers, classes and rooms into a one-to-one relationship. Each room, that is, was intended to house a single class; and each class was to be left in the overall charge of its own certificated (or provisionally-certificated) 'class' teacher.[44]

VI

In one sense, these changes merely marked a simple pedagogic substitution — the renaming of simultaneous instruction as class (or classroom) teaching (cf. Joseph Landon's bracketing of the 'simultaneous or classroom system' in *School Management*, 1883[45]). But there is another sense in which the substitution was not so simple. Something was left behind in the process. Simultaneous instruction lost the last remaining traces of its Englightenment rationale and, in exchange, became increasingly tainted with the negative connotations that already clung to 'unison' instruction.

It is perhaps no coincidence, then, that criticisms of Stow's work began to appear in the same decade. In *School Work* (1885), for instance, Frederick Gladman (a former 'Normal Master' at the Borough Road Training College) noted that it was 'generally thought' that 'oral gallery-teaching' had been 'overdone' by David Stow. By way of explanation, Gladman claimed that Stow's practice of combining pupils of 'very different powers' placed some of them at a 'disadvantage'.[46] Likewise, Gladman also sought to distance himself from Stow by eschewing the term 'simultaneous' teaching. Instead, he used 'collective' teaching — a term that, in its 'ordinary acceptation', was also known as 'class-teaching'. In these circumstances, collective teaching gained a new connotation. It embraced all the teaching that could be practised in a single classroom: viz. 'Telling and eliciting, teaching and training, giving information and testing, analysis and synthesis, simultaneous and individual teaching, interrogation, inductive and deductive teaching, and repetition'.[47]

By the 1890s, Stow's reputation seems to have reached a low point.
He was not forgotten, but his ideas were remembered only in the past
tense. In *The Principles of Oral Teaching and Mental Training* (1894), for
instance, Joseph Cowham (one time Master of Method at Westminster
Training College, London) built an argument on the (erroneous) basis
that 'simultaneous intellectual effort' was qualitatively different from the
'simultaneous answers of Mr Stowe (sic)'. Similarly, he conceded that
Stow's 'main principles' were 'excellent', yet also maintained that a
'simultaneous answer' (viz. the 'same for an entire class') was 'rarely
successful' in advancing the intellectual aims of class teaching. 'Today',
Cowham concluded, such a method was 'practically abandoned'[48].

Gladman's and Cowham's criticisms are historically-significant: not
because they were built around a caricature of Stow's thinking but,
rather, because they focused upon a single aspect of simultaneous
instruction — its presumed promotion of pupil uniformity. 'Individuality ought to be considered', Gladman protested. Children in a class may
have *'much in common'*, yet no two are *'exactly alike'*:

> Study your scholars [he continued], that you know how best to
> reach and deal with every one. Every class teacher must
> differentiate his pupils . . . Give as much attention as you
> possibly can to individuals, without damaging the class as a
> whole. The progress of the class as a whole, depends on the
> progress of its individual members.[50]

And, in a similar vein, Cowham accepted that a 'united and simultaneous
effort' was valuable to groups of pupils; yet still felt that unison
answering conflicted with the view that children 'naturally express their
thoughts in a variety of ways'.[51]

These sentiments about individualism and individual differences
brought a new dimension to pedagogic discussion. The net, if
paradoxical, result was that class(room) teaching rose to prominence
alongside the advancement of pedagogic individualization. The individual pupil became regarded as the fundamental pedagogic unit of
teaching while, over the same period, the class became the dominant
organizational unit of teaching. This latter trend is marked, for instance,
in the appearance of 'class' in such titles as Joseph Landon's *The Principles
and Practice of Class Teaching and Class Management* (1894)[52]; John Gunn's
Class Teaching and Class Management (1895)[53]; and Frederick Hackwood's
The Practical Method of Class Management (1897)[54].

One of the earliest juxtapositions of these two notions appears in the
multi-author *Teachers Manual of the Science and Art of Teaching* produced
by the National Education Society in 1879. The section on class teaching

— written by 'a lecturer on Method at one of the large training colleges'[55] — began by describing the advantages of class instruction as 'manifold'. Not only could 'twenty' pupils 'be instructed at one time', but even 'greater advantages' could be obtained through the release of the group-related 'forces' of 'sympathy, emulation and competition'. Thereafter, however, the *Manual* moderated its enthusiasm. Class teaching could 'economize time and labour' and it could 'utilize the forces which are found inseparable from the group', but there was also a danger, the *Manual* warned, that class teaching would '*sink the individual in the group*':

> Each must be as well cared for as though the instruction was to him alone. This is often overlooked. The class is addressed as a whole and if there is a fair amount of attention, the teacher is satisfied, which is a fatal mistake. The class must not be dealt with as a compound but made up of individuals. It must be dealt with as a skilful gardener deals with his garden, where each plant has the culture it needs, to the manifest advantage of the whole.[56]

These two trends — the endorsement of classes and the celebration of the individual pupil remained in parallel for another twenty years. They eventually merged, it seems, in a further book with 'class' in its title: Joseph Findlay's *Principles of Class Teaching* (1902).[57] Although Findlay — Headmaster of the Cardiff Intermediate School for Boys — shared with Owen, Stow and others the belief that the 'presence of comrades' was a positive educational 'stimulus', he preferred to build his theory of teaching upon the pedagogical premise that 'the *unit in education* is not the school, or the class, but *the single pupil*'[58].

Clearly, Findlay was not the first educationist to highlight the place of the individual in schooling. Rousseau, for instance, had claimed 140 years previously, that 'one man can only educate one pupil'[59]. Findlay's originality derived from a different source — the seriousness with which he (and other contemporaries) tackled the problem of resolving the interests of the individual with those of the social group.[60] Within the timescale of this book, therefore, Findlay's work — greatly extended following his appointment to the Chair of Education at the University of Manchester — was as much a point of historical departure as it was a point of historical convergence. It was certainly a revised expression of nineteenth-century 'collective' or 'class' teaching, but it was also a major contribution to the 'New Education' movement, itself a forcing house of the 'progressive' and 'child-centred' ideals of the twentieth century.[61]

Thus, if the classroom system was a child of the technological and ideological revolutions of the late eighteenth century, the closing decades of the nineteenth century saw it married off into a different intellectual community — one that owed as much, for instance, to Charles Darwin's notions about the evolutionary importance of individual differences as it did to Adam Smith's ideas about the economic importance of the division of labour. Throughout, however, the issue of pupil grouping remained permanently upon the pedagogic agenda. It also remained unresolved as, among other things, contrasting images of group structure, group dynamics and group development competed for the attention of schoolroom practitioners. For Jacob Abbott in 1833, the 'whole business' of public instruction hinged upon the development of methods for acting upon 'numbers at once'[62]; whereas for equivalent teacher trainers in the 1920s (for example, Percy Nunn in London and Woutrina Bone in Sheffield), the 'true aim' of the school was to 'cultivate individuality'[63], a goal that placed the design of 'individual occupations' at the very 'heart'[64] of teaching.

VII

In a 1967 account of 'Classification and streaming: A study of grouping in English Schools, 1860-1960', Brian Simon wrote that 'so far as I am aware there are no monographs on the internal evolution of the (nineteenth and twentieth century) schools'.[65] In a more general overview published ten years later — 'Aspects of neglect: the strange case of Victorian popular education'[66] — Harold Silver pointed to a similar omission, noting at the same time that the all-round development of educational studies had suffered accordingly. This chapter has tried — albeit in a preliminary fashion — to fill the gap identified by Simon and Silver. Inevitably, it remains a provisional account. My selective attention to the writings of a small cadre of (male) Masters of Method[67] still leaves plenty of scope for the incorporation of further data and for the resultant revision of the interpretations I have offered.[68]

Nevertheless, certain saliences seem to be relatively well-marked. For instance, the provisional periodization remains intact: the 1830s and the years around the turn of the twentieth century can, indeed, be regarded as decades of major pedagogic transformation. On the other hand, there appears to have been another historically-significant turning point — the 1860s decoupling of class teaching from its previous associations with group size and instructional setting.

This chapter has also indicated some of the processes that helped to shape the pedagogic topography of nineteenth century Britain. These include the increased attention given to writing in the elementary school curriculum; variations in the supply of 'certificated' and 'uncertificated' teachers; and developments in building, heating and lighting techniques that made possible the multi-room multi-storey urban school. Further, it should be noted that these processes did not operate in an independent or random fashion. Rather, constant attempts were made to control and to orchestrate them through the *Minutes* and *Memoranda, Acts* and *Codes* of the Committee of Council and its successor, the Education Department (established in 1856).

But even these state-led attempts at pedagogic regulation had, themselves, a wider context. Each was shaped, for instance, by changing patterns of urban and rural employment; by changing assumptions about the social role of women; and, not least, by changing beliefs about the state's responsibility towards the individual. Writ large, then, the pedagogic history of the nineteenth century is unbounded. Thus, to examine the careers of simultaneous instruction and class teaching is to explore merely a small part of the accessible terrain. Nonetheless, this chapter does have a general message for pedagogical map makers. Through an exploration of the year-by-year continuities and disconti-nuities of nineteenth-century schooling, its broad conclusion is that the labels left by earlier explorers give a false account of the stability of pedagogic phenomena. Indeed, as shown in the next chapter, such labelling may even smooth out periods of 'revolutionary' pedagogic change.

Notes

1 Abbott, J. (1833) *The Teacher,* quoted in Dunn, H. (n.d.) *Principles of Teaching,* London, p.2 (quotation abridged). Abbott's original wording can be found in *The Works of Jacob Abbott,* London (1851) p.423. Abbot was an American Congregational clergyman and a noted educational innovator.

2 Dick, T. (1836) *On the Mental Illumination and Moral Improvement of Mankind,* Glasgow, pp.206-7.

3 Tate, T. (1854) *The Philosophy of Education,* London, p.115 (quotation abridged).

4 Papers relating to Glasgow Grammar School are held in the Glasgow Room of the Mitchell Library, Glasgow.

5 The new social conditions of the industrial revolution and an appeal for a 'general national education' were the background to an unsuccessful Poor Law Bill presented to Parliament in 1807 (see Sturt, M. (1967) *The Education of the People: a History of Primary Education in England and Wales in the Nineteenth Century,* London, 47ff).

6   Bell, A. (1829) *Letters to Sir John Sinclair* (no.5), reprinted in Bell, A. (1832) *Complete Works,* Edinburgh.

7   Owen, R. (1814) 'A New View of Society' (3rd essay) in Simon, B. (Ed) (1972) *The Radical Tradition in Education in Britain,* London, p.75.

8   Kay-Shuttleworth, J. *The Moral and Physical Condition of the Working Classes of Manchester in 1832,* in Tholfsen, T.R. (Ed) (1974) *Sir James Kay-Shuttleworth on Popular Education,* New York, p.69.

9   Kay-Shuttleworth, J. (1839) Recent Measures for the Promotion of Education in England, pp.91-2.

10 *Minutes of the Committee of Council on Education* (1839-1840), p.27. See also Seaborne, M. (1971) *The English School: Its Architecture and Organisation 1370-1870,* London, pp.199-202.

11 Few commentators, it seems, have noted the contemporaneous emergence of equalized classes in educational, biological and social theory. In all cases, the shift was from individuals considered in 'ranks' to groups considered in 'classes'. This convergence is illustrated, for instance, in the work of Robert Owen. Besides being an educational innovator, he met the French biologist Cuvier in Paris, taught the 'Linnaean system of classification' at New Lanark and 'probably' provided the 'first English use' of the phrase 'working class' (see, respectively, Podmore, F. (1906) *Robert Owen: A Biography,* London, pp.225 and 145; and Williams, R. (1976) *Keywords: A Vocabulary of Culture and Society,* London, p.54). Further examination of these taxonomic parallels forms the basis of continuing research by Norman Bett and myself.

12 Andrew Bell's references to 'simultaneous' instruction occur, respectively, on pages 76 and 77 of the versions of *Elements of Tuition (Part II)* and *Mutual Tuition* reprinted in his *Complete Works.*

13 *Glasgow Herald,* 22 November 1819. Twentieth century studies that refer to 'simultaneous' instruction without acknowledging that it might have more than one meaning include Birchenough, C. (1925) *History of Elementary Education in England & Wales,* London, p.280; Smith, F. (1931) *A History of English Elementary Education,* London, pp.184 and 187; Rich, R.W. (1972) *The Training of Teachers in England and Wales During the Nineteenth Century,* Bath, pp.2, 12 and 38; Hurt, J. (1971) *Education in Evolution,* London, p.206; and Wardle, D. (1970) *English Popular Education 1780-1970,* Cambridge, p.88.

14 *Minutes of Committee of Council in Education* (1839-1840), p.31.

15 Stow, D. (1836) *The Training System,* Glasgow, p.123 (quotation abridged).

16 For evidence of Stow's retention of the term 'simultaneous answers' see *The Training System,* London (1850) pp.221ff. and 419.

17 For a concise summary of nineteenth-century changes in school design, see McNicholas, J. (1974) *The Design of English Elementary and Primary Schools,* Windsor.

18 Dick, T. (1836) *op cit,* p.170. For further information on Dick's writings see Smith, J.V. (1983) 'Manners, morals and mentalities: reflections on the popular enlightenment of early nineteenth-century Scotland' in Humes, W. and Paterson, H. (Eds). *Scottish Culture and Scottish Education 1800-1980,* Edinburgh, pp.25-54.

19 Stow, D. (1839) *Supplement to Moral Training and the Training System*, Glasgow, p.15.

20 Symons, J. (1852) *School Economy*, London, pp.72-3.

21 *Ibid.*, p.72.

22 *Ibid.*, p.73.

23 [W. Meston], *Practical Essay on the Manner of Studying and Teaching in Scotland*, Edinburgh (1823) 211 (Meston's authorship was revealed in a subsequent edition). Meston's work in northern France merits further investigation. Did he, for instance, have any direct experience of the teaching methods used by the Brothers of the Christian Schools (see chapter 3)?

24 Wilderspin, S. (1840) *A System for the Education of the Young*, London, p.xiv.

25 Symons, J. (1852) *op cit*, p.74.

26 Tate, T. (1854) *op cit*, p.118. It should be noted that a reference to the upward (rather than outward) elevation of pupils' hands appears in an earlier American manual: Page, D.P. (1848) *Theory and Practice of Teaching*, Syracuse, p.90.

27 Tate, T. (1854) *op cit*, pp.151-2.

28 Tate's connection with Kay-Shuttleworth is reported in Smith, F. (1923) *The Life and Work of Sir James Kay-Shuttleworth*, London, p.106.

29 *Memorandum Respecting the Organisation of Schools in Parallel Groups of Benches and Desks* (1851), quoted in Seaborne, M. (1971) *op cit*, p.207. The historical/pedagogical significance of this memorandum is also discussed in Rich, R.W. (1972) *op cit*, pp.129-30 (for example, 'previously, the elementary school had been looked upon as essentially a one-man place').

30 Between 1849 and 1859 the number of pupil teachers in England and Wales rose from 3580 (32 per cent female) to 15224 (46 per cent female); while the numbers of certificated teachers rose from 930 (24 per cent female) to 6999 (39 per cent female) (see Tropp, A. (1957) *The School Teachers*, London, pp.21-2; and Hurt, J. (1971) p.96). For more recent comment on gender ratios in nineteenth-century schooling see Corr, H. (1983) 'The sexual division of labour in the Scottish teaching profession, 1872-1914' in Humes, W. and Paterson, H. (Eds) *op cit*, pp.137-50; and Widdowson, F. (1983) *Going Up into the Next Class: Women and Elementary Teacher Training 1840-1914*, London.

31 *Memorandum Respecting the Organisation of Schools* (1851) p.207.

32 Gill, J. (1858) *Introductory Textbook to Method and School Management*, London, p.59.

33 Currie, J. (1857) *The Principles and Practice of Early and Infant-School Education*, Edinburgh, p.157.

34 Joyce, P.W. (1864) *A Handbook of School Management and Methods of Teaching*, Dublin, p.102.

35 *Handbook to the Borough Road Schools*, London (1854) p.5.

36 Gill, J. (1858) *op cit*, p.61.

37 Unwin, W.J. (1962) *The Primary School*, London, p.25.

38 Collins, G. (n.d.) *Notes on School Management*, London, p.18.

39 Robinson, R. (1869) *Teacher's Manual of Method and Organisation*, London, p.275.

40 *The Teacher's Manual of the Science and Art of Teaching,* London (1879), pp.215-49.
41 Seaborne, M. and Lowe, R. (1977) *The English School: Its Architecture and Organisation 1870-1970,* London, p.7.
42 Currie, J. (n.d.) *The Principles and Practice of Common-School Education,* Edinburgh, p.156.
43 Kennedy, W. (1879) *Large Schools and their Educational and Economic Advantages,* Glasgow, p.4.
44 During the last part of the nineteenth century and the early part of the twentieth century, the provision of separate classrooms was far from universal: 'In 1924 there were still over 145,000 rooms in elementary schools in England and Wales accommodating two or more classes, with a role of 1,027,000 children [i.e. 18 per cent] . . . In London, on the other hand, all but 1.5 per cent were in separate rooms' (Birchenough, C. (1925) *op cit,* p.393).
45 Landon, J. (1893) *School Management,* London, p.150.
46 Gladman, F. (1885) *School Work,* Norwich, p.24.
47 *Ibid.,* pp.134-5.
48 Cowham, J.H. (1894) *The Principles of Oral Teaching and Mental Training,* London, pp.106-7.
49 Gladman, F. (1885) *op cit,* p.135.
50 Ibid., pp.135-6 (emphasis removed).
51 Cowham, J.H. (1894) *op cit,* pp.106-7.
52 Landon, J. (1894) *The Principles and Practice of Class Teaching and Class Management,* London.
53 Gunn, J. (1895) *Class Teaching and Class Management,* London.
54 Hackwood, F. (1897) *The Practical Method of Class Management: a Ready Guide of Useful Hints to Young Class Teachers,* London.
55 *The Teacher's Manual of the Science and Art of Teaching,* p.iv.
56 *Ibid.,* pp.215-6. The influence of Froebel is suggested by the *Manual's* horticultural metaphor. Froebel societies had been founded in Manchester (1873) and London (1874) during the early years of the same decade (see Lawrence, E. (Ed) (1969) *Friedrich Froebel and English Education,* London, p.46).
57 Findlay, J.J. (1902) *Principles of Class Teaching,* London.
58 *Ibid.,* pp.12-13.
59 Rousseau, J.J. (n.d.) *Emile,* London, p.19.
60 For late nineteenth-century discussion of the relationship between individuals, communities and the state, see Gordon, P. and White, J. (1979) *Philosophers as Educational Reformers: The Influence of Idealism on British Educational Thought and Practice,* London, *passim.*
61 Findlay's contribution to the New Education and Progressivism has been described as follows: 'Findlay came into prominence as a Herbartian, transferred his allegiance to Dewey, and helped to publicize the scientific educationists' (Selleck, R.J.W. (1968) *The New Education 1870-1914,* London, p.333).
62 Abbott, J. (1851) *op cit,* p.423.
63 Nunn, T.P. (1923) *Education: Its Data and First Principles,* London, p.198 (chapter 15).

64 Bone, W. (1924) *Individual Occupations in the Three Rs*, London, p.2. For discussion of the twentieth century resurgence of educational individualism see various contributions to the *British Journal of Educational Studies*, (1980) 28, 3.

65 Simon, B. (1971) 'Classification and streaming: A study of grouping in English schools 1860-1960' reprinted in Simon, B. (Ed) *Intelligence, Psychology and Education: a Marxist Critique*, London, p.201.

66 Silver, H. (1977) 'Aspects of neglect: The strange case of Victorian popular education', *Oxford Review of Education*, 3, pp.57-69.

67 Rich reports that the first use of the term 'master of method' probably occurred in the 1840s at Kay-Shuttleworth's Battersea training school (*The Training of Teachers in England and Wales*, 78).

68 It should be noted, in particular, that my account omits any discussion of European and American influences upon school organization in nineteenth-century Britain. Certain elements of the European influence are examined in Pollard, H. (1956) *Pioneers of Popular Education 1760-1850*, London.

Chapter 6

The Recitation Revisited

The modern movement toward a return to the older mode of individual instruction as a means of 'breaking the lockstep' dates from about 1890.

(Bagley and Keith (1924) *An Introduction to Teaching*)[1]

Such terms as the individual and the social conception of education are quite meaningless . . . apart from their context.

(Dewey, (1916) *Democracy and Education*)[2]

I

In March 1969 the *American Educational Research Journal* published a pioneering article on the history of pedagogy. The article's message was carried by its title — 'The persistence of the recitation'. The authors — James Hoetker and William Ahlbrand — reported that a 'question-answer' form of class teaching, known in the USA as the 'recitation', had shown 'remarkable stability' since the 1890s.[3]

The breadth and originality of Hoetker and Ahlbrand's work set the standard for subsequent investigators. Indeed, even their original title persisted — finding echoes in such papers as Larry Cuban's 'Persistence of the inevitable: The teacher-centred classroom' (1982)[4]; and Susan Stodolski, Teresa Ferguson and Karen Wimpelberg's 'The recitation persists, but what does it look like?' (1981)[5].

If other investigators have taken the Hoetker/Ahlbrand claim on trust[6], Stodolski and Cuban subjected it to varying degrees of scrutiny. Stodolski and her colleagues, for instance, recognized that the term 'recitation' could be a 'gross characterization'[7] masking a variety of pedagogic forms. Similarly, Cuban has pointed out in another paper that the Hoetker/Ahlbrand evidence for stability might also be set against his own finding that 'at least one-third of all teachers' between 1900 and 1980 had made some kind of break with established practice'.[8]

By raising these issues Stodolski and Cuban point to two recurrent difficulties with the Hoetker/Ahlbrand argument. First, is the recitation concept sufficiently fine-grained to allow unambiguous claims about stability and change? For instance, if teachers systematically shift their class questioning in favour of girls, would that count as a change in the recitation? And second, what degree of disruption is required before 'stability' is transformed into 'change'? Should we, for instance, give our attention to the small number of teachers who rehearse the future, or should we be swayed by those who, it seems, carry on regardless?

In addition, the Hoetker/Ahlbrand debate has also raised — as most participants have recognized — a set of wider issues about the dynamism of twentieth-century American schooling. Are the schools, in fact, a set of conservative institutions? Or is their 'conservatism' merely a function of the theories and methods we use to judge them?

Setting aside these general measurement problems, my own initial reaction to the Hoetker/Ahlbrand claim was largely one of disbelief. Given my growing historical knowledge of other pedagogic forms, I was sceptical that the recitation could be so impervious to the changes that penetrated other areas of American life. Also, Hoetker and Ahlbrand's claim about the dominance of class-based recitations did not readily square with my own (and Bagley and Keith's) prior assumption that the end of the nineteenth century witnessed an important switch towards more individualized pedagogic forms. Clearly, to resolve these apparent contradictions, I needed to become much more sophisticated in my appreciation both of individualized instruction and of the recitation.

In practical terms, then, I decided to turn Hoetker and Ahlbrand's argument on its head. I started, that is, by assuming that the recitation is an historically-sensitive pedagogic form. Further, to gain access to its historical sensitivity, I knew that I would also need to strengthen my appreciation of the economic and ideological context of the 1890s — the epoch when, so Hoetker and Ahlbrand claimed, the recitation took on its modern form. Finally, by extending Hoetker and Ahlbrand's account of the recitation — both chronologically and theoretically — I hoped to identify some of the assumptions and circumstances that, through time, gave different cultural meaning and form to such a 'persistent' pedagogic practice.

II

Between 1877 and 1890 the railway network of the United States grew from about 37,000 to 200,000 miles.[9] This never-to-be-repeated expansion — facilitated by the standardization of track gauges, freight rates and geographic time zones — changed the face of American economic life. In 1865 the cost of moving a barrel of flour 1000 miles to the seaboard was $3.45; in 1885 it was 68 cents.[10] Such changes meant that, on the one hand, commodities could be marketed over hitherto unprecedented distances; and, on the other hand, that production could be concentrated among fewer and fewer large-scale enterprises.

This standardization and systematization of distribution also had other effects upon production and consumption. First, the circulation of cheaper agricultural and industrial products led to unemployment in marginal areas. Secondly, movement of surplus labour towards the remaining centres of production hastened the urbanization of American life. And, finally, price-cutting competition in a saturated market-place eventually provoked major innovations in the production process itself.

This last consequence of systematization was represented by the shift from 'factory' to 'mass' production. That is, labouring 'hands' were replaced not so much by a single machine — a much earlier substitution — as by a series of sequentially-coordinated, machine-based operations.[11] In turn, this streamlining of production recast the division of labour. Relatively autonomous industrial workers gradually became exposed to a new external discipline — a 'drive' system shaped jointly by machine-paced production and white-collar supervision.[12]

As might be expected, industrial innovations of this kind were not without their problems. For a start, long-run, high-speed production created difficulties in the design of reliable machines and in the search for raw materials that could withstand such treatment. As a result, the take-up of mass production lagged far behind the dissemination of its images. But such technical difficulties were only part of the story. Profitability was also jeopardized by the willingness of American industrial workers to regroup among themselves in defence of their living standards. Between 1884 and 1886, for instance, membership of the 'Knights of Labor', an early association of working men and women, rose fourteen-fold from 50,000 to 700,000.[13] And in 1887 and 1890 the number of establishments affected by strikes was five times greater than the number affected in 1882[14]. Indeed, one historian has recently commented that the 1880s were a period when the 'labor problem threatened to outweigh the technological and economic advantages of the factory'.[15]

Among certain industrial engineers, such a redefinition of the profitability issue prompted a shift of focus from the mechanical problems of 'technology' to the social problems of 'organization'.[16] But such attention to organizational efficiency — which marked the beginnings of 'scientific' management — did not stop at the factory gate. The labour problem — marshalling and restructuring a productive work force — was also tied to the contemporaneous social issues of unemployment, poverty and immigration. For instance, Grover Cleveland, President from 1884 to 1886, not only gave the first Presidential message on 'labor', he was also the first President to make official reference to any kind of 'immigration problem'.[17]

The 1880s, then, were a period when the question of social order embraced not only industrial organization but also social welfare and the supply of labour. The restructuring of production, that is, interfered with the structure of the labour market. It created a category of workers — the 'unskilled' — who were not easily accommodated within the existing social fabric.[18] Some ideologues of the day 'solved' these problems in one sweep: they made the laissez faire claim that social evolution should be left to the self-adjusting mechanisms of the market place (cf. the 'survival of the fittest'). Such early neo-Darwinian arguments may have offered intellectual comfort to industrialists keen to roll back the limiting powers of state legislatures, but they had little impact upon those squeezed out by the expansionist corporations or upon those (for example, trustees of local charities) who felt unreasonably burdened by the welfare consequences of unemployment, poverty and immigration.[19]

Theorists of this second constituency, who were later joined by industrialists who had witnessed the disorder of the 1880s, held a different view of social evolution. They believed that, unlike its biological counterpart, society could be beneficially influenced by conscious human design. Accordingly, such commentators claimed that unrestrained laissez faire was not the way ahead. Instead, social progress was to be rationally guided by a set of superordinate federal agencies — the organs of the state. 'Positive legislation'[20] (for example, the Sherman Antitrust Act of 1890) was to provide the political impetus; the social sciences (for example, welfare economics) were to furnish the policy guidelines; and the expanding universities (with suitable financial investment and curriculum reform) were to train the appropriate 'professionals'.[21]

To the extent that this view became dominant, the servants of the state began to take on the same kind of 'progressive' interventionist role as the servants of industrial production. By the 1890s social engineering was to the rationalization of the labour market as production engineering was to the rationalization of the workplace.

While scientific management enthusiasts restructured the factory, so their educational colleagues — of the same 'new middle class outlook'[22] — set about the reorganization of schooling. The common school system that had been reformed between about 1840 and 1860 was, at its cutting edge in the cities, swept up in a wider interest in organizational streamlining and administrative efficiency. After 1890, public schooling was no longer to be envisaged as a single (if rickety) ladder from which students fell at succeeding levels. Rather, it was to be a sturdy and increasingly branching structure that both celebrated and, as important, delimited opportunities for individual variation.

Against this general background, early American progressivism was a two-sided philosophy. In its Darwinian commitment to individual variation as the well-spring of social evolution it stood opposed to the 'lock-step' pedagogy of the common school. But, equally, in its belief in the virtues of state intervention (for example, compulsory school attendance for the working class)[23], it paid as much tribute to the eventual 'needs' of the labour market as it did to the immediate 'needs' of the individual.

This tension, which helped education to become 'the principal arena in which the issues of modern capitalism were joined'[24], faced all variants of progressive thinking and progressive action. And it was the same tension — i.e. between the fulfilment of the individual and the progress of the wider social group — that, no less, lay at the heart of debates about the reform of pedagogic practice.

III

Before, throughout and after the period reviewed above, the recitation was a mainstay of American schoolroom life. Yet, at the same time, it also attracted all kinds of qualifying adjectives. Should any historical significance, for instance, be read into labels like 'simultaneous' recitation (1848), 'class' recitation (1871) and 'socialized' recitation (1915)?[25] Or should the 'individual' recitation of the 1840s be chronologically bracketed with the 'individual' recitation of the 1890s?[26]

Whatever its ultimate origins, the recitation began to feature as a 'new' pedagogic technique in the latter half of the 1840s. It emerged alongside the systematization of the common school. Until that time, schools for the majority of the American people were relatively marginal social institutions. They were staffed by young men and women for whom teaching was often a seasonal or transient occupation; they were housed in cold, draughty and ill-equipped buildings; and they were irregularly attended by children who could easily be distracted by other activities. In 1846, for instance, the Superintendent of common schools in the state of New York reported that more than 75 per cent of the state's teachers had taught in the same school for two years or less; that more than 60 per cent of the teachers were under 25 years of age; that 30 per cent of schoolhouses were in a 'bad' state of repair (56 per cent without 'privies'); and that 76 per cent of pupils (over the age of 5 and under 16) had attended for less than six months in the previous year.[27]

Conditions such as these had a direct impact upon the pedagogic options open to teachers. For instance, the formation of stable classes was undermined both by irregular pupil attendance and frequent teacher turnover.[28] Further, teachers had to accept the lesson books that their pupils brought to school. Thus, since classes were formed around such books, a proliferation of texts also yielded a superabundance of classes. In 1844, for instance, the Superintendent of Cayuga County (New York) reported that with over 100 different kinds of books in use across 210 schools, the average class size was less than two pupils.[29]

In these circumstances, much instruction was, by necessity, a matter of one-to-one or near one-to-one tuition. But even these recitations, conducted 'individually',[30] commonly took place alongside up to ten or more other classes.[31] 'While the class is reading' wrote the Superintendent of Hamilton (New York), 'the teacher is attending to the other business of the school; and where the school is large, frequently he is not able at the close of the lesson, to tell of what the class has been reading'.[32]

The claimed ineffectiveness of such 'memoriter' recitations — widely discussed in the New York County Superintendent's reports (and elsewhere) — became one of the major justifications for pedagogic reform in the 1840s. In the north-eastern states the common school was failing to imbue sufficient American citizens with the economic and social attributes appropriate to an emergent manufacturing economy.[33] Faced with dislocation within the family structure (for example, parents working away from home in factories) and faced with a breakup of religious orthodoxy (cf. an increase in Roman Catholic influence)[34], reformers turned to the (secular) school system as a likely agency for promoting better moral supervision. In the words of the Cayuga (New York) Superintendent, E.G. Storke, universal school provision (if not universal school attendance) would fashion not only 'well ordered minds' but also 'well ordered social, religious and political institutions'.[35]

In these terms, universal schooling was a necessary but not

sufficient condition for the promotion of reform. Within-school changes were also required. Thus, approved or recommended texts were to be introduced; normal schools were to be founded for the training of teachers; a variety of regulations — largely exhortatory — were to be introduced to increase school attendance; and, finally, the schoolroom was to be brought under the influence of a more 'rational'[36] pedagogic system. If children could be grouped in 'masses instead of singly'; if they could be instructed orally via 'incidental questions' from the teacher's own 'well stored mind'; and if they could be subjected to the 'enlivening power of emulation'[37] then, so the argument ran, educational benefits would accumulate in the same degree to the learners, as financial savings (derived from larger classes and fewer books) would accrue to those who paid the bills.[38]

In the common schools of the 1840s, therefore, talk of oral instruction and classification appealed to a variety of social, intellectual, political and economic interests. The issues were never purely pedagogic. Nevertheless, oral instruction and classification became the sharp end of the reformers' programme — the channels through which, in terms used by Horace Mann (Secretary of the Massachusetts Board of Education) 'redeeming influences' could be injected into the 'whole mass of the children'.[39]

IV

If the designation of approved books helped to underwrite the standardization of schooling, the advent of sequentially-ordered texts provided for schooling's systematization.[40] By 1848, for instance, Henry Barnard (Commissioner of Public Schools in Rhode Island) could argue that school children would derive the 'highest degree of benefit' if, at school, they passed through a 'regular course of training' in a 'succession of classes'.[41] Claiming that such a system — the first and second McGuffey Readers had been published in 1836 — was 'almost universal in New England and other states'[42], Barnard further believed that 'success in the operation of a system of public schools' required that teachers act upon 'numbers [of pupils] at once', carrying them forward 'effectually together' for 'years in succession'.[43]

This programme of systematization took on further refinements in more populous areas. Rationalization affected both within-school and between-school structures. In the Cincinnati common schools of 1846, for instance, Barnard's 'progressive'[44] course of instruction was further sub-divided, administratively and pedagogically, into 'divisions', 'departments' and 'years'.[45] And, as early as 1841, the primary schools, grammar schools and the High School of Philadelphia were rearranged into a 'compact and connected frame'[46] of school governance wherein each type of school constituting a different 'grade'. As this last example suggests, the 'gradation'[47] of schools in the 1840s and 1850s was something quite different from the 'classification' of schools: 'grades' related specifically to a type of school, whereas 'class' usually referred to the sub-divisions employed within each school.

By the late 1850s, however, the terms 'gradation' and 'classification' began to converge; that is 'grade' also began to be used for within-school organizational units. This convergence, it seems, arose from the further consolidation of different grades of school (for example, primary, secondary) into a single organizational unit. Thus, an 1855 report on school architecture in Pennsylvania could note that a 'union graded system' brought 'all the different grades [into] . . . the same building and united [them] under one chief teacher or superintendent'.[48]

Superficially, then, hierarchical grading might appear to have been an inevitable consequence of the creation of multi-teacher schools. In fact, this does not seem to have been the case. In the American experience, multi-teacher (and multi-room) schools seem to have emerged in the 1820s and 1830s, not in the 1850s. In this respect Boston's experience may have been typical. A municipal recommendation had led, in 1819, to the creation of 'double-headed' schools in that city. Reading and writing were taught in two separate rooms, yet, according to a recent history of Boston schooling, both teachers retained 'equal' jurisdiction over all 'matters of instruction and discipline'.[49] By the 1850s, however, an alternative or 'single-headed' form of organization had begun to appear in Boston. The Chapman Grammar School, which had been set up on the double-headed plan in 1849, was 'united' in 1856 under the charge of 'one master assisted by a submaster, two female head assistants and seven assistants'.[50]

These administrative alterations had something to do, no doubt, with the 1852 appointment of Nathan Bishop, Boston's first school superintendent. In his inaugural report, Bishop spelled out his managerial aspiration. It was to organize 'a system . . . on one uniform plan', thereby 'bringing the whole into harmony with the great practical principles on which the best managed business enterprises are carried forward'.[51]

In these terms the move to graded schools can be directly linked to a general shift in managerial theory. It was not, therefore, an inevitable (or even unchallenged)[52] organizational response. Rather, it was a deliberate attempt to merge new ideas about overarching control (or 'harmony') with earlier notions about the productive benefits of the social and technical division of labour. Hence, despite opposition from community groups and teacher's organizations (for example, over curriculum control), it was the operationalization of these hierarchical values within a centralized administrative machinery that most clearly marked out the emergence of graded schooling.

One of the leading publicists for this innovation was W.H. Wells, Superintendent of the Chicago public school system. In *The Graded School* (1861) Wells not only endorsed the division of labour within 'all well-regulated establishments', he also recognized the value of careful standardization — viz. 'due classification and grading' — to the successful internal articulation of a multi-unit enterprise (cf. a school system).[53] 'The more perfect . . . the grading', he wrote quoting J.M. Gregory (State Superintendent of Michigan), 'the more certain and marked will be the success of the schools'.[54]

To create such perfection, Wells also recommended that each grade should be further sub-divided into classes. But such classes were not allocated according to the diversity of subjects or texts, as had been the case in earlier times. Instead, they were built around the general proficiency of the students.[55] The net result was a new set of pedagogic circumstances: classes were reorganized into a linear progression that, itself, fitted within an ascending ladder of grades. As another of Wells' sources (H. F. Cowdery, District Superintendent of Sandusky, Ohio) put it, 'The closer the classification, the better the school system'.[56]

Thus, from Barnard's 'progressive' course of instruction to Wells' 'graded' course of study, the class remained the basic recitation unit. Yet, insofar as Wells was able to achieve his goal of close classification, the composition of recitation classes changed significantly. In contrast to earlier reformers (like Mann) who recognized that diversity within classes could be harnessed to a variety of civilizing goals, Wells sought to partition diversity among different classes (albeit within the same grade). As an educationist who believed that industrial inefficiency arose from the use of poorly-selected components, and as a superintendent responsible for one of the largest schools systems in the USA, it is perhaps not surprising that Wells found homogeneous grouping educationally defensible, administratively desirable and demographically possible.

With grades sub-divided into classes; with 'fixed and known standards' attached to each grade; and with system-wide grade boundaries 'plainly and sharply defined'[57], Wells' ideas were, to use a modern term, a clear expression of batch processing in education. That is, children were to stay together in their given class; were to be taught

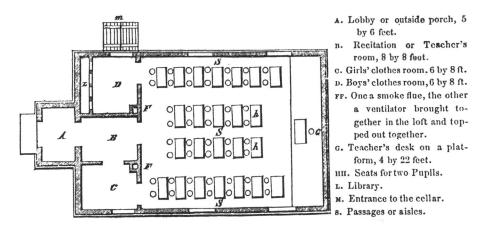

A. Lobby or outside porch, 5 by 6 feet.
B. Recitation or Teacher's room, 8 by 8 foot.
C. Girls' clothes room. 6 by 8 ft.
D. Boys' clothes room, 6 by 8 ft.
FF. One a smoke flue, the other a ventilator brought together in the loft and topped out together.
G. Teacher's desk on a platform, 4 by 22 feet.
HH. Seats for two Pupils.
L. Library.
M. Entrance to the cellar.
S. Passages or aisles.

Figure 10
United States schoolroom with adjacent 'recitation' room. Taken from T. H. Burrowes, *Pennsylvania School Architecture,* Harrisburg, 1855. (Glasgow University Library)

collectively to the required standard; and, thereafter, were to be promoted, as a class, from grade to grade.

V

Given the arguments and evidence deployed by Wells, it seems reasonable to claim that the imagery (if not the reality) of 'lockstep teaching' in the American common school dates at least from the 1860s.[58] Yet, even as certain common school systems, like Chicago, espoused such 'perfection of grading'[59], complaints were raised that such a 'mechanism' operated against the interests of individual children.[60] By the 1870s, these questioning voices had identified their pedagogic target: grading practices in general, and promotion practices in particular were moved up the educational agenda.

The general dilemma was clearly stated in 1874 by Emerson White, the School superintendent of Cincinnati. Accepting that the graded system tended to 'force uniformity', he recognized that the 'great difficulty' facing administrators was to 'secure a necessary degree of uniformity without ignoring or forcibly reducing differences' in pupils and teachers.[61] If White merely posed the problem, other commentators were ready to offer solutions. Division of labour enthusiasts like William Payne (Professor of the Science and Art of Teaching at the University of Michigan), believed that individual differences could be honoured through more stringent classification. 'Once put in their proper places',

Payne wrote in *School Supervision* (1875), 'it will not be necessary save under exceptional circumstances to give [pupils] a reclassification before the close of the year'.[62]

Perhaps the most sophisticated proposal, however, came from William T. Harris, the St Louis School Superintendent and a noted hegelian philosopher. From at least the beginning of the 1870s Harris argued in the St Louis *Annual Reports* for a more 'elastic' and 'mobile' school system.[63] To this end, he suggested that, in the lower grades, within-grade promotion (i.e. from class to class) be allowed; and that, in the upper reaches of the school system, pupils should be free to take 'one branch of study' in the 'class above'.[64]

Nevertheless, despite proposing greater flexibility, Harris still gave priority to the class over the individual. He indicated that, for the populous lower grades of the St Louis school system, up to 'one-third' of each class should be 'sent forward' leaving 'two-thirds or more' behind.[65] Harris' social arithmetic was by no means arbitrary. His explicit concern to 'preserve the identity of the class'[66] (i.e. by keeping back the majority of the pupils) was strictly in accord with the hegelian idea that social aggregations (cf. societies, communities and states) have a formative (cf. regulative) influence upon the lives of their constituents. Indeed, not only did Harris argue that 'COMBINATION (sic) is the principle which is instrumental in all that is good in civilization or culture',[67] he also believed that 'perhaps the very best thing in pedagogy is to be found in that principle of combination whose instrument is the CLASS (sic)'.[68]

Like the early Enlightenment pioneers of oral teaching, Harris regarded the class as something more than an aggregation of pupils. Yet his own formulation of its positive features owed as much to Charles Darwin as it did to George Hegel or Adam Smith. For Harris (but not, seemingly, for division of labour ideologues like Payne or Wells) the class was a 'social organism' whose heterogeneity could be validly mobilized in the interests of social evolution. That is, the 'mite' proferred by each individual could be added to a 'common fund' from which all, through a 'circular movement', could repeatedly withdraw an intellectual and moral dividend.[69] Thus, if 'self-activity' could be embedded within the collective processes of the class recitation, Harris believed that each member of the group would 'ascend' above 'idiosyncracy' and attain the 'universal forms of activity' that would make them a 'free man or woman'.[70]

But as Harris' social arithmetic also indicated, the wish to preserve the stability of classes had to be compromised with the furtherance of organizational elasticity. If, at times, Harris wrote as a social philosopher, it should not be forgotten that he was hired as an educational administrator. Harris' managerial task was, in effect, to resolve his hegelian beliefs with the exigencies of schooling in St Louis. In this last respect, he faced an organizational difficulty that Wells' *The Graded School* had failed to confront; namely, that any cohort entering the first year of a school system was rapidly reduced in size as it passed up through the grades. In the early 1870s, for instance, Harris reported that only about 10 per cent of St Louis pupils survived the eight-year programme that preceded their admission to the High School.[71] Such attrition — Payne called it a 'universal law' in 1875[72] — was sufficient to disrupt even the most rigid lockstep system since it required a constant reallocation of pupils to fewer and fewer classes per grade. As Harris put it, the organizational problem was to create a fluid system such that 'at all times' a 'full quota of pupils' could be passed to the high school grades of the 'ablest and highest-paid teachers'.[73]

In these terms, then, flexible promotion procedures were, for Harris, as much an economic imperative as any kind of tribute to individual pupil differences.[74] By comparison with the school systems of Barnard and Wells, Harris' model paid as much attention to the problems of system throughput as it did to issues of system structure. If earlier innovators had fashioned the graded school into a machine, Harris' generation transformed it into a carefully-synchronized delivery system. In this respect, Harris could usefully be regarded as one of the founding theoreticians of mass- as opposed to factory-production thinking in schooling.[75]

Whatever the subsequent fate of Harris' hegelian notions, his managerial prescriptions resonated harmoniously with the urbanization of the 1880s. As cities increased in size, more and more school systems could be built around a linear arrangement of (up to thirty) classes[76], each comprising pupils 'substantially at the same stage of advancement'.[77] As one later commentator put it, the uneven progress of the pedagogic 'stairway' or 'succession of terraces' was transformed into the perpetual ascendency of the 'inclined plane'.[78]

One feature of these promotion practices was that the class recitation could be retained without compromising anyone's belief in the importance of individuality. Indeed, homogeneous classification strengthened the claim that teaching directed towards an equalized class would be no different from teaching directed to each member of the class. For instance, J.L. Pickard (one-time Superintendent of Chicago public schools) seemed quite happy to report, in *School Supervision* (1890), that conditions of 'utmost mobility' in schools meant that the 'class remains though its membership changes'[79]. Likewise, the School Superintendent of Elizabeth (New Jersey), W.J. Shearer, felt no contradiction in meeting the 'needs of . . . individuals' by combining them into classes of 'very nearly equal ability' and exposing them collectively to the 'power of emulation'.[80]

In the 1890s, this individualization process was taken even further, boosted by a new claim about the social benefits of disaggregation. Looking back on a decade or so of civil unrest, influential commentators identified 'mass' behaviour as socially undesirable. In 1895, for instance, David Starr Jordan, President of Leland Stanford Junior University, believed that 'The civilization we enjoy today is . . . slipping from our hands'. The 'need of the hour', he claimed, was to 'break up the masses'. Further, Jordan believed that schools could meet such a need if each one took 'the student as its unit' and treated boys and girls as 'individuals not classes'.[81]

Although Jordan claimed that, by these means, the 'man' could be raised above the 'masses'[82], his general view of individualization had very little to offer the population at large. Individualization in the schoolroom, like its counterpart on the production line, was designed to meet the managerial prescriptions of system architects. The 'intellectual lockstep' — as Shearer called it — was not so much broken as divided into many pieces.

VI

Another new development of the 1890s was the downward penetration of curriculum 'electives' (i.e. options) into the upper reaches of the elementary school.[83] Again, this restructuring of the pedagogic ladder was tied to assumptions about the diversity of individuals. In 1890, for instance, one of the most active supporters of electives, C.W. Eliot (President of Harvard), claimed that the 'grouping together of children whose capacities are widely different' was not only 'flying in the face of nature' but also the 'worst feature of the American school'.[84] Returning to the same theme two years later, Eliot proposed a solution. To fulfil their democratic mission, schools should take the 'utmost possible account of individual instruction'; should grade 'according to capacity'; and should promote pupils, not 'by battalions', but by the most 'irregular and individual way possible'.[85]

But Eliot's and Jordan's assumption that diversification and individualization were essential to social progress did not go entirely unchallenged. It was countered, for instance, by Nicholas M. Butler, a philosophy professor at Columbia University. While Butler shared their belief in the virtues of social progress, he was doubtful of the measures they advocated. Indeed, in 1900 he claimed — in a speech to the National Education Association's Department of Superintendence — that individualism had gone 'too far'. In an effort to force its 'fullest flower' — viz. the 'early and complete adaptation of the individual to his appropriate career' — the individualism movement, so Butler believed, had 'torn itself up by the roots'. To set 'every man's hand against his fellow' was, he regarded, a 'sham individualism'. 'True individualism' was something else — a philosophy rooted in 'enrich[ing] the life of each with the possessions of all'. Furthermore, Butler claimed that this idea had already found expression among innovations that emphasized the 'social aspect of education' and that, accordingly, had reconstructed the school as a 'social center'.[86]

The contrasting visions of individual progress and social harmony advanced by Eliot and Butler were not restricted to the world of university professors. They were also evident in debates about pedagogic practice. For instance, one of the most prominent figures on Eliot's side was Preston W. Search, Superintendent of Pueblo, Colorado — later to be called the 'leader of individualism' by G. Stanley Hall.[87] Search's model of schooling — deemed particularly relevant to 'mass' education — required that the 'class recitation' be 'abolished' and replaced, instead, by recitations conducted with individual pupils. On the 'Pueblo Plan', as Search had named it by 1894, the pupil 'works as an individual, is promoted as an individual and is graduated (sic) as an individual'. No one is held back: 'all excepting the [pupil reciting] are uninterrupted in continuous advance (sic) work'.[88]

Like most of his contemporaries, Search emphasized the preciseness of individualization. If pupils could be placed 'purely' [i.e. precisely], they could 'get the most good' for themselves; and, in addition, their 'rises and falls' could be entirely attributed to their 'own efforts'. On the other hand, Search was also aware of a possible flaw in the logic of hyper-individualization. He recognized that if the organization of a school was subordinated to the needs of every pupil, then the school's overall 'mechanical excellence' could be jeopardized. In the event, Search overcame this counter-argument: such an 'apparent' loss of efficiency would, he believed, be more than off-set by greater pupil satisfaction and improved school retention rates.[89] Like many of his social-engineering contemporaries, Search was well aware that, in schools as well as factories, social efficiency need not be the same thing as mechanical efficiency.

Other pedagogical theorists, however, took the counter-argument seriously claiming, with Butler, that individualism itself was socially inefficient. One such opponent of mechanical individualization was

Samuel T. Dutton of Teachers College, Columbia University (and a former Superintendent of Brookline, Massachusetts). Echoing Butler's (and Dewey's) interest in the 'social conception' of education[90], Dutton made the claim in *School Management* (1903) that the 'greatest change' in twentieth century schooling had been the substitution of 'moral' for 'scholastic' purposes.[91] For such reasons, Dutton proposed a resuscitation of the class recitation — believing that, compared to the 'individual or Pueblo method', it was better suited to the social purposes of schooling. If groups could be assembled 'for a reasonable length of time', Dutton felt that the class recitation, by building upon 'cooperation' and 'social consciousness', would 'check' the 'reigning evil' in the world — 'selfishness'.[92]

Dutton was not the only pedagogue who believed that the class recitation might accommodate the new moral agenda. For instance, in 1898 J.H. van Sickle, originator of the 'North Denver Plan', had even drawn W.T. Harris into the argument:

> Is it not possible to retain the manifest advantages of the class recitation, so often set forth by Dr Harris, and yet as the recitation progresses allow individual pupils to drop out and do other work more profitable than simply maintaining the semblance of attention?[93]

As the quotation indicates, however, Sickle was careful to dissociate himself from the presumed inadequacies of 'lockstep' teaching. In doing so, he annexed a measure of Eliot-type 'electives' philosophy. The resultant amalgam marked an important turning point in curriculum thinking: the transformation of the pedagogic ladder into the pedagogic tree. Whereas the children in Shearer's 'Elizabeth Plan' of 1895 had merely been allowed to move 'forward or back'[94], Sickle's pupils were allowed to branch out and do 'other work'. If this interpretation of Sickle and Dutton is correct, it seems that the early twentieth-century group recitation could be used in two different ways. It could be retained with the sole purpose of serving social harmonization; or it could be used intermittently as a gathering station on a branching network of social differentiation.

As time passed, there seems to have been a blurring (or overlapping) of the boundaries between these two uses. In part, this probably followed from a wider acceptance of the idea that the branching curriculum was, itself, the royal road to social harmony. 'Class-individual' methods reached their maturity in *School Organisation and the Individual Child* (1912), a compendium of organizational forms compiled by W.H. Holmes, Superintendent of Westerly, Rhode Island. Building his argument on extensive correspondence — conducted in 1910 — with 'many of the leading superintendents and normal school principals in every state'[95], Holmes sought a 'synthesis' whereby 'self-respecting, successful' American citizens would combine 'a common study in the fundamentals' with 'optional topics' for the 'abler pupils'.[96] He believed that although 'normal' boys and girls — by which he included more than 90 per cent of the population[97] — could follow a core curriculum, individual (and remedial) methods were occasionally necessary to bring the 'different members of the class into line' so that, thereafter, all could 'participate profitably in the class work'.[98] Holmes was well aware that his proposals differed from those, like the 'Pueblo or Search Plan', where 'the recitation and examination' were 'wholly individual' and where pupils were 'promoted each day'.[99] But he did not reject individual instruction outright: he merely allocated it a secondary role. He recognized that the net result of his proposals would be a 'somewhat differentiated' course, but he believed that such a compromise was preferable to the irrevocable 'breaking up' of class-based instruction.[100]

One factor, perhaps, shaping this American interest in the moral potential of instruction was the 'alarming'[101] resurgence, over the same period, of industrial unrest and union activity. Membership of the American Federation of Labor doubled between 1898 and 1900, and trebled again between 1900 and 1904.[102] And in a thirty-three month period leading up to 1904, 198 union pickets and sympathizers were killed, 1966 wounded and 6114 arrested.[103]

In part, this labour problem was a consequence of the spread of manufacturing that used electricity in place of steam or water. As organizational constraints upon the use of steam engines, shafts and belts were removed, new 'institutional reforms' — shaping a 'new factory system'[104] — gradually became possible. Mass production entered a new phase after 1900. A less mechanistic efficiency rationale came into being — one that could give as much attention to the 'relationship between men'[105] as its predecessors had given to the relationship between machines (cf. the wider replacement of engineering management by personnel management).[106]

Within education, this welfare view of management was codified in *Education and Social Efficiency* (1913), a general educational treatise written by Irving King of the State University of Ohio. King offered four propositions that updated the Progressive viewpoint. First, that the economic and social upheavals of the late nineteenth century had created new residential complexes in place of the 'old-time neighbourhood'. Secondly, that the associated patterns of 'production distribution and consumption' brought with them difficulties of 'social adjustment'.

Thirdly, that such maladjustment could not be corrected without a new 'social morality'. And finally, that schools were in need of major reform if they were to play their part in the consolidation of the 'new social order'.[107]

The new patterns of production touched upon by King were, typically, associated with the breaking down of skilled trades into a series of machine-aided unskilled tasks. Yet, unlike the craft workers they replaced, the new generation of unskilled operatives did not understand where their own operation fitted into the overall design. Clearly, this particular productivity problem could not be solved by even greater use of specialisation. A new attitude to work was required.

One person who recognized the educational implications of this management/output problem was James H. Baker, Chairman of the National Council of Education Committee on the Economy of Time in Education, and President of the University of Colorado. In a 1911 submission to the Committee, he wrote that 'the lack of efficiency' in 'most industries and professions' was 'largely moral'. The solution he proposed was not a better drive (or reward) system in the hands of management but, rather, a better internal discipline in the minds of the workers. 'As machinery does more and more of the work of the world', Baker argued, the resultant 'waste and loss and accidents' could only be overcome if workers showed a greater 'responsibility' and 'sense of duty'. In Baker's educational economy, then, it was 'man's attitude toward work', rather than any 'lack in foundation education', that was in the shortest supply.[108]

VII

As the twentieth century took shape, more prominence seems to have been given to the view that schools should be charged with shaping social attitudes. One locus of this interest was the debate about the future of secondary education. By 1918 the high school population had increased, compared to 1890, by over 700 per cent.[109] And, as a major NEA commission on the *Reorganization of the Secondary School* noted in the same year, no longer was the high school a selective institution but, rather, one whose pupils were of 'widely varying capacities, aptitudes, social heredity and destinies in life'.[110]

The response of some social efficiency protagonists was to argue for a reorganization of secondary schooling into separate 'vocational' and 'liberal' strands. The NEA Commission, however, took a different view — that school organization should be responsive to the overriding (and controllable) task of 'unifying'[111] the American people. Accordingly, the social conception of education was given disproportionate attention in the Commission's deliberations. Eventually, the Commission concluded that, at all levels, schooling should have a common set of seven 'main objectives': (i) health; (ii) command of fundamental processes; (iii) worthy home membership; (iv) vocation; (v) citizenship; (vi) worthy use of leisure; and (vii) ethical character.[112] Indeed, insofar as the last was 'involved in all the other objectives', it was also held to be 'paramount'.[113]

The Commission, however, did not stop at the formulation of national goals. Its concern to help individuals find their 'place' in society and shape themselves to 'even nobler ends'[114] was further translated into the redesign of school systems, school curricula and school instructional methods. Thus, the 'comprehensive high school' — embracing 'all curriculums in one unified organization' — was to be the 'standard' secondary school[115]; 'household arts' for girls, and 'social studies' for all, were to figure prominently in all curricula[116]; and, not least, the 'socialized recitation' — whereby the 'class as a whole develops a sense of collective responsibility' — was to be the preferred method of 'developing attitudes and habits important in a democracy'.[117]

The NEA report made no further comment on the socialized recitation. Presumably it was treading ground already made familiar by William Whitney, Superintendent of Port Chester (Connecticut) in *The Socialized Recitation* (1913). Whitney prefaced his book with two tenets fundamental to the progressive viewpoint. First, that the child rather than the curriculum should be placed at the centre of the pedagogic exchange; and, secondly, that command of subject matter was not merely an end in itself but also the basis upon which children could develop their own powers of 'activity and responsibility'.[118] Building on these premises, Whitney went on to criticize existing pedagogic methods. In particular, he argued that the 'academized' recitation was not adequate to the needs of the twentieth century. Its 'ethical value'[119], that is, had been lost at some point in its post-renaissance history. Accordingly, Whitney sought to restore the balance. Recitations 'conducted by the teacher to the exclusion of the pupil' were to be replaced by 'conversations and discussion', fostered, in a 'class circle', by a teacher who was only 'occasionally drawn in'.[120]

In these terms, Whitney's ideas were to reach forward into the 1920s and beyond. Taken more generally, however, they were still very much a product of their own times. Confronted with the results of 'parental incapacity', 'unjust economic and industrial conditions' and 'family instability and inefficiency', schools needed to shoulder, so

Whitney believed, 'many of those responsibilities which formerly the home assumed'.[121] 'If the home neglects good manners', he continued; 'let the school teach manners and morals'.[122] Not surprisingly, then, 'moral training' was, for Whitney, 'by far the most important phase of education in the elementary school'.[123]

Given this diagnosis, Whitney identified the recitation as a pedagogic instrument that could compensate for social and familial shortcomings:

> If there are stubborn cases of discipline, the pride and honour of the room must settle them. If there are dirty boys and girls, the self-respect and humour of the class must attend to that. If there are members of the class whose conduct, speech, actions and manners are detrimental to good citizenship, the honour and respect of the class will remedy that. So the class and the recitation become one and the same thing.[124]

Whitney also believed — in much the same terms as James H. Baker — that the pursuit of citizenship had economic as well as social consequences. Moral training did not merely ensure social stability, it also had a role to play in the pursuit of social progress. If 'attitudes to life' also included 'attitudes to work' then there was no doubt in Whitney's mind that the future 'mechanic' would always be able to contribute to economic progress by doing 'effectively and efficiently . . . the thing in hand'.[125]

Whitney's version of the recitation stood at what Cremin has described as the 'great divide'[126] in progressive thinking. It was heavily influenced by contemporary diagnoses of society's economic malaise. Yet, in the terminology used beyond the great divide (i.e. after the First World War, and after the foundation of the Progressive Education Association in 1919) it was also strong on child-centred ideas about self-realization and self-control. In an important sense, then, Whitney's proposals were to schooling as innovations in 'human relations' thinking were to industrial management. Thus, it is with the history of human relations thought — beyond the scope of this chapter — that any discussion of post-war developments must, I suggest, begin.

VIII

This chapter has tried to link pedagogic practice to the changing economic and ideological climate of nineteenth- and early twentieth-century American life. Four waves of innovation can be discerned. First, the advancement of 'oral' instruction as a means of meeting the new civilizing circumstances (viz. technological republicanism) of the common schools of the 1830s and 1840s. Secondly, the integration of the common school recitation into the streamlining (or mass production) practices of graded school systems. Thirdly, the weakening of the class recitation in the 1880s and 1890s under the impact of an alliance between social-Darwinian individualism and unwanted mass social behaviour. And finally, the re-establishment (and recasting) of the recitation in response to early twentieth-century notions about social adjustment and economic productivity. Throughout, I would suggest, there is evidence of a close functional relationship between changing pedagogic practices, changing conceptions of the labour process, and changing assumptions about the individual and the state. In short, neither the school, nor the factory were unchanging phenomena. Both were centres of production and both responded dialectically to each other and to the wider circumstances in which they found themselves.

This being said, certain questions necessarily remain unanswered. No claim, for instance, is made about the uptake of these ideas; nor that their prominence in the minds of influential people matched their prevalence in the schoolroom. To answer such questions requires a different kind of study — one that follows, through time, educational institutions rather than a pedagogic idea. Nevertheless, I believe this enquiry does complement both Hoetker and Ahlbrand's original investigation and, more widely, the recent literature on the history of nineteenth- and twentieth-century American schooling. Besides responding, for instance, to Stanley Schultz's observation that 'there is no adequate history of the evolution of graded schools'[127], besides sharing Barbara Finkelstein's evaluation that 'there is no study which focuses specifically on the conduct of classrooms using the pedagogical process itself as an index of educational change'[128], and besides addressing Michael Katz's question 'did pedagogy change during the progressive era?'[129], this chapter has tried not only to reveal the diversity of pedagogical thinking that suffused the recitation label, it has also tried to provide some kind of the theoretical structure — the evolution of labour management — against which that diversity might reasonably be appreciated.

Notes

1 Bagley, W.C. and Keith J.H. (1924) *An Introduction to Teaching*, New York, p.198

2   Dewey, J. (1916) *Democracy and Education,* New York, p.112.

3   Hoetker, J. and Ahlbrand, W.P. (1969) 'The persistence of the recitation', *American Educational Research Journal,* 2, p.163. I could find only one definition of the recitation in the source literature of this chapter: 'The word recitation . . . [is] used in the United States for a class exercise or lesson conducted by the teacher and requiring the critical attention of the entire class' (*Report of the Committee of Fifteen on Elementary Education,* New York, 1895, p.86).

4   Cuban, L. (1982) 'Persistence of the inevitable: The teacher-centred classroom', *Education and Urban Society,* 1, pp.26-41.

5   Stodolski, S., Ferguson, T. and Wimpelberg, K. (1981) 'The recitation persists but what does it look like?', *Journal of Curriculum Studies,* 13, pp.121-30.

6   See, for example, Dunkin, M.J. and Biddle, B.J. (1974) *The Study of Teaching,* New York. Dunkin and Biddle go so far as to assume that the classroom and the recitation are 'natural' pedagogic forms (p.12).

7   Stodolski, S. *et al* (1981) *op cit,* p.121.

8   Cuban, L. (1982) *Teacher as Leader and Captive: Continuity and Change in American Classrooms 1890-1980,* Stanford University School of Education research report, mimeo, p.318.

9   Hinkle, R.C. (1980) *Founding Theory of American Sociology 1881-1915,* London, p.35.

10 Kirkland, E.G. (1956) *Dream and Thought in the Business Community 1860-1900,* Ithaca, NY, p.155; see also chapter 3 of the same work: 'The political economy of the public school'. For the social, political and demographic background to late nineteenth-century educational reforms see Violas, P.C. (1978) *The Training of the Urban Working Class (A History of Twentieth Century American Education),* Chicago, IL, chapter 1.

11 'Mass production differed from existing factory production in that machinery and equipment did not merely replace manual operation . . . Machinery was placed and operated so that several stages were integrated and synchronized technologically and organisationally within a single industrial establishment' (Chandler, A.D. (1978) *The Visible Hand: The Managerial Revolution in American Business,* London, p.24).

12 'In the United States . . . giant industrial enterprises staffed by salaried managers first appeared during the 1880s' (Chandler, A.D. and Daems H. (Eds) (1980) *Managerial Hierarchies: Comparative Perspectives on the Rise of the Modern Industrial Enterprise,* Cambridge, MA, p.207). For discussion of the links between the reconstitution of production and the reorganization of labour see, variously, Braverman, H. (1974) *Labor and Monopoly Capital: the Degradation of Work in the Twentieth Century,* New York; Gordon, D.M., Edwards, R. and Reich, M. (1982) *Segmented Work, Divided Workers: The Historical Transformation of Labor in the United States,* London; Clawson, D. (Ed) (1980) *Bureaucracy and the Labor Process: the Transformation of United States Industry 1860-1920,* New York; and Zimbalist, A. (Ed) (1979) *Case Studies on the Labor Process,* New York.

13 Weibe, R.H. (1967) *The Search for Order 1877-1920,* New York, p.45.

14 'The strike frequency index at the end of the 1880s climbed to roughly three times its levels at the beginning of the decade. The average number

of workers per strike did not increase through these years but the number of establishments affected each year increased substantially, with the average number of establishments affected in the peak years 1887 and 1890 climbing to five times the number affected in 1882' (Gordon, D.M. *et al* (1982) *op cit,* pp.98-9, quotation abridged).

15 Nelson, D. (1980) *Frederick W. Taylor and the Rise of Scientific Management,* Madison, WI, pp.9-10

16 'When the prolonged economic depression of the 1870s brought a continuing drop in demand and with it unused capacity in metal working, manufacturers began to turn their attention from technology to organisation. The new interest led to the beginnings of the scientific management movement in American Industry' (Chandler, A.D. (1978) *op cit,* p.272). For the claim that, in turn, scientific management drew upon earlier educational innovations (viz. those adopted in the 1820s at West Point Military Academy) see Hoskin, K.W. and MacVe, R.M. (1986) 'Accounting and the examination: a genealogy of discipline and power', *Accounting Organisations and Society,* 11, p.130.

17 Weibe, R.H. (1967) *op cit,* pp.45 and 54.

18 If events in late nineteenth-century America brought about a reconstitution of the labour market, it is important to note that the general impact of the labour market pre-dates the Civil War. Cf. 'The shift in the nature of social organization consequent upon the emergence of a class of wage laborers, rather than industrialisation or urbanisation, fueled the development of the public institutions' (Katz, M. (1976) 'The origins of public education: A reassessment', *History of Education Quarterly,* 16, p.391); and 'The great upheavals of the 1880s "signalled the appearance on the scene of a new class which had not hitherto found a place in the labour market, namely the unskilled"' (Gordon, D.M. *et al* (1982) *op cit,* p.125, quoting Perlman). It has also been estimated that whereas about 20 per cent of the non-slave labour force were wage and salaried employees in 1776, the same group has risen to 62 per cent of the labour force by 1876 (see Hogan, D. (1982) 'Making it in America: Work, education and social structure' in Kantor, H. and Tyack, D. *Work, Youth and Schooling: Historical Perspectives on Vocationalism in American Society,* Stanford, CA, p.154).

19 For differing views on the impact of laissez faire ideas in American politics, see Kolko, G. (1963) *The Triumph of Conservatism: a Reinterpretation of American History 1900-1916,* New York; and Hofstadter, R. (1955) *Social Darwinism in American Thought,* Boston, MA.

20 *Ibid.,* p.72.

21 For the connections between progressivism, legislation, social science and higher education see Crunden, R.M. (1982) *Ministers of Reform: the Progressives' Achievement in American Civilisation 1889-1920,* New York (for example, 'For at least fifteen years [i.e. after the foundation of the American Social Science Association in 1865] . . . the profession of social science did not properly exist: the men (sic) had no social mission beyond a vague idea of reform, no systematized body of knowledge, no legally sanctioned authority or role, no code of ethics, and no sense of themselves as a separate group. In the early 1880s, the same forces that had opened Johns Hopkins University in 1876 were working both in the universities

and in the larger culture to end this amateur status for social science',
pp.68-9); Silver, H. (1983) *Education as History,* London, chapters 5 and 6
(for example, 'In Europe and America, mainly from the 1880s, the
discrete social sciences as we know them established their autonomy in
academic and professional arenas, and with new institutional machineries',
132); and Haskell, T.L. (1972) *The Emergence of Professional Social Science,*
Urbana, IL. (for example, 'My principle concern is to investigate the rise
of a distinctively modern perspective on human affairs, one that has been
institutionalized and greatly elaborated in academic social science
disciplines, but which pervades many other areas of modern thought',
preface).

22 Weibe, R.H. (1967) *op cit,* p.112 ('Consciousness of unique skills and
functions . . . characterized all members of the new middle class. They
demonstrated it by a proud identification as lawyers and teachers, by a
determination to improve the contents of medicine or the procedures of a
particular business, and by an eagerness to join others like themselves in a
craft union, professional organisation, trade association, or agricultural
cooperative').

23 Cf. 'One of the progressive movement's greatest triumphs was the success
of the compulsory school movement' (Cohen, S. (1964) *Progressives and
Urban School Reform: The Public School Association of New York City
1895-1954,* New York, p.71); and 'Pre- [first World] War progressivism
was largely an affair of the public schools, particularly those attended by
working class children' (Graham, P.A. (1967) *Progressive Education: From
Arcady to Academe (A History of the Progressive Education Association
1919-1955),* New York, p.8). See also Tiffin, S. (1982) *In Whose Best
Interest?: Child Welfare Reform in the Progressive Era,* London.

24 Gilbert, J.B. (1977) *Work Without Salvation: America's Intellectuals and
Industrial Alienation 1880-1910,* Baltimore, MD, p.110. See also
Whitaker, R. (1979) 'Scientific management theory as political ideology',
Studies in Political Economy, 2, pp.75-108.

25 See, respectively, Page, D.P. (1848) *Theory and Practice of Teaching,*
Syracuse, NY, p.116; Harris, W.T. (1871) 'Advantages of class
recitation', *Western Educational Review,* 2, pp.3-6; and Whitney, W.T.
(1915) *The Socialized Recitation,* New York.

26 McLintock, J. and R. (Eds) (1970) *Henry Barnard's School Architecture*
(reprint of the 1848 edition), New York, p.84; and Search, P.W. (1894)
'Individual teaching: The Pueblo Plan', *Educational Review,* pp.154-70.

27 *Annual Report of the Superintendent of Common Schools of the State of New York,*
1846. For comparable circumstances elsewhere on the Eastern seaboard of
the USA, see Kaestle, C.F. and Vinovskis, M. (1980) *Education and Social
Change in Nineteenth Century Massachusetts,* Cambridge, MA.

28 Irregular attendance and teacher turnover were to trouble country schools
for many years. As late as 1875, for instance, William Payne could write
that 'the two things which make it very difficult to sustain a graded course
of instruction in such [i.e. country] schools are great irregularity of
attendance, and the frequent change of teachers' (*Chapters on School
Supervision,* Cincinnati, 1875, p.91). See also Kaestle, C.F. (1983) *Pillars
of the Republic: Common Schools and American Society 1780-1869,* New York,
pp.110-11.

29 *Annual Report of the Superintendent of the Common Schools of the State of New York,* 1844, p.157. For other counties in the same state, see pp.166-7, 247, 270, 298, 497-9 and 565.

30 *Ibid.,* p.247.

31 *Ibid.,* p.498.

32 *Ibid.,* p.310.

33 See, for instance, Kasson, J.F. (1977) *Civilizing the Machine: Technology and Republican Values in America 1776-1900,* Harmondsworth, chapters 1 and 2; and Kaestle, C.F. (1983) *op cit,* pp.63 and 66-7 (for example, 'By the late 1840s, the Northeast had become unmistakably a manufacturing region', and 'Schoolteachers have always been concerned with discipline and moral character, yet there seems to have been a quantum shift in the purposes, methods and importance of school discipline in ante-bellum America . . . Antebellum school reports emphasized discipline for orderly procedure in schools as well as for the production of model citizens'.

34 See, for instance, Schultz, S. (1973) *The Culture Factory: Boston Public Schools 1789-1860,* New York, pp.55ff. and 63ff.

35 *Annual Report of the Superintendent of the Common Schools of the State of New York,* 1844, 168.

36 *Ibid,* p.573. See also Kaestle, C.F. (1983) *op cit,* chapter 6 ('The common school reform program').

37 *Annual Report of the Superintendent of the Common Schools of the State of New York,* 1844, pp.138, 516, 245 and 183. It is important to note that the spread of oral instruction was linked to the spread of blackboards (for example, 'Eight-tenths of the school houses are furnished with a blackboard, a perfect *sine qua non* at this day, since that old memoriter and uninteresting method of teaching, has commenced receding into an undisturbed, and we hope, long continued repose', Superintendent of Franklin, p.270). Further, school districts in New York State could, from 1841, levy a tax to purchase 'maps, globes, blackboards and other school apparatus' (*Laws Relating to Common Schools,* New York, (n.d.) copy in Glasgow University library).

38 One New York educationist who identified the joint pedagogical and economic benefits of common school reform was the Superintendent of Allegany County (Northern section), R.H. Spencer: 'One of the principal advantages of classification of pupils in schools is the great saving of the time of the teacher . . . for instance, suppose the teacher has twenty scholars studying arithmetic or geography, by classing them in two classes, as will generally be proper on account of age, capacity, etc. he will save nine-tenths of the time devoted to that science, which will enable each pupil to receive ten times the amount of oral instruction which he would were no attention paid to classification; this will appear the more important, when we consider that oral instruction constitutes an indispensible and by far the most important part of the pupils' means of acquiring knowledge' (*Annual Report of the Superintendent of the Common Schools of the State of New York,* 1844, p.138).

39 *3rd Annual Report of the Massachusetts Board of Education,* quoted in Mann, H. (1844) *Reply to the 'Remarks' of Thirty-one Boston Schoolmasters,* Boston, MA, p.27.

40 Cf. 'After 1840, reading books were produced almost entirely in graded series' (Reeder, R. (1900) *The Historical Development of School Readers and Methods of Teaching Reading,* New York, p.49).

41 McLintock, J. and R. (Eds) (1970) *op cit,* p.82.

42 *Ibid.*

43 *Ibid,* pp.87-8.

44 *Ibid,* p.83.

45 *Eighteenth Annual Report of the Trustees and Visitors of Common Schools to the City Council of Cincinnati,* 1846.

46 *Twenty-third Annual Report of the Controller of the Public Schools of the City and County of Philadelphia,* 1841, p.4.

47 Burrowes, T.H. (1855) *Pennsylvania School Architecture,* Harrisburg, p.15; and McLintock, J. and R. (Eds) (1970) *op cit, Henry Barnard's School Architecture,* p.82. It should also be noted, however, that while the 'classification' of schools did not mean the same as the 'gradation' of schools, a 'class' of school seems to have been synonymous with a 'grade' of school (*ibid,* 97 and 92). In general the graded system comprised three units — primary, grammar (or secondary) and high schools; but other ancillary labels also appeared in the 1840s (for example, 'central', 'intermediate' and 'district' schools). See, for instance, *ibid,* pp.92, 97 and 108; and the *Nineteenth Annual Report of the Trustees and Visitors of Common Schools to the City Council of Cincinnati,* 1847, p.11.

48 Burrowes, T.H. (1855) *op cit,* p.15.

49 Schultz, S. (1973) *op cit,* p.107. Schultz also reports that the opening attack upon the double-headed system came in 1845 (p.338). For a further example of the introduction of hierarchical rationalisation see Kaestle, C.F. (1973) *The Evolution of an Urban School System: New York City 1750-1850,* Cambridge, MA, chapter 6. The separate development of the division of labour and of hierarchical rationalization also seems to have obtained in industry. In both cases the development of centralized administration took place, not because it necessarily increased technical efficiency but, rather, because it allowed greater (cf. more stable) managerial control (see, for instance, Marglin, S.A. (1974) 'What do bosses do?: The origins and functions of hierarchy in capitalist production', *Review of Radical Political Economics,* pp.60-112).

50 *Annual Report of the School Committee of the City of Boston,* 1857, p.51. Philadelphia also seems to have followed the Boston pattern. It began to abandon one-room, one-teacher public schools in the 1830s, indicating its intention by building extra classrooms and employing, 'as an experiment', extra adult teachers, both male and female (*Twentieth Annual Report of the Controller of Public Schools,* 1838, p.9).

51 Quoted in Schultz, S. (1973) *op cit,* p.131.

52 Various challenges to the centralization of graded schools are described in Kaestle, C.F. (1983) chapter 7.

53 Wells, W.H. (1862) *The Graded School: A Graded Course of Instruction for Public Schools,* New York, p.7. For later reviews of graded schooling see White, E.E. (1891) *Promotions and Examinations in Graded Schools,* Washington, DC; and Adams, F. (1875) *The Free School System of the United States,* London, p.199ff.

54 Wells, W.H. (1862) *op cit,* p.9

55 The changing language of nineteenth-century pupil categorization ('capacity', 'attainment' etc.) deserves further attention.

56 Wells, W.H. (1862) *op cit,* p.9.

57 *Ibid,* pp.9, 7, and 8.

58 Cf. 'By 1860 grading was the rule in nearly all the cities and large villages', *Annual Report of the U.S. Commissioner of Education* (hereafter: *US Annual Report*), 1890-91, p.982.

59 Fraser, J. (1866) *Report on the Common School System of the United States and of the Provinces of Upper and Lower Canada,* London, Ontario, p.108.

60 Exceptional promotions were not disallowed in the 1860s but, generally, they seemed to have been frowned upon — largely because teachers had been reported as advancing pupils simply to claim their own superior efficiency (*ibid,* p.88).

61 Quoted in Pickard, J.L. (1902) *School Supervision,* New York, pp.108-9.

62 Payne, W. (1875) *op cit,* p.34.

63 Extracts from the St Louis Superintendent's *Annual Reports* of the 1870s, reprinted in the *US Annual Report,* 1891-2, p.611.

64 *Ibid,* pp.605-8.

65 *Ibid,* pp.606-7.

66 *Ibid,* p.606.

67 Harris, W.T. (1870) *St Louis School Report,* p.173. (I am grateful to Louis Smith of Washington University (St Louis) for copies of both this report and Harris's related article on 'Advantages of class recitation'.)

68 Harris, W.T. 'Advantages of class recitation', p.4.

69 Harris, W.T. (1870) *op cit,* p.172.

70 Harris, W.T. 'Advantages of class recitation', p.5.

71 *St Louis School Report,* 1872-3; reprinted in *US Annual Report,* 1891-2, p.615.

72 Payne, W. (1875) *op cit,* p.97.

73 *St Louis School Report,* 1872-3; reprinted in *US Annual Report,* 1891-2, pp.615-6.

74 Cf. 'The school should be a living process, continually readjusting itself to the want of the organization as well as to the capacities of the pupils', *ibid,* p.616.

75 My belief that Harris was a managerial innovator differs, perhaps, from the judgment of S.K. Troen: 'Harris . . . was not responsible for creating the efficient system [in St Louis]. Rather he rationalized and advertized what had already been accomplished during the 1850s' (*The Public and the Schools: Shaping the St Louis System 1838-1920,* Columbia, MO, 1975, p.142). My contrasting view is that Harris' rationalization was, in fact, prompted by what he regarded as the organizational inefficiency of earlier schemes.

76 'Thirty classes between the first and the eighth grade are possible in large schools in cities' (Harris, W.T. (1897), quoted in *US Annual Report,* 1898-9, p.332); and 'Experience alone can determine what this interval should be and the frequency with which pupils should be promoted. It is possible that both of these facts may depend somewhat upon the number of pupils included in a graded system, a much more complete classification

being possible in large cities than in small towns' (White, E.E. (1874) quoted in *US Annual Report,* 1896-7, p.1508). It should also be noted that from the 1870s, if not earlier, a separate literature emerged in respect of the management of non-city schools (see, for instance, Holbrook, A. (1871) *School Management,* Lebanon, OH; Phelps, W.F. (1874) *The Teachers Handbook for the Institute and the Classroom,* New York; and Baldwin, J. (1892) *The Art of School Management,* New York.

77   *US Annual Report,* 1896-7, p.875.

78   Pickard, J.L. (1902) pp.70 and 92.

79   *Ibid,* p.92 (originally published in 1890).

80   Shearer, W.J. 'The Elizabeth Plan of grading', *US Annual Report,* 1898-9, pp.331-2.

81   Jordan, D.S. (1904) *The Care and Culture of Men: A Series of Addresses on the Higher Education,* San Francisco, CA, pp.70-1 (original address, 1895). When speaking of 'schools' Jordan was, in fact, speaking of college education. Nevertheless, it was ideas such as these that, among other things, attracted a range of influential educators to Stanford (for example, Cubberley and Sneddon) whose own support for individualization and differentiation helped shape the thinking of generations of future school administrators (see, for instance, Tyack D. and Hansot, E. (1982) *Managers of Virtue: Public School Leadership in America 1820-1980,* New York, pp.114ff.; Drost, W.H. (1967) *David Sneddon and Education for Social Efficiency,* Madison, WI; and Berman, B. (1983) 'Business efficiency, American schooling, and the public school superintendency: A reconsideration of the Callahan thesis', *History of Education Quarterly,* Fall, pp.297-321).

82   Jordan, D.S. (1904) *op cit,* p.16 (original address, 1892).

83   In an address to the NEA in 1892, C.W. Eliot spoke of 'the recent introduction of heretical options into the sacred grammar school grades' (reprinted in Eliot, C.W. (1898) *Educational Reform: Essays and Addresses,* New York, p.284). Much earlier mention of high school curriculum electives can be found in Fraser, J. (1866) *op cit,* p.128. Electives were also associated with the practice of specialized teaching by elementary teachers. Known as 'departmental teaching', this procedure of instructing 'in one subject or in one group of related subjects only' had, by 1908, become the 'prevailing' method of teaching in the last two years of the New York elementary school system (see Kilpatrick, V.E. (1908) *Departmental Teaching in Elementary Schools,* New York, pp.1 and v).

84   Eliot, C.W. (1898) *op cit,* pp.191-2.

85   *Ibid,* p.262.

86   Butler, N.M. 'Status of education at the close of the century', *US Annual Report,* 1899-1900, pp.566-8.

87   Hall, G.S. quoted without source in Burstall, S.A. (1909) *Impressions of American Education in 1908,* London, p.165. Hall's judgment was probably based on the publicity surrounding Search's book, *An Ideal School* (New York, 1902). Hoetker and Ahlbrand also cite Sara Burstall's *Impressions* as a source. In their commentary, however, Hoetker and Ahlbrand dismiss Burstall's observations — claiming that they differ not only from earlier sources (for example, Joseph Rice) but also from 'all later

observers' ('Persistence of the recitation', p.150). In fact, Burstall's account (for example, her description of a recitation where the teacher acted as the 'chairman of a meeting', p.108) is strongly reminiscent of the 'socialized' recitation.

88   Search, P.W. (1894) *op cit,* pp.170, 157, 154 and 158.

89   *Ibid,* pp.166 and 167.

90   For an early and seemingly influential discussion of the social conception of education see Howerth, I.R. (1902) 'Education and the social idea', *Educational Review,* 24, pp.150-65.

91   Dutton, S.T. (1911) *School Management: Practical Suggestions Concerning the Conduct and Life of the School,* New York (original printing, 1903), p.77.

92   *Ibid,* pp.78, 84 and 144.

93   *US Annual Report,* 1898-99, p.342.

94   Quoted in Holmes, W.H. (1912) *School Organisation and the Individual Child,* Worcester, MA, p.32. Besides data from other countries, Holmes' book also details many other organizational innovations that received attention in the first decade of twentieth-century America.

95   *Ibid,* p.62.

96   *Ibid,* pp.84 and 86.

97   *Ibid,* pp.84 and 11.

98   *Ibid,* p.96.

99   *Ibid,* pp.66-8.

100 *Ibid,* p.84.

101 Wirth, A.G. (1972) *Education in the Technological Society: the Vocational-Liberal Studies Controversy in the Early Twentieth Century,* Scranton, N.J. p.27.

102 *Ibid.*

103 Gonzalez, G.G. (1977) 'The relationships between monopoly capitalism and progressive education', *Insurgent Sociologist,* 7, p.30 (quoting Lens).

104 Gordon, D.M. *et al* (1982) *op cit,* pp.14-15 (i.e. 'Employers responded to the problem of labor productivity in the late nineteenth century with mechanization, greater use of foremen to supervise workers, and decreasing reliance on skilled labor. Part of the early explorations with [this] drive system also contributed to labor unrest as the turn of the century approached. Consolidation required some further institutional reforms', quotation abridged). See also, Nelson, D. (1980) *op cit,* pp.10ff.

105 Haber, S. (1964) *Efficiency and Uplift: Scientific Management in the Progressive Era 1890-1920,* Chicago, IL, p.x ('Efficiency not only signified a personal quality, a relationship between materials, and a relationship between investment and revenue, but, most important, it signified a relationship between men. Efficiency meant social harmony and the leadership of the "competent". And it is this meaning that has particular importance for the understanding of the progressive era').

106 'The number of . . . personnel management programs grew rapidly in the decade before World War One — a reflection of the increased public interest in the "labor problem" and of the belief that welfare would reduce or eliminate it . . . [However] personnel management, like the engineer's revisions of traditional production management, underwent a

substantial gestation period. Businessmen often accepted the reformers' arguments long before they were prepared to attack the *status quo'* (Nelson, D. (1980) *op cit,* p.19).

107   King, I. (1915) *Education for Social Efficiency: A Study in the Social Relations of Education,* New York, pp.16-18.

108   Reprinted in the *Report of the Committee of the National Council of Education on Economy of Time in Education* (US Bureau of Education, Bulletin No. 38), Washington, DC, 1913, p.57 (Baker was Chairman of the Committee). Baker's view that inefficiency was a moral problem should be contrasted with a more narrow drive-based outlook on social efficiency: for example, 'Every pupil should at every minute be doing something'; 'The teacher like the engineer must determine pace and speed by keeping close track of time'; 'How long before we rid ourselves of the idea that all of a given class must be doing the same tasks'; 'By the better use of ground space, by better setting of machinery, by better placing of raw material, by the cutting down of labour motions, by simplifying the adjustment of interchangeable parts, by producing harder and more lasting cutting tools . . . the factories have increased their output . . . And we teachers ought to do the same' (Mitchell, T.C. (1913) 'Loss of efficiency in the recitation', *Educational Review,* 45, pp.14, 15, 21 and 28). For a history of this technocratic approach to educational efficiency see Callahan, R.E. (1962) *Education and the Cult of Efficiency,* Chicago, IL. In my view, the relative impact of these two strands has still to be adequately assessed.

109   Tyack, D. (1974) *The One Best System: A History of American Urban Education,* London, p.183. Over the same period the total US population rose by only 68 per cent.

110   *Cardinal Principles of Secondary Education,* Washington, DC, 1918, p.8. (I am grateful to Larry Cuban of Stanford University for sending me a copy of this report, unobtainable at that time in the U.K.) For a wider review of high school reform, see Krug, E.A. (1969) *The Shaping of the American High School 1880-1920,* Madison, WI.

111   *Cardinal Principles of Secondary Education,* p.22.

112   *Ibid,* pp.10-11.

113   *Ibid,* pp.10 and 15.

114   *Ibid,* p.9.

115   *Ibid,* p.24.

116   *Ibid,* p.20.

117   *Ibid,* p.14. Cf. Joel Spring's comment that in the early stages of the comprehensive high school system 'democracy did not involve choice but rather doing that which you were best able to do' (*Education and the Rise of the Corporate State,* Boston, MA, 1972, p.107).

118   Whitney, W.T. (1915) *op cit,* p.i.

119   *Ibid,* p.x.

120   *Ibid,* p.2.

121   *Ibid,* p.9.

122   *Ibid,* pp.9-10.

123   *Ibid,* p.15.

124   *Ibid,* p.14.

125 *Ibid*, p.17. See also John Dewey's views on social morality and social efficiency in chapter nine of *Democracy and Education*.

126 Cremin, L. (1964) *The Transformation of the School: Progressivism in American Education 1876-1957*, New York, p.179. Cremin's characterization of the 'great divide' should be compared with Patricia Graham's judgment that 'Although post-war educational innovations differed in certain important respects from those of the prewar period, both had their source in the shifting currents of pedagogical change in the late nineteenth century' (*Progressive Education: from Arcady to Academe*, p.1).

127 Schultz, S. (1973) *op cit*, p.343.

128 Finkelstein, B.J. (1970) *Governing the Young: Teacher Behavior in American Primary Schools 1820-1880*, EdD thesis, University of Columbia, 1970, p.1 (thesis now produced as a book entitled *Governing the Young*, Lewes).

129 Katz, M. (1975) *Class, Bureaucracy and Schools*, New York, p.120.

Chapter 7

Notes Towards a Theory of Schooling

Schools and houses, as places where living and learning occur, are not revealed by procedures that dismantle them.
> (Barker and Gump, (1964) *Big School, Small School*)[1]

There is every ground for believing that . . . the capacity for setting and achieving goals is the chief feature inherent in the life activity of creatures endowed with a psyche.
> (Davydov, (1982) *'Much learning does not teach understanding'*)[2]

I

The foregoing chapters have used a range of conceptual prisms to display some of the forms that schooling has taken over the last 1000 years. The prisms were chosen to break up the undifferentiated 'white light' of the educational record, rendering its constituents more accessible to investigation and explanation. In this final chapter, I reverse the prisms and recast the original record in a transposed and attenuated form. In doing so, I seek to re-view the problematic relationship between 'schooling', 'society' and 'pedagogic change'.

Typically, discussion of the relationship has revolved around two contrasting reference points: (i) the idea that schools merely 'reproduce' predetermined social structures (cf. some of the arguments in Bowles and Gintis' *Schooling in Capitalist America*);[3] and (ii) the contrasting claim that schools can shake themselves free of social structure and become autonomous sites of educational innovation (cf. some of the assumptions made by contributors to Young's *Knowledge & Control*).[4] From the first standpoint, pedagogic change originates outside schools (for example, in the industrial sector of society); whereas from the second perspective, it stems from the ability of teachers to construct new educational relationships within the status quo.[5]

Such analyses are helpful. Yet, they exact a price for their contribution. The elements of schooling are disentangled to such a degree that they cannot be put back together again. Wittingly or unwittingly, 'school in society' is reconceptualized as 'school and society'. This chapter seeks to avoid such a dualism. It starts from the opposite premise — that schooling and society must be examined in terms of the reciprocal relationships that hold them together across time and space. From such a perspective, the day to day practices of schooling are deemed to be both socially-constructed and historically-located. Their shape derives as much, for instance, from the changing expectations of priests and politicians as it does from the pre-given circumstances of school architecture and textbook availability. Necessarily, then, the practices of schooling are both 'in' and 'of' society.[6]

II

In such terms schooling is inherently tension-laden. The web of anticipations that holds it in place also serves as a seedbed of ideas for the transformation of schools, curricula and schoolteachers. Clearly, such conditions of instability (viz. the uneasy coexistence of 'what is' with visions of 'what might be') provide a stimulus for pedagogic change. But they are only part of the story. The will to change is not the same as the capacity to change.

Equally, reform is a more sophisticated concept than change. In a profound sense, reform is inconceivable until such time as the goals of change can be harnessed to a rationale for the 'delivery' of such change. Like 'advancement' and 'progress', the political notion of reform presumes that appropriate routemaps and appropriate vehicles are made available. Deprived of such resources, social change remains — quite literally — a disorderly affair.[7]

From this perspective, then, the history of successful pedagogic innovation is part of a much broader historical movement — the gradual extension of humankind's capacity to transform its own social, psychological and material circumstances. During its early history, the human species had only a limited appreciation of its own capacities. Like other animals it lived a vulnerable existence. The alternative futures that it dreamed about — and stored in myth and legend — remained little more than distant, unreachable heavens.

Through time, however, socio-technical innovations have brought some of these heavens within human reach. In the Middle Ages, for instance, developments in literacy and accounting rendered the mysterious ways of God open to logical scrutiny and rational interpretation. Likewise, the recasting of classical conceptions of method gave credence to Renaissance dreams about the perfectibility of the human condition. And, not least, the curriculum-related rationales that emerged in the late sixteenth century served to strengthen the 'hearing of the Word' that was a central tenet of the Reformed churches. Together, these developments helped schooling to become a delivery system in its own right. Without a programme of educational delivery, so the political/theological argument ran, there could be no prospect of spiritual deliverance.[8]

Refinement of schooling as an instrument of church and state policy continued through the seventeenth and eighteenth centuries. In particular, state officials were attracted to the cartesian notion that, suitably redesigned, schools could operate as efficiently as machines (cf. the municipal adoption of De la Salle's *Conduite de l'École Chrétienne,* 1720). In turn, these images of social engineering fuelled the political aspirations of the Enlightenment. Schooling was to be reformed in accordance with the new notions of equality and inequality that came to a head in the French and American revolutions. And one of the key assumptions underpinning such reform was 'Education can do everything' — a maxim attributed to the French philosopher Claude-Adrien Helvetius (1715-1771).[9]

Finally, the organizing principles of schooling were transformed once again as the eighteenth-century Enlightenment shaded into the nineteenth-century industrial revolution. The self-evident success and social efficiency of steam power raised fresh hopes for the salvation and deliverance of humankind. Beneath the relative inexactitudes of engineering were to be found, so Andrew Bell and others claimed, the eternal laws of science. If schooling could be brought into line with these 'natural truths' then the future of civil society would be assured. In short, science was deemed to be the ultimate delivery system.[10]

III

For such reasons, discussions about school reform were gradually colonized by ideas from the emergent sciences of psychology, sociology and administration. At the same time, too, a new discipline emerged: the selective transposition of knowledge about education into a codified theory of schooling meant that, henceforth, theorists of schooling became distinguishable from theorists of education.[11]

Since the eighteenth century, theorists of schooling have been found among the ranks of government inspectors, school superintendents, textbook authors, architects, and teacher-trainers. Throughout, their official concern has been to maintain a functional correspondence between the organization of schooling and the aims of the political state. In turn, state servants (for example, James Kay Shuttleworth and William T. Harris) have used pedagogic innovations as a means of coopting teachers, learners, taxpayers (etc.) to a state-sponsored model of the future. Currently, then, state-led schooling attempts a two-pronged intervention in the social fabric of society.[12] On the one hand, curricula are disseminated to promote a clearly-specified vision of the future (viz. the beliefs and dispositions deemed appropriate to the next generation of citizens); and on the other hand, a cluster of assessment practices are promulgated to shape teaching and learning in accordance with that normative vision.[13]

Through such penetrating practices, the state pursues its political mission. It influences the ways that schooling articulates with other social institutions (for example, the family, the labour market, the military); it shapes a variety of intra-school articulations (for example, teacher/teacher, learner/learner and subject/subject relationships); and, not least, it endorses social beliefs (for example, male/female stereotypes and 'nature'/-'nurture' distinctions) that, in their turn, suffuse the self-regulation of teachers and learners.

IV

The dream, however, is not the deed. Theorists of schooling regularly acknowledge that state intervention falls short of its goals. Yet, their accompanying diagnoses remain firmly within the realm of systems engineering. As a result, the pedagogical delivery system is not so much re-examined as retuned. Targets are reset, resources are reallocated and managers are retrained. School reform becomes a permanent solution. Yet, in the process, deliverance is reduced to delivery.

If this book has any message, it is that the officially acknowledged inadequacies of pedagogical practice do not derive from the shortcomings of systems engineers. Rather, their origins lie elsewhere — in a destabilizing contradiction that is inherent to the technocratic dream. At root, technocratic thinking is driven by a vision of control and standardization. It succeeds, therefore, to the degree that it is able to create teacher-proof and learner-proof curricula, and to the degree that it can ignore the differences among schools and schoolrooms. But, in its denial of the goal setting capacities of teachers and learners, and in its denial of variations among school settings, technocratic thinking is ultimately self-defeating. Schooling designed to its specifications is alienated from the social, economic and political anchor-points that, hitherto, have held it in place. It remains 'of' society but ceases to be 'in' society. Beyond history, it is no longer schooling; it is something else.[14]

V

Throughout the preparation of this book and these concluding notes, I have struggled with two views about schools and schooling. On the one hand I have identified schooling as an agency of state-led social regulation; and on the other hand, I have identified schools as potential sites of autonomous social change. At first glance, these contrasting accounts of schooling suggest a logical weakness in my own thinking. How can I justify the claim that schooling is simultaneously a site of social regulation and a site of social redefinition? In this final chapter, I have tried to show that this apparent contradiction can be resolved if teachers and learners are acknowledged to be, at one and the same time, both the social target of schooling and the active medium through which that target can be reached. If a curriculum is to be effective, the active engagement of teachers and learners is required. Yet, in their activity, teachers and learners also have a reactive effect upon the curriculum (and beyond). Regulation and redefinition are not, therefore, mutually-exclusive outcomes. They are inseparable aspects of the same social process.[15]

Despite this eventual resolution, however, I am also aware that much of this book gives a disproportionate amount of attention to social regulation — a function, doubtless, of my early decision to focus upon the schooling of those who are less powerful in society. An exhaustive account of schooling would, I accept, need to accumulate a more rounded appreciation of the contrasting social possibilities of schooling. In the meantime, however, this book might serve as a prologue to that task.

Notes

1 Barker, R.G. and Gump, P.V. (1964) *Big School, Small School,* Palo Alto, CA, p.45.
2 Davydov, V. (1982) 'Much learning does not teach understanding', quoted in Levitin, K. (Ed) *One is Not Born a Personality: Profiles of Soviet Education Psychologists,* Moscow, p.312.
3 Bowles S. and Gintis, H. (1976) *Schooling in Capitalist America: Educational Reform and the Contradictions of Economic Life,* London.

4   Young, M.F.D. (Ed) (1971) *Knowledge and Control: New Directions for the Sociology of Education,* London, 1971.

5   For a cogent review of recent Anglo-American debates about the links between 'schooling', 'society' and 'educational change' see Whitty, G. (1985) *Sociology and School Knowledge: Curriculum Theory, Research and Politics,* London, chapters 1 and 2.

6   For a detailed analysis of the dialectical (or mutually-constitutive) relationships that create social practices see Henriques, J., Holloway, W., Urwin, C., Venn, C. and Walkerdine, V. (1984) *Changing the Subject: Social Regulation and Subjectivity,* London.

7   The notion that information might be 'delivered' has a long history. It is used, for instance, by Francis Bacon (1640) in *The Advancement of Science,* Book 6, chapter 2 ('as knowledges have hitherto been delivered'). Note, too, that the word 'progress', like the terms 'advancement' and 'reform', took on its political meaning in the sixteenth and seventeenth centuries (see, for instance, the *Oxford English Dictionary*).

8   For the general transformation of sixteenth-century social policy-making into a manipulative rather than an ethical discipline see MacIntyre, A. (1981) *After Virtue: A Study in Moral Theory,* London, chapters 5-8; and for further details of the seventeenth-century institutionalization of schooling see Hamilton, D. (1987) 'The pedagogical juggernaut', *British Journal of Educational Studies,* 35, pp.18-29.

9   Cumming, I. (1955) *Helvetius: His Life and Place in the History of Educational Thought,* London, chapter 15.

10   Note, for instance, that one of the most important 'scientific' constructs used in schooling — the normal curve — dates from the early nineteenth century.

11   The split between educational theory and schooling theory is evident, for instance, among eighteenth and early nineteenth century writers — like Jean Jacques Rousseau, Wilhelm von Humboldt, Johann Pestalozzi, and Elizabeth Hamilton — who switched backwards and forwards from a concern with education to a concern with the management of schooling (see variously, Vernon, R. (1986) *Citizenship and Order: Studies in French Political Thought,* Toronto; Sorkin, D. (1983) 'Wilhelm von Humboldt: The theory and practice of self-formation (*Bildung*), 1791-1810', *Journal of the History of Ideas,* 44, pp.55-73; Silber, K. (1960) *Pestalozzi: The Man and His Work,* London; and Russell, R. (1986) 'Elizabeth Hamilton: Enlightenment educator', *Scottish Educational Review,* 18, pp.23-30).

12   My argument about the double intervention implied in pedagogic practice owes much to Ulf Lundgren of the Stockholm Institute of Education.

13   If state-led curricula and state-led assessment practices ran in parallel in the nineteenth century, twentieth century schooling seems to be marked by a convergence of curriculum theory and assessment theory (see, for instance, Hamilton, D. (1987) 'How the curriculum idea was grounded', Glasgow University Department of Education, mimeo).

14   Contradictory elements in curriculum implementation are explored, for instance, in Berlak, A. and Berlak, H. (1981) *Dilemmas of Schooling: Teaching and Social Change,* London; and Popkewitz, T.S., Tabarchnick, B.R. and Wehlage, G. (1982) *The Myth of Educational Reform: a Study of*

School Responses to a Program of Change, Madison, WI.

15   In addressing the object/agent and regulation/redefinition problems, I have been greatly assisted by E.V. Ilyenkov's two books: *Dialectical Logic: Essays in its History and Theory* (Moscow, 1977); and *The Dialectics of the Abstract and Concrete in Marx's Capital* (Moscow, 1982). Further, my attention to Ilyenkov's work owes much to the encouragement and example of Jack Whitehead of the University of Bath.

Bibliography

Manuscript Sources

Committee Book of the Glasgow Infant School Society (Jordanhill College of Education).

Glasgow Grammar School Papers (Mitchell Library, Glasgow).

Letters from George Jardine to Robert Hunter (University of Glasgow Special Collections).

Letters between Robert Owen, David Stow and Thomas Chalmers (New College Library, Edinburgh).

New Lanark Cash Book (University of Edinburgh Library).

New Lanark Visitors Books (University of Glasgow Archives).

Papers relating to the Academy of Geneva (University of Geneva).

Newspapers

Glasgow Advertiser and Evening Intelligencer (which subsequently became the *Glasgow Herald*) 1789-1840.

Books and Articles

ABBOTT, J. (1851) *The Works of Jacob Abbott,* London, Griffin.

ADAMS, F. (1875) *The Free School System of the United States,* London, Chapman & Hall.

ADAMSON, J.W. (1971) *Pioneers of Modern Education in the Seventeenth Century,* New York, Teachers College Press.

ALEXANDER, H.G. (1945) *Time as Dimension and History,* Alberquerque, NM, University of New Mexico Press.

ALLEN, P. (1922) *Letters of Erasmus,* Oxford, Clarendon Press.

ALT, R. (1960) *Bilderatlas zur Schul- und Erziehungs Geschichte* (vol. 1), Berlin, Volk und Wissen Volkseigener.

ANDERSON, P. (1979) *Lineages of the Absolutist State,* London, Verso.

ANDERSON, W.I. (1902) *Prize Lists of the University of Glasgow from Session 1777-8 to Session 1832-3,* Glasgow, Carter & Pratt.

Annual Report of the School Committee of the City of Boston, 1857.

Annual Report of the Superintendent of the Common Schools of the State of New York, 1844.

Annual Report of the Superintendent of the Common Schools of the State of New York, 1846.

Annual Reports of the· US Commissioner of Education, Washington, DC, 1873-1916.

ANSCOMBE, E. and GEACH, P.T. (Eds) (1970) *Descartes' Philosophical Writings,* London, Nelson.

ARIES, P. (1962) *Centuries of Childhood: A Social History of Family Life,* New York, Vintage.

ARMYTAGE, W.H.G. (1970) *400 Years of English Education,* Cambridge, Cambridge University Press.

ASTON, T. (Ed) (1965) *Crisis in Europe 1500-1660,* London, Routledge.

AVERY, G. (Ed) (1967) *School Remembered: an Anthology,* London, Gollancz.

BAGLEY, W.C. and KEITH, J.H. (1924) *An Introduction to Teaching,* New York, Macmillan.

BAILYN, B. (1960) *Education and the Forming of American Society* (reprinted New York, Norton, 1972)

BAILYN, B. (1982) 'The challenge of modern historiography', *American Historical Review,* 87, pp.1-24.

BALDWIN, J. (1892) *The Art of School Management,* New York, Appleton.

BALDWIN, J.W. and GOLDTHWAITE, R.A. (Eds) (1972) *Universities in Politics: Case Studies from the Late Middle Ages and Early Modern Period,* Baltimore, MD, Johns Hopkins University Press.

BARKER, R.G. and GUMP, P.V. (1964) *Big School, Small School,* Stanford, CA, Stanford University Press.

BARNARD, H.C. (1954) *Girls at School Under the Ancien Regime,* London, Burns & Oates.

BATTERSBY, W.J. (1949) *De la Salle: A Pioneer of Modern Education,* London, Longmans.

BATTLES, F.L. and MILLER, C. (1972) *A Computerised Concordance to Institutio Christianae Religionis (1559) of Ionnes Calvinus,* Pittsburgh, PA, Pittsburgh Theological Seminary.

BELL, A. (1832) *Complete Works,* Edinburgh, Oliver & Boyd.

BENSON, R.L. and CONSTABLE, G. (Eds) (1982) *Renaissance and Renewal in the Twelfth Century,* Oxford, Clarendon Press.

BERLAK, A. and BERLAK, H. (1981) *Dilemmas of Schooling: Teaching and Social Change,* London, Methuen.

BERMAN, B. (1983) 'Business efficiency, American schooling, and the public school superintendency: A reconsideration of the Callahan thesis', *History of Education Quarterly,* 23, pp.297-321.

BERNSTEIN, A. (1978) *Pierre D'Ailly and the Blanchard Affair: University and Chancellor of Paris at the Beginning of the Great Schism,* Leiden, Brill.

BIETENHOLZ, P.G. (1971) *Basle and France in the Sixteenth Century: The Basle Humanists and Printers in their Contacts with Francophone Culture,* Geneva, Droz.

BIRCHENOUGH, C. (1925) *History of Elementary Education in England and Wales*, London, University Tutorial Press.

BONE, W. (1924) *Individual occupations in the Three Rs*, London, Pitman.

BOURGEAUD, C. (1900) *Histoiré de l'Université de Genève: l'Academie de Calvin*, Geneva, Georg.

BOWLES, S. and GINTIS, H. (1976) *Schooling in Capitalist America: Educational Reform and the Contradictions of Economic Life*, London, Routledge & Kegan Paul.

BRAVERMAN, H. (1974) *Labor and Monopoly Capital: The Degradation of Work in the Twentieth Century*, New York, Monthly Review Press.

BRENNER, R. (1976) 'Agrarian class structure and economic development in pre-industrial Europe', *Past and Present*, 70, pp.30-75.

BRENNER, R. (1982) 'Agrarian class structure and economic development in pre-industrial Europe', *Past and Present*, 97, pp.17-113.

BROBY-JOHANSEN, R. (1974) *Skolen i Kunsten, Kunsten i Skolen*, Copenhagen, Gyldendal.

BROCKLISS, L.W.B. (1976) 'The University of Paris in the sixteenth and seventeenth centuries', PhD thesis, University of Cambridge.

BROUDY, H. and PALMER, J.R. (1965) *Exemplars of Teaching Method*, Chicago, IL, Rand McNally.

BROWN, J.H. (1933) *Elizabethan Schooldays*, Oxford, Blackwell.

BUCHDAHL, G. (1961) *The Image of Newton and Locke in the Age of Reason*, London, Sheed & Ward.

BUISSON, F. (1882) *Dictionnaire de Pédagogie et d'Instruction Primaire*, Paris, Hachette.

BURROWES, T.H. (1855) *Pennsylvania School Architecture*, Harrisburg, PA, Boyd Hamilton.

BURSTALL, S. (1909) *Impressions of American Education in 1908*, London, Longmans.

BUTLER, J. (1828) *Outlines of Practical Education*, London, Hamilton.

BUTLER, N.M. (1899-1900) 'Status of education at the close of the century', *Annual Report of the US Commissioner of Education*, pp.566-8.

CALLAHAN, R.E. (1962) *Education and the Cult of Efficiency: a Study of the Social Forces that have Shaped the Administration of the Public Schools*, Chicago, IL, University of Chicago Press.

CALVIN, J. (1833-34) *Commentaries* (in latin), Berlin, Thome.

CAMPBELL, R.H. and SKINNER, A.S. (1982) *Adam Smith*, London, Croom Helm.

CAMPBELL, T.D. (1971) *Adam Smith's Science of Morals*, London, Allen & Unwin.

Cardinal Principles of Secondary Education, Washington, DC, Government Printing Office, 1918.

CARNOY, M., LEVIN, H.M. and KING, K. (1980) *Education, Work, Employment II*, Paris, UNESCO.

Cassell's Latin Dictionary, London, Cassell, 1893.

CHANDLER, A.D. (1978) *The Visible Hand: The Managerial Revolution in American Business*, London, Belknap Press.

CHANDLER, A.D. and DAEMS, H. (Eds) (1980) *Managerial Hierarchies: Comparative Perspectives on the Rise of the Modern Industrial Enterprise*, Cambridge, MA, Harvard University Press.

CHARMOT, F. (1943) *La Pédagogie des Jésuites*, Paris, Editions Spes.
CHARTIER, R., JULIA, D. and COMPÈRE, M. (1976) *L'Éducation en France du XVIe au XVIIIe Siècle*, Paris, SEDES.
CHILL, E. (1962) 'Religion and mendicity in seventeenth century France', *International Review of Social History*, 7, pp.400-25.
CHURCH, W.F. (Ed) (1969) *The Impact of Absolutism in France*, London, Wiley.
CIPOLLA, C.M. (Ed) (1973) *The Fontana Economic History of Europe*, vol.3, London, Fontana.
CLAGETT, M., POST, G. and REYNOLDS, R. (Eds) (1966) *Twelfth Century Europe and the Foundations of Modern Society*, Madison, WI, University of Wisconsin Press.
CLANCHY, M.T. (1979) *From Memory to Written Record*, London, Edward Arnold.
CLARKE, W.K.L. (1959) *A History of the SPCK*, London, SPCK.
CLAWSON, D. (Ed) (1980) *Bureaucracy and the Labor Process: The Transformation of United States Industry 1860-1920*, New York, Monthly Review Press.
CLOUATRE, D.L. (1984) 'The concept of class in French culture prior to the revolution', *Journal of the History of Ideas*, 45, pp.219-44.
COBBAN, A.B. (1975) *The Medieval Universities: their Development and Organisation*, London, Methuen.
COHEN, G.A. (1984) *Karl Marx's Theory of History: A Defence*, Oxford, Clarendon Press.
COHEN, S. (1964) *Progressives and Urban School Reform: The Public School Association of New York City 1895-1954*, New York, Teachers College, Columbia University.
COLLINS, G. (n.d.) *Notes on School Management*, London, Moffatt & Paige.
COLLINS, J. (1971) *Descartes' Philosophy of Nature*, Oxford, Blackwell.
COMENIUS, J.A. (1896) *The Great Didactic* (1632) London, Adam & Charles Black.
COMENIUS, J.A. (1969) *A Reformation of Schools* (translated by S. Hartlib, 1642), Menston, Scolar Press.
Commission Internationale pour l'Histoire des Universités (1967) *Les Universités Européenes du XIVe au XVIIIe Siècle: Aspects et Problèmes*, Geneva, Droz.
COMPÈRE, M. and JULIA, D. (1981) 'Les collèges sous l'ancien régime', *Histoire de l'Education*, 13, pp.1-27.
CONNELL, R.W. (1987) *Gender and Power: Society, the Person and Sexual Politics*, Cambridge, Polity Press.
CORRIGAN, P. and SAYER, D. (1985) *The Great Arch: State Formation, Cultural Revolution and the Rise of Capitalism*, Oxford, Blackwell.
COURTENAY, W.J. (1987) *Schools and Scholars in Fourteenth-century England*, Princeton NJ, Princeton University Press.
COWHAM, J.H. (1894) *The Principles of Oral Teaching and Mental Training*, London, Westminster School Book Depot.
CRAIGIE, J. (1970) *A Bibliography of Scottish Education before 1872*, London, University of London Press.
CRAIGIE, J. (1974) *A Bibliography of Scottish Education 1872-1972*, London, University of London Press.
CREMIN, L. (1964) *The Transformation of the School: Progressivism in American Education 1876-1957*, New York, Vintage.

CRUNDEN, R.M. (1982) *Ministers of Reform: the Progressives' Achievement in American Civilisation 1889-1920,* New York, Basic Books.

CUBAN, L. (1982a) 'Persistence of the inevitable: The teacher-centred classroom', *Education and Urban Society,* 1, pp.26-41.

CUBAN, L. (1982b) *Teacher as Leader and Captive: Continuity and Change in American Classrooms 1890-1980,* Stanford, CA, Stanford University School of Education research report.

CURRIE, J. (1857) *The Principles and Practice of Early and Infant-School Education,* Edinburgh, Laurie.

CURRIE, J. (n.d.) *The Principles and Practice of Common-School Education,* Edinburgh, Laurie.

DALE, R., ESLAND, G., FERGUSSON, R. and MACDONALD, M. (Eds) (1981) *Education and the State* (vol. 1), Lewes, Falmer Press.

Deeds Instituting Bursaries, Scholarships and Other Foundations in the College and University of Glasgow, Glasgow, Richardson, 1850.

DEWEY, J. (1916) *Democracy and Education,* New York, Macmillan.

DHOTEL, J.C. (1967) *Les Origines du Catéchisme Moderne d'après les Premiers Manuels Imprimés en France,* Paris, Aubier.

DICK, T. (1836) *On the Mental Illumination and Moral Improvement of Mankind,* Glasgow, Collins.

DICKENS, A.G. (1968) *The Counter Reformation,* London, Thames & Hudson.

DICKENS, A.G. (1976) *The German Nation and Martin Luther,* London, Fontana.

DOBB, M. (1946) *Studies in the Development of Capitalism,* London, Routledge.

DROST, W.H. (1967) *David Snedden and Education for Social Efficiency,* Madison, WI, University of Wisconsin Press.

DUBY, G. (1968) *Rural Economy and Country Life in the Medieval West,* London, Edward Arnold.

DUBY, G. (1980) *The Three Orders: Feudal Society Imagined,* Chicago, IL, University of Chicago Press.

DUBY, G. and LE GOFF, J. (Eds) (1977) *Famille et Parenté dans l'Occident Médiévale,* Rome, École Française de Rome.

DUNKIN, M.J. and BIDDLE, B.J. (1974) *The Study of Teaching,* New York, Holt, Rinehart & Winston.

DUNLOP, O.J. and DENMAN, R.D. (1912) *English Apprenticeship and Child Labour: A History,* London, Fisher Unwin.

DUNN, H. (n.d.) *Principles of Teaching,* London, Sunday School Union.

DUNN, R.S. (1970) *The Age of Religious Wars 1559-1689,* London, Weidenfeld & Nicolson.

DURIG, W. (1952) 'Disciplina: Eine Studie zum Bedeutungsumfang des Wortes in der Sprache der Liturgie und des Vater', *Sacris Erudiri,* 4, pp.245-79.

DURKAN, J. and KIRK, J. (1977) *The University of Glasgow 1451-1577,* Glasgow, University of Glasgow Press.

DURKHEIM, E. (1905) 'The evolution and the role of secondary education in France', reprinted in DURKHEIM, E. (1956) *Education and Sociology,* London, Free Press.

DURKHEIM, E. (1985) *The Evolution of Educational Thought,* London, Routledge.

DUTTON, S.T. (1911) *School Management: Practical Suggestions Concerning the Conduct and Life of the School,* New York, Scribners.

Eighteenth Annual Report of the Trustees and Visitors of Common Schools to the City Council of Cincinnati, Cincinnati, OH, 1846.

ELIAS, N. (1978) *The Civilising Process,* Oxford, Blackwell.

ELIOT, C.W. (1898) *Educational Reform: Essays and Addresses,* New York, Century.

ERASMUS, D. (1969-) *Opera Omnia* (in Latin), Amsterdam, North-Holland.

ERASMUS, D. (1978-) *Collected Works* (in English), Toronto, University of Toronto Press.

FINDLAY, J.J. (1902) *Principles of Class Teaching,* London, Macmillan.

FINKELSTEIN, B.J. (1970) *Governing the young: Teacher behavior in American primary schools 1820-1880,* EdD thesis, Columbia University, now printed by Falmer Press (1989).

FITZPATRICK, E.A. (1951) *La Salle: Patron of All Teachers,* Milwaukee, WI, Bruce.

FLANDRIN, J. (1979) *Families in Former Times,* Cambridge, Cambridge University Press.

FOUCAULT, M. (1979) *Discipline and Punish: The Birth of the Prison,* Harmondsworth, Penguin.

FOULQUIE, P. (1971) *Dictionnaire de la Langue Pédagogique,* Paris, PUF.

FRASER, J. (1866) *Report of the Common School System of the United States and of the Provinces of Upper and Lower Canada,* London, HMSO.

GALL, J. (n.d.) *The Effects of the Lesson System of Teaching on Criminals, General Society, and the Lowest Orders of the Human Intellect,* Edinburgh, Gall.

GANSS, G.E. (1956) *Saint Ignatius's Idea of a Jesuit University,* Milwaukee, WI, Marquette University Press.

GARDINER, D. (1929) *English Girlhood at School,* Oxford, Oxford University Press.

GAUFRES, M.J. (1880) *Claude Baduel et la Réforme des Études au XVIᵉ Siècle,* Paris, Hachette.

GAUKROGER, S. (Ed) (1980) *Descartes: Philosophy, Mathematics and Physics,* Hassocks, Harvester Press.

GIBSON, J. (1977) *The History of Glasgow,* Glasgow, Chapman & Duncan.

GILBERT, J.F. (1977) *Work Without Salvation: America's Intellectuals and Industrial Alienation 1880-1910,* Baltimore, MD, Johns Hopkins University Press.

GILBERT, N. (1960) *Renaissance Concepts of Method,* New York, Columbia University Press.

GILL, J. (1858) *Introductory Textbook to Method and School Management,* London, Longmans.

GLADMAN, F. (1885) *School Work,* Norwich, Jarrold.

GONZALEZ, G.G. (1977) 'The relationships between monopoly capitalism and progressive education', *Insurgent Sociologist,* 7, pp.25-41.

GOODRICH, M. (1983) 'Encyclopedic literature: Childrearing in the Middle Ages', *History of Education,* 12, pp.1-8.

GOODSON, I. (1988) *The Making of Curriculum,* Brighton, Falmer Press.

GORDON, D.M., EDWARDS, R. and REICH, M. (1982) *Segmented Work, Divided Workers: The Historical Transformation of Labor in the United States 1860-1920,* New York, Cambridge University Press.

GORDON, P. and WHITE, J. (1979) *Philosophers as Educational Reformers: The*

Influence of Idealism on British Educational Thought and Practice, London, Routledge.

GOSDEN, P.H.J.H. (Ed) (1969) *How They Were Taught: An Anthology of Contemporary Accounts of Learning and Teaching in England 1800-1950*, Oxford, Blackwell.

GOULET, R. (1928) *Compendium on the University of Paris*, Philadelphia, PA, University of Philadelphia Press, [translation of 1517 edition].

GRAFTON, A.T. and JARDINE, L. (1982) 'Humanism and the school of Guarino: A problem of evaluation', *Past and Present*, 96, pp.51-80.

GRAHAM, P.A. (1967) *Progressive Education: From Arcady to Academe (A History of the Progressive Education Association 1919-1955)*, New York, Teachers College Press.

GUNN, J. (1895) *Class Teaching and Class Management*, London, Nelson.

HABER, S. (1964) *Efficiency and Uplift: Scientific Management in the Progressive Era 1890-1920*, Chicago, IL, University of Chicago Press.

HACKWOOD, F. (1897) *The Practical Method of Class Management: A Ready Guide of Useful Hints to Young Class Teachers*, London, Philip.

HAIG, T. (n.d.) *Advantages to be Derived from Equalized Classification*, London, Gilbert & Piper.

HAMILTON, D. (1977) *In Search of Structure: A Case Study of a New Scottish Open Plan Primary School*, London, Hodder & Stoughton.

HAMILTON, D. (1978) *Classroom Research and the Evolution of the Classroom System: Some Interim Papers*, Glasgow, University of Glasgow Department of Education, mimeo.

HAMILTON, D. (1980) 'Adam Smith and the moral economy of the classroom system', *Journal of Curriculum Studies*, 12, pp.281-98.

HAMILTON, D. (1981a) 'On simultaneous instruction and the early evolution of class teaching', Glasgow, University of Glasgow Department of Education, mimeo.

HAMILTON, D. (1981b) 'Simultaneous instruction and the changing disciplines of eighteenth and nineteenth century schooling', Glasgow, University of Glasgow Department of Education, mimeo.

HAMILTON, D. (1983) 'Schooling and capitalism 1100-1800: Some points of departure', Glasgow, University of Glasgow Department of Education, mimeo.

HAMILTON, D. (1987a) 'The pedagogical juggernaut', *British Journal of Educational Studies*, 35, pp.18-29.

HAMILTON, D. (1987b) 'How the curriculum idea was grounded', Glasgow, University of Glasgow Department of Education, mimeo.

HAMILTON, D. and GIBBONS, M. (1980) 'Notes on the origins of the educational terms class and curriculum', Glasgow, University of Glasgow Department of Education, mimeo.

Handbook to the Borough Road Schools, London, British and Foreign Schools Society, 1854.

HARRIS, W.T. (1870) *St Louis School Report*, St Louis, MO.

HARRIS, W.T. (1871) 'Advantages of class recitation', *Western Educational Review* (St Louis), 2, pp.3-6.

HASKELL, T.L. (1972) *The Emergence of Professional Social Science*, Urbana, IL, University of Illinois Press.

HEER, F. (1963) *The Medieval World,* New York, Mentor.

HELD, D. (Ed) (1985) *States and Societies,* Oxford, Blackwell.

HENDERSON, B.L.K. (n.d.) *Schoolboys of Other Days,* London, Allman.

HENRIQUES, J., HOLLOWAY, W., URWIN, C., VENN, C. and WALKERDINE, V. (1984) *Changing the Subject: Social Regulation and Subjectivity,* London, Methuen.

HIGSON, C.W.J. (1967) *Sources for the History of Education,* London, Library Association.

HIGSON, C.W.J. (1976) *Supplement to Sources for the History of Education,* London, Library Association.

HILL, C. (1969a) *Society and Puritanism in Pre-Revolutionary England,* London, Panther.

HILL, C. (1969b) *Reformation and Industrial Revolution,* Harmondsworth, Penguin.

HILTON, R. (Ed) (1978) *The Transition from Feudalism to Capitalism,* London, Verso.

HINKLE, R.C. (1980) *Founding Theory of American Sociology 1881-1915,* London, Routledge.

HOETKER, J. and AHLBRAND, W.P. (1969) 'The persistence of the recitation', *American Educational Research Journal,* 2, pp.145-7.

HOFSTADTER, R. (1955) *Social Darwinism in American Thought,* Boston, Beacon Press.

HOLBROOK, A. (1871) *School Management,* Lebanon, OH, Holbrook.

HOLMES, W.H. (1912) *School Organization and the Individual Child,* Worcester, Davis Press.

HOOYKAAS, R. (1958) *Humanisme, Science et Reforme: Pierre de la Ramee,* Leiden, Brill.

HOPFL, H. (1982) *The Christian Polity of John Calvin,* Cambridge, Cambridge University Press.

HOSKIN, K.W. and MACVE, R.M. (1986) 'Accounting and the examination: A genealogy of discipline and power', *Accounting Organisations and Society,* 11, pp.105-36.

HOWERTH, I.R. (1902) 'Education and the social idea', *Educational Review,* 24, pp.150-65.

HUFTON, O. (1974) *The Poor of Eighteenth Century France 1750-1789,* Oxford, Clarendon Press.

HUGHES, D.O. (1975) 'Urban growth and family structure in medieval Genoa', *Past and Present,* 66, pp.2-28.

HUMES, W. and PATERSON, H. (Eds) (1983) *Scottish Education and Scottish Culture 1800-1980,* Edinburgh, John Donald.

HUPPERT, G. (1984) *Public Schools in Renaissance France,* Urbana, IL, University of Illinois Press.

HURT, J. (1971) *Education in Evolution,* London, Granada.

HYMA, A. (1950) *The Brethren of the Common Life,* Grand Rapids, MI, Eerdmans.

ILYENKOV, E.V. (1977) *Dialectical Logic: Essays in its History and Theory,* Moscow, Progress.

ILYENKOV, E.V. (1982) *The Dialectics of the Abstract and Concrete in Marx's Capital,* Moscow, Progress.

IRVINE, T.A. (1982) 'Number consciousness and the rise of capitalism: Some preliminary considerations', MEd thesis, University of Glasgow.

JACOB, E.F. (1963) *Essays in the Conciliar Epoch,* Manchester, Manchester University Press.

JANSSEN, J. (1887) *L'Allemagne et la Réforme,* Paris, Plon.

JARDINE, G. (1797) *Synopsis of the Lectures on Logic and Belles Lettres Read in the University of Glasgow,* Glasgow, Glasgow University Press.

JARDINE, G. (1825) *Outlines of Philosophical Education Illustrated by the Method of Teaching the Logic Class in the University of Glasgow,* Glasgow, Glasgow University Press.

JARDINE, L. (1974) *Francis Bacon: Discovery and the Art of Discourse,* Cambridge, Cambridge University Press.

JOHNSON, R. (1970) 'Educational policy and social control in early Victorian England', *Past and Present,* 49, pp.96-119.

JONES, K. and WILLIAMSON, K. (1979) 'The birth of the schoolroom', *Ideology and Consciousness,* 6, pp.59-110.

JORDAN, D.S. (1904) *The Care and Culture of Men: a Series of Addresses on the Higher Education,* San Francisco, CA, Whitaker & Ray.

JORDAN, W.K. (1959) *Philanthropy in England 1480-1660: A Study of the Changing Pattern of English Social Aspirations,* London, Allen & Unwin.

JOYCE, P.W. (1864) *A Handbook of School Management and Methods of Teaching,* Dublin, McGlashan & Gill.

JUNOD, L. and MEYLAN, H. (1947) *L'Académie de Lausanne au XVIe Siècle,* Lausanne, Rouge.

JURRIAANSE, M.W. (1965) *The Founding of Leiden University,* Leiden, Brill.

KAESTLE, C. (Ed) (1973a) *Joseph Lancaster and the Monitorial School Movement,* New York, Teachers College Press.

KAESTLE, C.F. (1973b) *The Evolution of an Urban School System: New York City 1750-1850,* Cambridge, MA, Harvard University Press.

KAESTLE, C.F. (1983) *Pillars of the Republic: Common Schools and American Society 1780-1869,* New York, Hill & Wang.

KAESTLE, C.F. and VINOVSKIS, M. (1980) *Education and Social Change in Nineteenth Century Massachussetts,* Cambridge, Cambridge University Press.

KANE, W. (1938) *An Essay Toward a History of Education,* Chicago, IL, Loyola University Press.

KANTOR, H. and TYACK, D. (Eds) (1982) *Work, Youth and Schooling: Historical Perspectives on Vocationalism in American Society,* Stanford, CA, Stanford University Press.

KARIER, C., VIOLAS, P.C. and SPRING, J. (1973) *Roots of Crisis: American Education in the Twentieth Century,* Chicago, Rand McNally.

KASSON, J.F. (1977) *Civilizing the Machine: Technology and Republican Values in America 1776-1900,* Harmondsworth, Penguin.

KATZ, M. (1975) *Class, Bureaucracy and Schools,* New York, Praeger.

KATZ, M. (1976) 'The origins of public education: A reassessment', *History of Education Quarterly,* 16, pp.381-407.

KEARNS, E.J. (1979) *Ideas in Seventeenth Century France,* Manchester, Manchester University Press.

KEEN, M. (1969) *A History of Medieval Europe,* Harmondsworth, Penguin.

KENNEDY, W. (1879) *Large Schools and their Educational and Economic Advantages,* Glasgow, Cameron.

KENT, A. (Ed) (1950) *An Eighteenth Century Lectureship in Chemistry,* Glasgow, Jackson.

KIERNAN, V.G. (1980) *State and Society in Europe 1550-1650,* Oxford, Blackwell.

KIERSTEAD, R.F. (Ed) (1975) *State and Society in Seventeenth Century France,* New York, New Viewpoints.

KILPATRICK, V.E. (1908) *Departmental Teaching in Elementary Schools,* New York, Macmillan.

KING, I. (1915) *Education for Social Efficiency: A Study in the Social Relations of Education,* New York, Appleton.

KIRKLAND, E.G. (1956) *Dream and Thought in the Business Community 1860-1900,* Ithaca, NY, Cornell University Press.

KLIEBARD, H. (1986) *The Struggle for the American Curriculum 1893-1958,* London, Routledge.

KNOWLES, D. (1962) *The Evolution of Medieval Thought,* New York, Vintage.

KOLKO, G. (1963) *The Triumph of Conservatism: a Reinterpretation of American History 1900-1916,* New York, Free Press.

KRUG, E.A. (1969) *The Shaping of the American High School 1880-1920,* Madison, WI, University of Wisconsin Press.

LAMB, R.B. (1974) 'Adam Smith's system: Sympathy not self-interest', *Journal of the History of Ideas,* 35, pp.671-82.

LANCASTER, J. (1806) *Improvements in Education,* London, printed and sold by the author.

LANDON, J. (1893) *School Management,* London, Kegan Paul.

LANDON, J. (1894) *The Principles and Practice of Class Teaching and Class Management,* London, Holden.

LA SALLE, J.B. (1935) *The Conduct of Christian Schools,* New York, McGraw Hill.

LA SALLE, J.B. (1965) *Conduite des Écoles Chrétiennes,* Rome, Maison Saint Jean-Baptist de la Salle [reprint of 1670 ed].

La Scuola nell'Occidente Latino dell Alto Medioevo (vol. 19 of the Settimani di Studio del Centro Italiano di Studi sull'Alto Medioevo), Spoleto, Presso la Sede del Centre, 1972.

LASS, A.H. and TASMAN, N.L. (Eds) (1981) *Going to School: An Anthology of Prose about Teachers and Students,* New York, Mentor.

LAWRENCE, E. (Ed) (1969) *Friedrich Froebel and English Education,* London, National Froebel Foundation.

Laws Relating to Common Schools, New York, n.d.

LEACH, A.F. (1911) *Educational Charters and Documents 598-1909,* Cambridge, Cambridge University Press.

LEACH, A.F. (1915) *The Schools of Medieval England,* London, Methuen.

LE COULTRE, J. (1926) *Maturin Cordier et les Origines de la Pédagogie Protestante dans le Pays de la Langue Française (1530-1564),* Neuchatel, Secretariat de l'Université.

Leidsche Universiteit 1574-1871, The Hague, Government Historical Publications, 1913-24.

LEVITIN, K. (Ed) (1982) *One is Not Born a Personality: Profiles of Soviet Education Psychologists,* Moscow, Progress.

LIS, C. and JOLY, H. (1979) *Poverty and Capitalism in Pre-Industrial Europe,* Hassocks, Harvester Press.

LITTLETON, A.C. and YAMEY, B.S. (Eds) (1956) *Studies in the History of Accounting,* London, Sweet & Maxwell.

LOCKE, J. (n.d.) *Some Thoughts Concerning Education,* London, National Society.

LUNDGREN, U.P. (1979) *School Curricula: Content and Structure and their Effects on Educational and Occupational Careers,* Stockholm Institute of Education Department of Educational Research, Reports on Education and Psychology No.2.

LUNDGREN, U.P. (1983) *Between Hope and Happening: Text and Context in Curriculum,* Geelong, Deakin University Press.

LYNCH, J.H. (1976) *Simoniacal Entry into Religious Life from 1000 to 1260: A Social, Economic and Legal Study,* Columbus, OH, Ohio State University Press.

MCCANN, P. and YOUNG, F.A. (1982) *Samuel Wilderspin and the Infant School Movement,* London, Croom Helm.

MCDONNELL, M. (1959) *The Annals of St Pauls,* printed privately.

MCINTYRE, A. (1981) *After Virtue: A Study in Moral Theory,* London, Duckworth.

MACKIE, J.D. (1954) *The University of Glasgow 1451-1951,* Glasgow, Jackson.

MCLAREN, D.J. (1983) *David Dale of New Lanark,* Milngavie, Heatherbank Press.

MCLINTOCK, J. and MCLINTOCK, R. (Eds) (1970) *Henry Barnard's School Architecture,* New York, Teachers College Press.

MCMAHON, C.P. (1947) *Education in Fifteenth Century England,* Baltimore, MD, Johns Hopkins University Press.

MCNICHOLAS, J. (1974) *The Design of English Elementary and Primary Schools,* Windsor, National Foundation for Educational Research.

MALAND, D. (1970) *Culture and Society in Seventeenth Century France,* London, Batsford.

MANN, H. (1844) *Reply to the "Remarks" of Thirty-one Boston Schoolmasters,* Boston, Fowle & Capen.

MARGLIN, S.A. (1974) 'What do bosses do?: The origins and function of hierarchies in capitalist production', *Review of Radical Political Economics,* pp.60-112.

MARKUS, T.E. (Ed) (1982) *Order and Space in Society: Architectural Form and its Context in the Scottish Enlightenment,* Edinburgh, Mainstream.

MARROU, H. (1948) *Histoire de l'Education dans l'Antiquite,* Paris, Editions de Seuil.

MASON, J. (1954) 'Scottish charity schools of the eighteenth century', *Scottish Historical Review,* 33, pp.1-13.

MASSEBIEAU, L. (1886) *Schola Aquitana: Programme d'Etudes de Collège de Guyenne au XVIᵉ Siècle,* Paris, Delagrave.

MATHEW, W.M. (1966) 'The origins and occupations of Glasgow students 1740-1839', *Past and Present,* 33, pp.74-94.

MAYNES, M.J. (1985) *Schooling in Western Europe: A Social History,* Albany, NY, State University of New York Press.

MEAGHER, P.K., O'BRIEN, T.C. and AHERNE, C.M. (1979) *Encyclopaedic Dictionary of Religion,* Washington, Corpus Publications.

MELLON, P. (1913) *L'Academie de Sedan,* Paris, Fischbacher.

MESTON, W. (1823) *Practical Essay on the Manner of Studying and Teaching in Scotland,* Edinburgh, McReadie Skelly.

Minutes of the Committee of Council on Education 1839-1840, London, 1840.

MIR, G.C. (1968) *Aux Sources de la Pedagogie des Jesuites: le Modus Parisiensis,* Rome, Instituti Historici S.J.

MITCHELL, T.C. (1913) 'Loss of efficiency in the recitation', *Educational Review,* 45, pp.8-28.

MOLTMANN, V.J. (1957) 'Zur Bedeutung des Petrus Ramus für Philosophie und Theologie im Calvinismus', *Zeitschrift für Kirchengeschichte,* 68, pp.295-318.

MONROE, P. (1911) *A Cyclopedia of Education,* New York, Macmillan.

MONTMORENCY, J.E.G. (1902) *State Intervention in English Education: A Short History from the Earliest Times Down to 1833,* Cambridge, Cambridge University Press.

MORAN, J.H. (1979) *Education and Learning in the City of York 1300-1560,* York, St Anthony's Press.

MORAN, W. (1966) 'Development and evolution of the educational theory and practice of John Baptist de la Salle in the congregation of the brothers of the Christian schools in France in the eighteenth and nineteenth centuries', PhD thesis, University of London.

MORGAN, J. (1986) *Godly Learning: Puritan Attitudes Towards Reason, Learning and Education,* Cambridge, Cambridge University Press.

MORRIS, R.J. (1979) *Class and Class Consciousness in the Industrial Revolution 1780-1850,* London, Macmillan.

MOUSNIER, R. (1971) *Peasant Uprisings in Seventeenth Century France, Russia and China,* London, Allen & Unwin.

MOUSNIER, R. (1979) *The Institutions of France Under the Absolute Monarchy 1598-1789,* Chicago, IL, University of Chicago Press.

Munimenta Alma Universitatis Glasguensis (records of the University of Glasgow from its foundation till 1727), Glasgow, Maitland Club, 1854.

MURRAY, A. (1978) *Reason and Society in the Middle Ages,* Oxford, Clarendon Press.

NELSON, D. (1980) *Frederick W. Taylor and the Rise of Scientific Management,* Madison, WI, University of Wisconsin Press.

Nineteenth Annual Report of the Trustees and Visitors of Common Schools to the City Council of Cincinnati, Cincinnati, 1847.

NORRIS, N. (Ed) (1977) *Safari Papers II,* Norwich, University of East Anglia Centre for Applied Research in Education.

NUNN, T.P. (1923) *Education: Its Data and First Principles,* London, Edward Arnold.

OESTREICH, G. (1982) *Neostoicism and the Early Modern State,* Cambridge, Cambridge University Press.

ONG, W.J. (1958) *Ramus, Method and the Decay of Dialogue: from the Art of Discourse to the Art of Reason,* Cambridge, MA, Harvard University Press.

PAGE, D.P. (1842) *Theory and Practice of Teaching,* Syracuse, Hall & Dickson.

PARÉ, G., BRUNET, A. and TREMBLAY, P. (1933) *La Renaissance du XIIe Siècle: les Écoles et l'Enseignment,* Paris, Vrin.

PARKER, G. (1979) *Europe in Crisis 1598-1648,* London, Fontana.

PARKER, G. (1979) *The Dutch Revolt,* Harmondsworth, Penguin.

PARKER, G. and SMITH, L.M. (Eds) (1978) *The General Crisis of the Seventeenth Century,* London, Routledge.

PARKER, T.H.L. (1971) *Calvin's New Testament Commentaries*, London, SCM Press.

PARRY, A.W. (1920) *Education in England in the Middle Ages*, London, Clive.

PAYNE, W. (1875) *Chapters on School Supervision*, Cincinnati, OH, Van Antwerp.

PHELPS, W.F. (1874) *The Teacher's Handbook for the Institute and the Classroom*, New York, Barnes.

PICKARD, J.L. (1902) *School Supervision*, New York, Appleton.

PIRENNE, H. (1929) 'L'instruction des marchands au Moyen Age', *Annales d'Histoire Economique et Sociale*, 1, pp.13-28.

PODMORE, F. (1906) *Robert Owen: A Biography*, London, Hutchinson.

POLLARD, H. (1956) *Pioneers of Popular Education 1760-1850*, London, Murray.

POLLARD, S. (1965) *The Genesis of Modern Management: A Study of the Industrial Revolution in Great Britain*, London, Edward Arnold.

POPKEWITZ, T.S., TABARCHNICK, B.R. and WEHLAGE, G. (1982) *The Myth of Educational Reform: A Study of School Responses to a Program of Change*, Madison, WI, University of Wisconsin Press.

POST, R.R. (1968) *The Modern Devotion*, Leiden, Brill.

POTTER, G.R. and GREENGRASS, M. (Eds) (1983) *John Calvin*, London, Edward Arnold.

POUTET, Y. (1970) *Le XVIIᵉ Siècle et les Origines Lasalliens*, Rennes, Imprimerie Réunies.

POUTET, Y. (1971) 'L'Enseignement des Pauvres dans la France du XVIIᵉ Siècle', *Dixseptieme Siècle*, 90-91, pp.87-110.

QUEYRAT, F. (1919) *L'Émulation et son Rôle dans l'Éducation*, Paris, Alcan.

RABB, T.K. (1975) *The Struggle for Stability in Early Modern Europe*, New York, Oxford University Press.

RAIT, R.S. (1912) *Life in the Medieval University*, Cambridge, Cambridge University Press.

RASHDALL, H. (1936) *The Universities of Europe in the Middle Ages* (edited by F.M. Powicke and A.B. Emden), Oxford, Clarendon Press.

REEDER, R. (1900) *The Historical Development of School Readers and Methods of Teaching Reading*, New York, Columbia University.

REIN, W. (1903) *Encyklopädisches Handbuch der Pedagogik*, Langensalzer, Beyer.

RENAUDET, A. (1916) *Préréforme et Humanisme à Paris (1496-1517)*, Paris, Champion.

Report of the Committee of Fifteen on Elementary Education, Washington, Government Printing Office, 1895.

Report of the Committee of the National Council of Education on Economy of Time in Education, Washington, Government Printing Office, 1913.

Report of the Select Committee on the Education of the Lower Orders in the Metropolis, London, 1816.

REUSEN, E.J.H. (1967) 'Statuts primitifs de la Faculté des Arts de Louvain', *Comptes Rendus des Séances de la Commission Royale d'Histoire*, 9, pp.147-206.

RICH, R.W. (1972) *The Training of Teachers in England and Wales During the Nineteenth Century*, Bath, Cedric Chivers.

RICHARDSON, J.G. (1980) 'Variation in date of enactment of compulsory school attendance laws: An empirical enquiry', *Sociology of Education*, 53, pp.153-63.

RICHÉ, P. (1979) *Les Écoles et l'Enseignement dans l'Occident Chrétien de la fin du Ve au Milieu du XIe Siècle,* Paris, Aubier Montaigne.

ROBINSON, R. (1869) *Teacher's Manual of Method and Organisation,* London, Longmans.

ROUSSEAU, J.J. (n.d.) *Emile* (1762), London, Dent.

RUSSELL, R. (1986) 'Elizabeth Hamilton: Enlightenment educator', *Scottish Educational Review,* 18, pp.23-30.

SCHOENGEN, M. (1898) *Die Schule von Zwolle von ihren Anfangen bis zu dem Auftreten des Humanismus,* Friburg, printed doctoral thesis.

Schools and Scholars in History, London, Nelson, n.d.

SCHULTZ, S. (1973) *The Culture Factory: Boston Public Schools 1789-1860,* New York, Oxford University Press.

SCOTT, W.R. (1937) *Adam Smith as Student and Professor,* Glasgow, Jackson.

SEABORNE, M. (1971) *The English School: Its Architecture and Organisation 1370-1870,* London, Routledge.

SEABORNE, M. and LOWE, R. (1977) *The English School: Its Architecture and Organisation 1870-1970,* London, Routledge.

SEARCH, P.W. (1894) 'Individual teaching: The Pueblo Plan', *Educational Review,* pp.154-70.

SEARCH, P.W. (1902) *An Ideal School,* New York, Appleton.

SELLECK, R.J.W. (1968) *The New Education 1870-1914,* London, Pitman.

SHARP, R. and GREEN, A. (1975) *Education and Social Control,* London, Routledge.

SHEARER, W.J. (1898-99) 'The Elizabeth Plan of grading', *Annual Report of the US Commissioner of Education,* pp.331-2.

SILBER, K. (1960) *Pestalozzi: The Man and his Work,* London, Routledge.

SILVER, H. (1965) *The Concept of Popular Education: A Study of Ideas and Social Movements in the Early Nineteenth Century,* London, McGibbon & Kee.

SILVER, H. (1977) 'Aspects of neglect: The strange case of Victorian popular education', *Oxford Review of Education,* 3, pp.57-69.

SILVER, H. (1983) *Education as History,* London, Methuen.

SIMON, B. (Ed) (1968) *Education in Leicestershire 1540-1940,* Leicester, Leicester University Press.

SIMON, B. (1971) *Intelligence, Psychology and Education: A Marxist Critique,* London, Lawrence & Wishart.

SIMON, B. (Ed) (1972) *The Radical Tradition in Education in Britain,* London, Lawrence & Wishart.

SIMON, J. (1966) *Education and Society in Tudor England,* Cambridge, Cambridge University Press.

SMITH, A. (1974) *The Wealth of Nations* (1776), Harmondsworth, Penguin.

SMITH, A. (1976) *The Theory of Moral Sentiments* (RAPHAEL, D.D. and MCPHIE, A.L., (Eds), Oxford, Clarendon Press.

SMITH, F. (1923) *The Life and Work of Sir James Kay-Shuttleworth,* London, Murray.

SMITH, F. (1931) *A History of English Elementary Education,* London, University of London Press.

SNYDERS, G. (1965) *La Pédagogie en France aux XVIIe et XVIIIe Siècles,* Paris, PUF.

SORKIN, D. (1983) 'Wilhelm von Humboldt: The theory and practice of self-formation (*Bildung*), 1791-1810', *Journal of the History of Ideas*, 44, pp.55-73.

SOUTHERN, R.W. (1970) *Western Society and the Church in the Middle Ages*, Harmondsworth, Penguin.

SPRING, J. (1972) *Education and the Rise of the Corporate State*, Boston, Beacon Press.

STEWART, W.A.C. and MCCANN, W.P. (1967) *The Educational Innovators 1750-1880*, London, Macmillan.

STODOLSKI, S.S., FERGUSON, T.L. and WIMPELBERG, K. (1981) 'The recitation persists, but what does it look like?', *Journal of Curriculum Studies*, 13, pp.121-30.

STOW, D. (1833) *Infant Training*, Glasgow, Collins.

STOW, D. (1836) *The Training System*, Glasgow, McPhun.

STOW, D. (1839) *Supplement to Moral Training and the Training System*, Glasgow, McPhun.

STOW, D. (1850) *The Training System*, London, Longmans.

STRAND, K.A. (Ed) (1968) *Essays in the Northern Renaissance*, Ann Arbor, MI, Ann Arbor Publishers.

STRAUSS, G. (1978) *Luther's House of Learning: the Indoctrination of the Young in the German Reformation*, Baltimore, MD, Johns Hopkins University Press.

STURT, M. (1967) *The Education of the People: A History of Primary Education in England and Wales in the Nineteenth Century*, London, Routledge.

SYMONS, J. (1852) *School Economy*, London, Parker.

TATE, T. (1854) *The Philosophy of Education*, London, Longmans.

TAWNEY, R. (1942) *Religion and the Rise of Capitalism*, Harmondsworth, Penguin.

The Teacher's Manual of the Science and Art of Teaching, London, National Society's Depository, 1869.

THOLFSEN, T.R. (Ed) (1974) *Sir James Kay-Shuttleworth on Popular Education*, New York, Teachers College Press.

TIBBLE, J.W. (Ed) (1966) *The Study of Education*, London, Routledge.

TIFFIN, S. (1982) *In Whose Best Interest?: Child Welfare Reform in the Progressive Era*, London, Greenwood Press.

TIMBS, J. (n.d.) *Schooldays of Eminent Men*, London, Lockwood.

TOCANNE, B. (1978) *L'Idée de Nature en France dans la Seconde Moitié du XVIIe Siècle*, Paris, Klincksieck.

TOPOLSKI, J. (1976) *The Methodology of History*, Dordrecht, Reidel.

TROEN, S.K. (1975) *The Public and the Schools: Shaping the St Louis System 1838-1920*, Columbia, MO, University of Missouri Press.

TROPP, A. (1957) *The School Teachers*, London, Heinemann.

Twentieth Annual Report of the Controller of Public Schools, Philadelphia, 1838.

Twenty-third Annual Report of the Controller of the Public Schools of the City and County of Philadelphia, Philadelphia, 1841.

TYACK, D. (1974) *The One Best System: A History of American Urban Education*, London, Harvard University Press.

TYACK, D. and HANSOT, E. (1982) *Managers of Virtue: Public School Leadership in America 1820-1980*, New York, Basic Books.

UNWIN, G. (1904) *Industrial Organisation in the Sixteenth and Seventeenth Centuries*, Oxford, Clarendon Press.

UNWIN, W.J. (1862) *The Primary School,* London, Longmans.

VERGER, J. (1976) 'Les universités françaises au XVe siècle: Crise et tentatives de réforme', *Cahiers d'Histoire,* 21, pp.43-66.

VERNON, R. (1986) *Citizenship and Order: Studies in French Political Thought,* Toronto, University of Toronto Press.

VINCENT, W.A.L. (1950) *The State and School Education (1640-1660) in England and Wales,* London, SPCK.

VIOLAS, P.C. (1978) *The Training of the Urban Working Class (A History of Twentieth Century American Education),* Chicago, IL, Rand McNally.

VYGOTSKY, L. (1978) 'Problems of method', reprinted in VYGOTSKY, L. *Mind in Society: the Development of Higher Psychological Processes,* London, Harvard University Press, pp.64-5.

WADE, I.O. (1971) *The Intellectual Origins of the French Enlightenment,* Princeton, Princeton University Press.

WALKER, R. (1971) 'The social setting of the classroom: A review of observational studies and research', MPhil thesis, University of London.

WARDLE, D. (1970) *English Popular Education 1780-1970,* Cambridge, Cambridge University Press.

WATSON, F. (1916) *The Old Grammar Schools,* Cambridge, Cambridge University Press.

WATSON, F. (Ed) (1921) *The Encyclopedia and Dictionary of Education,* London, Pitman.

WEIBE, R.H. (1967) *The Search for Order 1877-1920,* New York, Hill & Wang.

WEIJERS, O. (1979) 'Terminologie des Universités Naissantes', *Miscellanea Mediaevalia,* 12, pp.258-80.

WELLS, W.H. (1862) *The Graded School: A Graded Course of Instruction for Public Schools,* New York, Barnes.

WHITAKER, R. (1979) 'Scientific management theory as political ideology', *Studies in Political Economy,* 2, pp.75-108.

WHITE, E.E. (1891) *Promotions and Examinations in Graded Schools,* Washington, DC, Government Printing Office.

WHITE, G.A. (1983) 'Silks and saints: David Stow and infant eduction 1816-1836', MEd thesis, University of Glasgow.

WHITNEY, W.T. (1915) *The Socialized Recitation,* New York, Barnes.

WHITTY, G. (1985) *Sociology and School Knowledge: Curriculum Theory, Research and Politics,* London, Methuen.

WIDDOWSON, F. (1983) *Going Up into the Next Class: Women and Elementary Teacher Training 1840-1914,* London, Hutchinson.

WILDERSPIN, S. (1823) *On the Importance of Educating the Infant Children of the Poor,* London, Goyder.

WILDERSPIN, S. (1840) *A System for the Education of the Young,* London, Hodson.

WILLIAMS, R. (1976) *Keywords: A Vocabulary of Culture and Society,* London, Fontana.

WILLS, G. (1976) 'Benevolent Adam Smith', *New York Review of Books,* 9 February.

WIRTH, A.G. (1972) *Education in the Technological Society: The Vocational-Liberal Studies Controversy in the Early Twentieth Century,* Scranton, Intext.

WITHRINGTON, D. (1970) 'What is and what might be: Some reflections on the writing of Scottish educational history', *Scottish Educational Studies,* 2, pp.110-8.

WOOD, J. (1828) *Account of the Edinburgh Sessional School,* Edinburgh, Wardlaw.

WOODWARD, W.H. (1904) *Desiderius Erasmus Concerning the Aim and Method of Education,* Cambridge, Cambridge University Press.

YOUNG, M.F.D. (Ed) (1971) *Knowledge and Control: New Directions for the Sociology of Education,* London, Collier Macmillan.

ZIMBALIST, A. (Ed) (1979) *Case Studies on the Labor Process,* New York, Monthly Review Press.

Index

Seaborne, M., 92, 116–8
Search, P.W., 133, 142, 146
section (group of pupils), 109–10
secular school subjects, 100
Selleck, R.J.W., 9, 28, 118
Sharp, R., 29
Shearer, W.J., 131–2, 134, 146
Sickle, J.H. van, 134
Silber, K., 155
Silver, H., 27, 96, 119, 142
Simon, B., 27, 114, 116, 119
Simon, J., 33, 55, 74
simony, 14, 30
simultaneous instruction, 2, 9, 21, 23, 34, 60, 91, 102–16
Sisters of the Common Life, 52
    of the Holy Child Jesus, 58
    of Charity of St Vincent de Paul, 64
Skinner, A.S., 92–3
Smith, A., 4–9, 32, 75–96, 114, 130
Smith, F., 116–17
Smith, L.M., 72
Smith, J.V., 116
Sneddon, D., 146
Snyders, G., 71
social
    adjustment, 22, 135, 139
    arithmetic, 130
    control, 10
    darwinism, 21, 139, 141
    efficiency, 11, 15, 19, 22, 26, 33, 47, 54, 133, 136
    engineering, 123, 133
    evolution, 20, 123–4
    harmony, 90, 127
    machine, 82
    morality, 136
    order, 18, 100, 123, 125, 136
    regulation, 17, 60, 154
    science, 123, 141–2
    structure, 69, 105
    unification, 22, 34, 137
    welfare, 19, 123
Sorbonne, 39, 68
Sorkin, D., 155
Southern, R., 13, 29, 50
Spenser, R.H., 143
Spring, J., 4, 28, 148
standardization, 128

Standonck, J., 41, 52
state, 10, 18, 22, 26, 29, 30, 33, 40, 43, 51, 63, 66, 69, 71, 72, 88, 91, 115, 118, 123, 139, 152, 154
    capitalist, 18
    intervention, 124
    local, 17
station (social), 83
Stewart, W.A.C., 96
Stodolski, S., 120, 140
Storke, E.G., 125
Stow, D., 2, 5–6, 14–15, 23, 28, 75–6, 85, 92, 95, 103, 105–6, 108, 111–13, 116
Strasburg, 46
Strauss, G., 55
streaming, 114
Sturm, J., 41–2, 46–7, 52
Sturt, M., 115
Sulpicians, 65, 68
superintendents, of schools, 20
survival of the fittest, 21
Symons, J., 106–7, 117
sympathy, 5, 84–5, 92, 105, 113
    of numbers, 106
systematization, 68–9, 73, 78, 92

Tabarchnick, B.R., 155
Tasman, N.L., 27
Tate, T., 97, 107, 115, 117
Tawney, R., 8, 28, 47, 54
Taylor, F.W., 141
Teneti, A., 31
textbooks, 75, 125–6, 144, 153
Theory of Moral Sentiments, The, 77, 82–3, 92, 94
Tholfson, T.R., 116
Tiffin, S., 142
Timbs, J., 27
Tocanne, B., 74
Toulouse, 65
Tremblay, P., 31
Trimmer, S., 82, 93
Troen, S.K., 145
Tropp, A., 117
tutorial teaching, 87
Tyack, D., 4, 28, 146, 148